THE BOOK OF BRITISH RAILWAYS STATION TOTEMS

THE BOOK OF BRITISH RAILWAYS STATION TOTEMS

DAVE BRENNAND & RICHARD FURNESS

First published in the United Kingdom in 2002 by
Sutton Publishing Limited · Phoenix Mill · Thrupp
Stroud · Gloucestershire GL5 2BU

A catalogue number for this book is available from the British Library

ISBN 0 7509 2997 9

We dedicate this 'Book of Totems'

Typeset in 8.5/11pt Helvetica.
Typesetting and origination by
Sutton Publishing Limited.
Printed and bound in England by
J.H. Haynes & Co. Ltd, Sparkford.

Contents

April 1974. (Alan Young)

Acknowledgements

The only book on totems before this work was the small paperback produced over a decade ago by the first-named author. Since then much photographic and historical information has come to light to enable us to compile this more definitive book. It seemed to us that the simple title *The Book of British Railways Station Totems* naturally suggested itself! During the preparation we have enlisted the help of many friends, fellow collectors and sympathisers. They have given us much material and information.

The desire to produce this ultimate totem book stems from a personal quest to educate both young and old alike about the astonishing array of signs that have been saved by an army of like-minded nostalgia freaks. There are literally thousands of these evocative little time capsules left over from the true heyday of our railway heritage. Even though they were used for a relatively short period (in railway history terms), they have become an integral part of collections and the modern railwayana scene. Totems (and their owners) are spread far and wide, not just within the British Isles, but also as far afield as Asia, Australia, Canada and the USA. There are people from many walks of life hooked on all aspects of railwayana (including enamel signs) and they have saved much for the benefit of future generations. Whether you are a seasoned collector, a novice or perhaps just plain curious, the simple totem is firmly fixed in British social history. They were installed throughout Great Britain, from the most grand of city stations to the most run-down and neglected country platforms.

It is most fitting that Andrew Dow, whose father George really started the ball rolling with the first totem sales in the 1960s, has kindly agreed to write our foreword. Through him, we sincerely thank the Dow family for the unique contribution that they have made to this area of railwayana, both in historical and collecting terms.

Our friend Alan Young, who has kindly supplied many of the *in situ* pictures, has also given us the benefit of his knowledge on the history and geography of the North Eastern region. He enlightened us both with major contributions to the Changing Regions and De-Totemisation chapters. Fortunately for all of us, Alan toured the BR system in the early 1970s recording just how many stations still retained totems, and taking some very evocative photos in the process. Alan, we salute you! An enormous amount of help, information, photo evidence and stimulus for our efforts also came from Ian Faulkner. Tim Clarke made available to us many old black and white photos of stations and totems from his library. We sincerely thank both of you for supporting our work.

We have spent simply thousands of hours assembling the data, and we take this opportunity to extend our sincere gratitude to the following friends and colleagues, without whose assistance there would be many more gaps in the databases than there are today. We acknowledge expertise and inputs from: Peter Allibone, Paul Arnold, Mark Bladwell, Rod Blencowe, Michael Brooks, Julian Brown, Paul Carter, David Chinnery, Jim Connor, George Devine, Brian Douglas, David and Michael Glynn, Mike Green, Chris Halsall, Mike Harris, Malcolm James, John Jolly, David Jones (Woodford), David Jones (Notts), the Kilvington family, Phil Kimbrey, Mark Koch, Malcolm Lamb, John Lancelot, Alan Lewis, Alf Miles, Steve Montgomery, Greg Norden, Dave Phillips, Julian and Christine Rider, Malcolm Root, Pete Sargieson, Tom Sherratt, Brian Shores, Neil Smith (South Devon Railway Trust, Buckfastleigh), Trevor Smith, Mike Soden, Trevor Thompson, Paul Tonkin, Simon Turner, Ed & Gayle Whalley, Bob Withers, David Wood, David Wright (NRM) and Ian Wright (also for his work in the railwayana field). We would also like to acknowledge super help from Simon Fletcher, Michelle Tilling and Glad Stockdale during final preparation.

Our greatest debt is owed to our wives (Belinda and Judi) who helped with a lot of the typing, a good deal of the background record keeping and proof reading. We also thank them for their real patience and understanding during the very long hours that we spent 'glued' to our books, maps and computers. Sorry!

Dave Brennand and Richard Furness
December 2001

We have adopted the practice throughout the book of highlighting stations that were fitted with totems in **bold** letters.

The Totem Study Group has been formed by the authors to gather and distribute new information that comes to light as a result of the research undertaken during this project. To subscribe or offer new information please contact either 'Rydal Water', The Old Pitch, Tirley, Gloucester, GL19 4ET or PO Box 2093, Wickford, Essex, SS12 0WP.

Foreword

Andrew Dow

Just over 50 years ago the newly created British Railways decided upon the design characteristics to be used for station signs. The task of getting the new signage into place on thousands of stations was given to the Public Relations and Publicity Officers of each region, and these six men were given substantial budgets for the task. The PR&PO of the largest region, the London Midland, was my father, George Dow. In his years on the LNER he had made a particular study of the design and layout of station signs and advertising, and he took a great interest in the new task of unifying these features of ex-LMS stations, some of which still had extensive pre-Grouping signs.

It was an urgent business. Thousands of name signs had been removed during the war, and many stations had only paper name signs, pasted under the roofs, where they could not be seen from low-flying aircraft. With only a few exceptions, the new signs (including those for directions, information and warnings) were made of vitreous enamel on steel. They were designed to last far longer than was ever required by the turn of history and among them was the now familiar totem, used for many purposes, including, particularly, station names. Standard sizing and lettering was prescribed and they were turned out in their thousands by specialist companies. One such was Gowshall, a leading manufacturer of road signs.

After all this effort and expense, it is extraordinary that all too soon, BR went through a re-design of their corporate image. This coincided with wholesale closures during the Beeching Era. So began a period of removing much work, done barely fifteen years before.

My father found this very depressing, particularly when stations around Stoke-on-Trent where he had his Divisional Headquarters, were closed. He mentioned to my mother Doris (also ex-LNER) his sense of wanton destruction, and she suggested that instead of sending vast quantities of material to the scrapyard, it should be sold in auction. Thus it was that at Stoke-on-Trent the first auction of railway memorabilia was organised by BR, but carried out by a professional firm of auctioneers to my father's instructions. It took place on 6 June 1964 and raised £964. Included in the 261 lots were 'station lamp totems' from Fenton (7 totems), Kidsgrove Liverpool Road (8), Newcastle (10), Newchapel & Goldenhill (8), Normacot (4), and Stafford (3). Contemporary press reports suggested that totems went for about 10*s* each. The sale made the national papers; and the £946 is about £12,000 in current values!

Since then the totem, in far greater variety than most of us ever expected, has become a most popular collector's item: more personal (from the home town or favourite holiday spot) than most other collectable items could be, and they are now very cherished. This is as it should be for a totem carries no fewer than four messages: the place name, the Regional colour, Eric Gill's noble typeface and BR's simple but highly effective design. All in all, we see the totem name sign as a classic example of excellent industrial design.

Andrew Dow
November 2001

Mr George Dow - the pioneer of railwayana auctions.

CHAPTER 1

Introduction

Opening comments

The formation of British Railways on 1 January 1948 was the beginning of a new era for the nation's railways. Without the moves taken by the post-war government, the network would have slowly ground to a halt. The devastation from the Second World War had left the industrial centres and ports of Britain crying out for funds to rebuild a near crippled economy. It was essential that these places were connected with each other to enable the importing of raw materials and the exporting of finished goods. As the road system was inadequate for the task, the bulk of supplies and goods had to be moved by rail.

The growth of the British economy during the mania years of railway building in the 19th century showed how central a good transport system was to a strong nation. At that time many brave and wealthy men risked fortunes to give birth to the age of railways. After the Second World War the Directors of the 'Big Four' realised the same injection of capital and effort was needed. Without the Nationalisation programme, some companies would have gone bankrupt, as their infrastructure needs were enormous. The cost of new locomotives, rolling stock, track, signalling and building refurbishment was beyond the capability of the companies and shareholders at that time. Following the physical battering that the nation took (especially the industrial cities), this new age of railways had to help rebuild national pride as well as a transport system. The picture below shows damage at Manchester Exchange after a German air raid. Such damage was typical of many British stations throughout the war. Coventry, St Pancras, York and others all suffered severe damage.

The country that gave railways to the world had to show that the furnaces had not gone cold and that a second industrial revolution was about to unfold. At railway headquarters in Marylebone, London, the Public Relations and Publicity Department was given the task of creating a new logo to bring all the 'Big Four' companies together. A modern design was needed to show strength and unity. It also had to be simple and instantly recognisable, so everybody would associate rail travel with it.

The birth of the totem logo

The now familiar lozenge-shaped sign was first shown at a Railway Executive press conference in February 1948 to an eager audience, where it was officially referred to as a British Railways Totem. Why this word was chosen is not at all clear because reference to the Oxford dictionary defines a totem as 'A natural object, especially an animal, adopted amongst North American Indians as an emblem of a clan or family'. We are all familiar with the totem pole, which is actually a tall pole where totems are carved as part of the clan emblem, usually erected in the centre of the village as the focal point. From these facts it is difficult to image why 'totem' was chosen for station signs, but we would surmise that it was maybe the family image that BR wanted to portray. The designer, Mr A.J. White, certainly hit on a winning logo; there is no doubt of that! We also think the original shape was first used by Bassett-Lowke, the model makers, in one of their early publications. We are still trying to track this down. The images below epitomise the sign.

Besides the name, we can only speculate why the shape was chosen. Whatever the reason, there is an undeniable attractiveness about the object that became so familiar as station signing throughout the '50s and '60s. They were first erected around or just before 1950 and some saw lifetimes of less than 10 years. A new white 'corporate' image was adopted in the mid-'60s, so by 1970 many totems had been removed. Upon removal they became sought after by collectors (whose numbers were few at first) but gradually they were sold from all parts of the country. In recent years they have become very desirable to historical collectors.

The totem shape also appeared on all BR publicity, on cap badges and on vehicles as well as the station signs themselves. Every handbill, timetable, poster and information sheet was re-issued in that first year and literally millions of totem-shaped images bombarded the public during the late 1940s. The new British Railways approved it as the central theme of publicity. Regional colours were adopted (Chapter 2) to reflect the heritage, and top artists of the day were commissioned to paint images, posters and carriage prints. Just two examples of the many wonderful posters that have survived are shown below. Others appear in the relevant chapters that follow. To us, posters and totems are a natural pairing.

(South Devon Railway Trust - Tindale Collection)

(South Devon Railway Trust - Tindale Collection)

Station direction signs were located in all cities, towns and country areas, so it was difficult to travel very far without coming across a totem image. The examples shown below are from suburban Liverpool and rural Hertfordshire.

Our research also shows that the intention was to use the design on the side of locomotives. It is well documented that a Schools class 4–4–0 locomotive No. 926 *Repton* turned up at Waterloo station in March 1948 in a publicity exercise carrying a 12ft×2ft totem logo on the sides of the tender. Inside this shape was painted 'BRITISH RAILWAYS'. It was not that attractive and was soon dropped in favour of the much smaller 'Lion over Wheel' emblem.

In the '50s and '60s the railways touched most people's lives. Today there are people who rarely travel by train, as they prefer the convenience of their car instead. The large number of trucks and lorries on the roads now is testament to how the movement of goods has changed substantially in fifty years. It is only the announcements of long overdue investment and the forced attention to track maintenance that has brought the railways back into focus. Railways can bring enormous benefits. It is gratifying that feasibility studies are underway for the Peak Line through Derbyshire and the Waverley route through southern Scotland as possible additions to aid the economy, as well as the community, in those areas.

Most of us remember our childhood and how things seemed better then, with much less stress and hassle in our lives. Those who remember it sorely miss the age of steam. In the late '50s many stations were grimy with an acrid atmosphere (look for example, at the condition of most totems from Bradford, Huddersfield or Leeds to see how polluted the environment must have been – see pages 12 or 170). Paint often flaked from windows and canopies, and the waiting rooms had real coal fires. Posters similar to those shown opposite looked down, beckoning the traveller to the Lake District, Cornwall, historic Windsor, Wales and the Scottish Highlands.

Whether you were commuting, visiting friends, going on holiday or just trainspotting, all journeys seemed to have one thing in common – they were just more enjoyable than the train travel today. Most stations, however small, seemed to have goods yards and much more activity than there is today. Clanking point rods, semaphore signals and constant movement created interest for the old and young alike! How many times have we asked the signalman if we could spend some time sitting in his box to get a better view? (Well, *we* did anyway!)

Today, however, powerboxes, coloured signals, complex gantries and largely faceless train control are a way of life. A visit to the NRM at York or one of the many preserved railways can give a flavour of what has disappeared. To take you there, your train will whisk you along at more than 100mph, controlled from a signalling castle that is maybe 100 miles away.

As soon as totems were installed in some places they were being removed from others. The Eastern Region was one such place, and here some collectable gems disappeared forever. Conversely, other stations maintained their treasures well into the late '70s, and pockets of resistance could still be found in the early '80s. During that period our contributor Alan Young spent a good deal of time travelling the country photographing this rapidly disappearing part of railway folklore, 'the station totem'. He has kindly written sections about his recollections of totems, and following are just a few of his nostalgic photos that can be found throughout the book.

January 1974. (Alan Young)

September 1973. (Alan Young)

The favoured place for a totem was under the many types of station lamp (also collectable today). These varied from region to region and many can be seen adorning gardens up and down the country. Some of the country stations had one or two lamps with totems towards the end of each platform and more totems in and around the station buildings. The larger stations positioned totems beneath most of the lights, so the name could be read more easily.

November 1974. (Alan Young)

(Dawlish Museum)

How many of us can remember standing on the end of platforms at dusk as the light first flickers into life and then slowly illuminates the station name? This wonderful painting by Peter Insole of the Guild of Railway Artists shows this to perfection!

'Spandrels and Capitals' by Peter Insole GRA. (courtesy of the artist)

The railways of our formative years were snatched away with haste in the modernisation era of the mid-'60s. Such changes accelerated with the appointment of Dr Beeching, as costs and economics began to rule. Plastic, steel and concrete replaced classic artefacts and even entire stations. The **Birmingham New Street** and **Manchester Exchange** of the early '60s are a far cry from what we have today.

If a regional colour was present it was invariably scrapped, replaced by fluorescent light strips and clinical-looking corporate black and white signs everywhere. Should you have been lucky enough to have witnessed the disappearance of totems (and then calmly walked up to the scrapman to offer a few shillings for a prized possession), you are fortunate indeed! The average collector today is faced, in some cases, with quite an outlay just to acquire one classic or evocative name in good condition.

The list of classic names will fill several pages and everybody has favourites. These could be your local station, a great junction, old holiday memories, steam shed locations, the old closed branch line or the majesty of the great stations or termini such as **Bristol Temple Meads**, **Carlisle**, **Kings Cross**, **Paddington**, St Pancras or **York**. Some of the other desirable names could be **Bassenthwaite Lake**, **Besses o' th' Barn**, **Blair Atholl**, **Evercreech Junction**, **Stalbridge** or **Whitby Town**. Of the great architectural masterpieces, we show two in carriage print form. The first is Carlisle Citadel (painted by Kenneth Steel), home to Duchesses and A3s alike. Following that is part of Claude Buckle's watercolour of the simply superb façade of St Pancras. It would have been wonderful if St Pancras had carried totems, but as compensation, a few from **Carlisle** have survived.

A carriage print - Carlisle Citadel by Kenneth Steel. (R. Furness Collection)

A carriage print - St Pancras by Claude Buckle. (R. Furness Collection)

There is a real sense of pride in owning a totem, whether it is a good **Buntingford** or a battered **Dewsbury Central** – you have an artefact from another era.

The colours remind us of the different aspects of our rail journey – the grime of an industrial centre or rolling pastures *en route* to the seaside. We can all remember the excitement of that first glimpse of the ocean when approaching our resort or the mounting excitement as the train enters some great city for the first time.

Totem collectors, whether from the steam, diesel or electric era, all share one thing – a love of railways and train travel. How many of us have stood on **Clapham Junction** station and raced from one platform to another as trains whizz by, or been lucky enough to have been on **Shap** or **Beattock** as steam giants struggle to the summit. The exhilaration of places where land meets sea (at such places as **Barmouth**, **Llandudno**, **Budleigh Salterton** or **Penzance**) can all be brought back to life just by owning such sought-after items.

Many of these memories have been captured on canvas. Just one of these (an original painting by Norman Elford GRA) shows Duchess No. 46238 *City of Carlisle* struggling up **Beattock** with a heavy express. The restoration of No. 6233, *Duchess of Sutherland* will one day allow us (we hope) to relive this sight.

City of Carlisle. (Original painting in acrylics by Norman Elford GRA)

The first 'totems'

Even before the appearance of the totem in the late '40s, stations had been fitted with signs to tell travellers where they were. These were often wooden boards or metal signs that were situated at the ends of the platforms and at various points on station buildings themselves. In earlier times stations had their identities displayed on rectangular signs. The colours of these also represented the regions, but they are not the colours you would have expected. The SECR area had dark blue and white signs, the North East had light cream coloured signs with brown lettering, while the old LMS station signs were yellow with black lettering. Some Scottish stations were fitted with dark blue signs but with different letter style to those in the South East. They were all termed 'lamp tablets' and are the forerunners of our redoubtable totem. A selection of these is shown alongside. Although not as colourful as the later BR totems they are attractive, and some lasted well into the totem era.

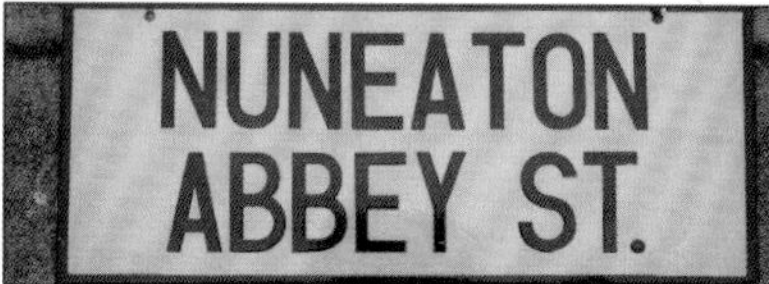

In the 1930s another form of sign (the hawkseye) became standard on the LMS and its constituent companies. An example is shown *in situ* at Abergavenny Junction, a joint GW/LNWR station. Strictly speaking they were 'running in boards', but may be classed as a form of totem.

(R. Blencowe)

Although an LMS sign (and therefore expected to be a shade of red), the hawkseye had a yellow background with black lettering. Some have been restored maroon and white, but the true original colours appear below on two signs.

Llandovery in mid-Wales is the ex-Vale of Towy Joint station and Godwin's Halt is an ex-Midland Railway station just north of Hemel Hempstead in Hertfordshire that closed in 1947. This is therefore the only 'totem' obtainable from that station.

The Southern Railway adopted another approach using metal sheets, enamelled with the station name. These are termed 'targets', presumably because of their shape, and are also now highly collectable. However, unlike the standard length totem, the actual size depended on the station name. Contrast the two stations below.

Such items from the Isle of Wight and from Dorset are much sought after these days. A study by Chris and Julian Rider indicates that at least 567 stations carried these items and about half of these names have appeared in auction. The treatment of the lower panel appendage was interesting: the wording appeared as curved names in the lower half of the sign, sometimes called the 'half moon'. However, the lettering size in the lower panel could be different. The short name below illustrates the strange look of some smaller targets.

Most of the commuter towns in Sussex, Kent, and Surrey had targets fitted and they extended right down to the extremities of the Southern Railway in Devon. We close this short look at targets (which are really outside the sphere of our research) with two examples from Dorking in Surrey.

The modern 'totem' arrives

Once British Railways had been formed in 1948, targets and all the other signs were under threat of removal. In the case of the old lamp tablets, this was largely the case but the targets lived on for many years into the totem era. Indeed, we can think of many stations in the south where totems were not fitted and the older targets were used until the black and white 'cleansing era' started. We doubt whether the black and white signs that replaced totems and targets will ever become as sought-after, as there is no mistaking that they are quite simply not as attractive. Even a desirable sign such as Euston (below) will probably never become a classic.

In the mid-'90s, we can remember piles of these signs (carrying early BR logos and Network Southeast colours) stacked at the former Collectors Corner in Coburg Street near Euston station. Each visit we made showed that the pile had not diminished much and only a few find their way into today's auction scene. They are simply stamped aluminium alloy sheets with a basic screening of each name and logo on to a plain white background – yuk!

The layout of the book

This book has been compiled with the help of many people. Collectors gave their photographs freely and supplied information to enhance our knowledge of the subject. We have also included a bibliography at the end of the book. We first describe the basic design parameters, the reasons for the regional colours, how totems were manufactured and then try to fathom some of the decisions behind resigning policy (Chapter 2). We then look at collecting pioneers (Chapter 3) and follow with an attempt to discuss some of the many and varied themes of collecting (Chapter 4). Next we look at just some of the unusual items, since there are quite a few totems that do not conform to the BR guidelines of 1948 (Chapter 5). The real meat of the book follows in Chapters 6 to 11. A chapter is devoted to each of the regions with a greatly enhanced database, as much new data has come to light in the past decade, since the publication of the original totem book (1991).

It was this book that prompted most of the new information. We have constructed all the databases so that the reader can make updates as more information surfaces. Each database page includes photos of some of the rarer items. Alan Young originally drafted the last two chapters (12 and 13). Chapter 12 looks at some of the boundary changes that occurred in the first twenty-five years of British Railways, and Chapter 13 reviews the time when totems were being removed. Some of us will have been lucky enough to start our collections when the humble totem was classed as lower grade railwayana. However, when the stations were undergoing change, just look how totems and other treasures of today were treated – at the end of their working lives – nothing more than scrap!

Gillingham station, Kent, October 1974. (Alan Young)

How much nicer they looked hanging proudly in place rather than thrown in a heap. Just soak up the atmosphere at the old **Crowborough** (SR) and **Dingwall** (ScR) stations in Tim Clarke's two black and white pictures taken in the early '70s.

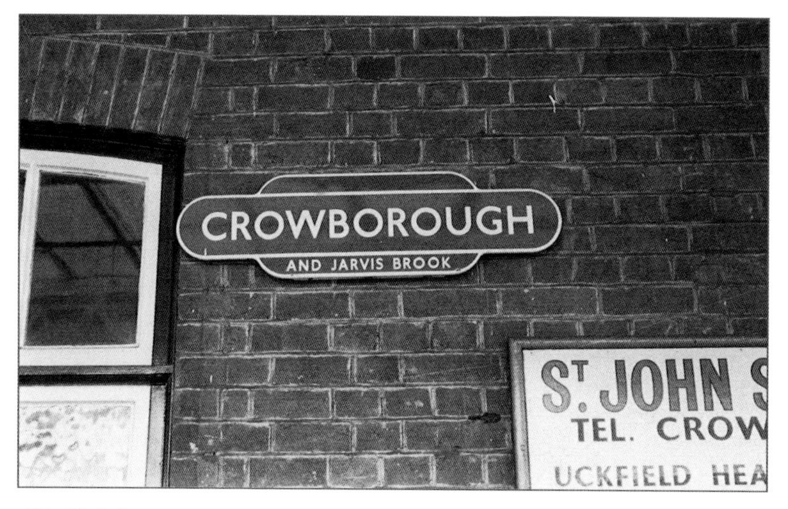

(Tim Clarke)

The interest is now many times what it was even a decade ago. We begin our fresh look at the subject by covering the design and manufacture.

CHAPTER 2

Totem Design, Manufacture, Colours and Signing Policy

Introduction

British Railways ordered the first totems during October 1948, after the Railway Executive published a document entitled *Code of Instructions for Station Name and Direction Signs*. This document appeared on 27 September 1948 and was sent to several potential suppliers for comment and bid. The document gave detailed instructions on the manufacturing process, materials to be used, and precise layout, design and sizes of the Gill Sans lettering to be used. It also contained instructions for the making of all ancillary signs, even down as far as humble doorplates. Those of you who regularly attend auctions and swap meets may be fully aware of the vast range of signs that this document covered – each carrying the regional colours. This chapter will show that these instructions were not fully adhered to and a good deal of subjective and indeed personal interpretation took place.

Basic instructions for manufacture

A section in the Railway Executive paper referred to above is shown below:

SECTION 3

SMALL NAME SIGNS (LAMP TABLETS)

Dimensions. 36" long.

Lettering. Standard 3". When the name contains more letters than can be accomodated in 3" size, the height of the letters may be reduced as far as necessary on the following scale :—

	Height of letters	Approximate maximum number of letters
Standard	3"	10
	2¾"	12
	2½"	14
	2¼"	16
Minimum	2"	18

Such words as "Junction," "Central" and "Halt" may be placed in the lower panel in 1" letters, if there is insufficient space in the centre panel.

For the comparatively few names which cannot be shown in a 36" sign within the foregoing rules, Gill Sans Condensed letters may be used.

NOTES :

(I) On very wide platforms at the largest stations, tablets with lettering larger than 3" may be required. Such signs should be exactly proportionate to the approved design and lettering scale : letters not to exceed 4".

(II) For illustrations, see Annexure "A."

The document states that the totems were to be rigidly suspended from platform roofs near to station lamps so they could be easily read. It does however leave the spacing open to interpretation and we suspect that the quantity of signs made for each station was also decided in consultation with local managers. Note (B) of the extract also states: 'The relative proportions will not be altered but the station name would be shown in the centre panel.' This made totems different from the Southern targets or the LMS hawkseyes, whose length changed according to the station name. Adjusting the letter height, spacing and number of rows for the title would accommodate the different station names. Therefore, we could have single-, double- or, in rare cases, triple-lined totems. The standard lettering was to be 3in high, but a scale was given for those cases where the number of letters exceeded defined values. Thus we have the following rules established:

	Height of letters (inches)	*Maximum number of letters*
Standard	3.0	10
	2.75	12
	2.5	14
	2.25	16
Minimum	2.0	18

'Words such as Junction, Central or Halt may be placed in the lower panel in 1in letters if there is insufficient space in the central panel. For the comparatively few names that cannot be shown in a 36in sign, within the foregoing rules, then Gill Sans condensed lettering may be used.'

It was also stated that on very wide platforms at the largest stations, signs with letters larger than 3in may be required. (The only region to actually use this option was the Eastern.) The rules went on to confirm that these signs should still be in the same proportion to the approved layout and lettering scale. This clause therefore allowed signs of 48in to be used at some locations. Another clause listed the number of signs for the small stations to be manufactured in 'reasonable quantities' – a subjective statement if ever there was one! This last note has allowed some obscure stations with only a few totems to be keenly fought over today, examples being **Colnbrook Estate Halt** (WR) or **Trench Crossing** (MR).

The document was sent to several sign companies. The most well known of these was Mead McClean of South London, since they had been responsible for the manufacture of 'targets' for the former Southern Railway. These high quality signs had given excellent service in the inclement British weather and McClean's were considered the clear favourite to supply the new station signs for BR. Other suppliers who were approached were Garniers of North London, the Patent Enamel Company of Birmingham, and Gowshall's, all of whom had experience in sign making for the road and railway industries. A whole range of signs of various sizes and types was required for every station. The smallest were doorplates for the various staff (station master, porter, ticket inspector, etc.) and the largest were the platform indicator boards, station running in boards and large directional placards. Even electrical substations in certain locomotive works were fitted with enamelled totem-like signs. The unusual object below came from Crewe Works.

Totems represented the middle size range, but all the signs used a common grade of material as the basis, VE CR4 grade steel. The thickness ranged from 16-gauge steel (for the large signs) down to 22-gauge steel for small plates. Tens of thousands of signs (examples below) were made.

It was interesting that, despite their quality, the first totems were sold for a few shillings, and even a decade later you could still pick up some future treasures for a few pounds.

The following list comes from a BR sale in Scunthorpe thirty years ago in 1971, with some choice treasures to be had for the Lincolnshire collectors!

Scunthorpe Auction at the BR Goods Shed, High Street East, Scunthorpe.
Saturday 16th January 1971

TOTEMS
Sutton -on-Sea £3
Sutton-on Sea with brackets £3.50p
1 Mablethorpe & 1 Sutton-on-Sea £5
1 Alford Town & 1 Sutton-on-Sea £4.50p
2 Sutton-on-Sea £5
Alford Town £4.50p
Mablethorpe £5.50p
1 Sutton-on-Sea & 1 Mablethorpe £5.50p
1 Sutton-on-Sea & 1 Alford Town £5
Sutton-on-Sea £5.50p
1 Mablethorpe & 1 Alford Town & 1 Sutton-on-Sea £9
2 Sutton-on-Sea & 1 Alford Town £9

TOTEMS
1 Sutton-on-Sea & 1 Alford Town £5.50p
1 Sutton-on-Sea & 1 Alford Town £7
1 Sutton-on-Sea & 1 Alford Town £5
1 Mablethorpe & 1 Sutton-on-Sea £7.50p
1 Skegness (price unrecorded)

Many cast iron seatbacks were on offer still in their seats eg Willoughby Jnc.

Many enamel boxboards also on offer.

Doorplates 3 to 4 in each lot 15/- to 3

Totem manufacture

The actual manufacture of totems involved some special processes. There was simply too much work for just one company, so the whole of the national re-signing was spread between several companies. This may account in part for some of the variations we now have today. One of the companies who made the signs, Garniers of London, used seven different operations to complete each totem. This description of the Garnier process was first published in the September 1996 edition of *Totem Exchange*. Other suppliers must have used very similar processes. The sign was first cut from sheet steel and pressed into shape. Once the final shape had been formed the vitreous enamelling process began (this is the fusing of glass to steel at high temperatures). The metal blanks were first pickled in acid tanks to ensure no dirt or grease was present, as this could seriously affect the quality if not fully removed. Once the pickling was complete the multi-layered coating process could start.

The first layer applied was always black or dark grey enamel. When this was dry, the enamelled blank was placed in a hot oven for a few moments so the base material could fuse with the steel. It was then left to cool naturally, and formed the basis for all enamel signs irrespective of use or size. The next stage was the application of a generous coating of white enamel, regardless of the final colour. Experience had taught the sign manufacturers that a black base with a good coat of white gave a very solid foundation and helped to intensify the colours. (If you look at some of the enamel chips on totems, you can see both these layers).

The final designs were created through the use of hand-prepared screens to the specific requirements for each sign. These screens (made from nylon) were stretched on to frames. Strong magnets were then used to hold the white enamelled blanks in place on the screening bed, while the printing was done. The screens were used for one colour at a time. After the first printing using the regional colour, the item was re-fired for a few moments at 800°C before more layers of colour were added.

These regional colours were hand-prepared to a tight specification (though you would never know this after reading Chapter 5!). We can only assume that the many companies who supplied enamel signs used slightly different mixtures during this part of the process, which may have contributed to the slightly different shades on the final items. The preparation was the responsibility of the mill room operators who ground the glass, oxides and other chemicals to produce the coating material. The screening enamel was brought in from other suppliers and mixed with the glass groundings to give the final spray coating. The range and variety of colours was large, with London Transport for example having 10 standard colours. The process then consisted of successive screening and fusing, with as many as 13 layers being required to build up the final thickness. A sign could be made from start to finish in three days, but the most usual cycle time was around four weeks. The finished totem was a sight to behold. Some examples of today's survivors were never hung (**Calne**, **Peak Forest** and the full flanged **York** are a few examples), so the full original beauty has been maintained. We believe that this, in some ways, makes them more desirable within a collection.

Design variations

The first totems produced were either flangeless or half-flanged. The half-flange refers to the part of the sign at the top and bottom that was bent at right angles to allow fixing to walls, posts, lamp brackets, etc. These were approximately 1in wide with three holes drilled in each flange. A few flangeless totems were made for the MR, NER and WR, and these have been identified in the appropriate section of the database. The majority of these flangeless totems were drilled prior to enamelling, though in some instances they were drilled as an afterthought. This method produced some unsightliness around the holes, and careful examination of some items reveals this form of manufacture. Over a period of time it turned out that these early designs were not so robust, with chipping and then corrosion occurring at the edges and around the holes. Some of the totems offered through auction show this type of deterioration. They also presented easy targets for vandals, who seemed to take great pleasure in bending the end section of the body at right angles, to render the longer named stations unreadable! Many of these have also appeared in auction after straightening and restoration (for example the double creased **Hertford East** totem alongside, sold at Kidlington). The question of whether or not to restore a totem is a purely personal one. Our opinion is that where a sign has large chips, creases or is just plain filthy, then restoration (if done properly) will always improve the appearance and in the majority of cases may increase the

value. (However, one note of caution: we have seen many cases over the years of varnished totems. This usually decreases the value, especially if done poorly.)

Fully-flanged totems were a later design change, with a ¼in lip being added all the way around the sign. This gave the signs more robustness. They were more expensive to produce (but fortunately now difficult to reproduce!). We believe these first appeared in the mid-'50s. Many stations were changed from the early half-flanged variety to the full-flanged version, and we have tried to list all the known variants for each station. This is where some readers may have more data than we have, so any corrections will be gratefully received. Some other totems were made with the full flanges reduced to fit flush to walls. These had four small holes drilled into the sign's face, and were known as 'face drilled' or 'wall mounted'.

We must assume that the various suppliers had to first install machinery and fully tool up for production, so it is fairly safe to say that the first totems appeared no earlier than the spring of 1949. Installation of the various designs progressed through the network for at least twenty years. During this period nearly 3,000 stations were re-signed. We estimate the average number could have been 8 to 10 per station (some halts had only four but large stations may have had several dozen). This means that 28 to 30,000 totems could have been made up to 1971, the last year of production.

The actual number that have survived is pure speculation; we would hazard a guess at maybe 50 per cent and possibly as many as 70 per cent. This would put the number in collections, museums and on public display at between 12,000 and 20,000. We also hesitate to estimate how many people have at least one in their possession, but it is at least a few hundred, and may be as many as a few thousand.

The regional colours

One of the sheer delights of totem collecting is the wonderful array of colours produced when they are placed together. The image on the next page is taken from the only previous book devoted purely to totems and shows the variants and colours to good effect. There is, however, nothing quite like seeing a wall full of totems from every region, and the displays at Derby in 1994, Sheffield in 2000, and Fawley in 2001 yielded some spectacularly colourful photos. We have included pictures from Derby and Fawley at the end of Chapter 5.

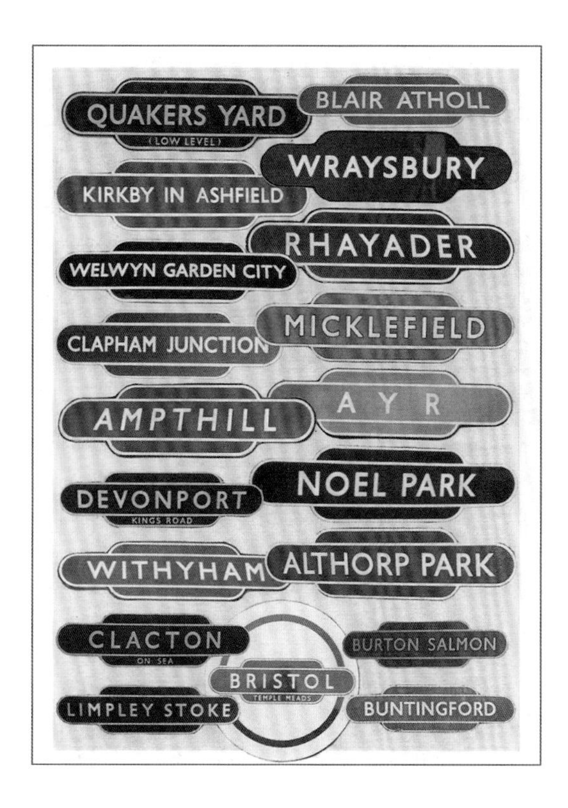

The colour schemes chosen were based on the old railway companies that existed before the post-war nationalisation in 1948. This regional colour policy only served to propagate the rivalry that existed in former times, and flew in the face of BR's attempt to create a national railway identity. It was almost as if the grouping policy was half-hearted when it came to station identities. However, we feel there is clear evidence that the BR Board tried to build their new identity on historical grounds; whether this was a good decision or not, it turns out to have been a super decision for the totem collector of today! The six regions that joined together to form British Railways (with the basic regional colour following in the brackets) were:

Eastern Region	(dark blue)	Southern Region	(green)
Western Region	(brown)	Midland Region	(maroon)
Scottish Region	(light blue)	North Eastern Region	(tangerine)

The basic totem colour for the Western Region was brown, based on GWR chocolate and cream. The totem lettering was cream, though variants in colour tone were common. A fine example of a Wiltshire totem is shown below alongside a section of a painting by Malcolm Root showing the gleaming Castle class No. 5078 *Beaufort* hauling the 'Capitals United Express' during 1958. The rake of coaches oozes pure GWR from Swindon at its zenith.

(Malcolm Root GRA)

The Midland Region totems were a deep red (maroon) based on the Crimson Lake so characteristic of the former Midland Railway. The station lettering was white, giving a good contrast that was readable at almost any speed. The two pictures below illustrate a Midland Region totem and a section of the painting, the evocative *Crimson Rambler* in **Kentish Town** shed, *c.* 1920, painted by Philip Hawkins in 1992.

(Philip Hawkins FGRA)

The **Blackpool South** totem (ex-LMS) comes from the famous seaside town in central Lancashire (the station opened in 1903 as Waterloo Road and was renamed by the LMS in 1932). Midland compound No. 1000 now forms part of the National Collection at the NRM, York. There is no denying the shades are very similar to each other.

The distinctive blue used on Scottish Region totems is a direct descendant of Caledonian Railway livery. The totems can vary in colour as discussed in Chapter 5. A totem from the ex-CR station at **Kentallen** is shown alongside a painting of the preserved CR locomotive No. 123, and there is no denying the comparison.

(Author's collection)

The Eastern Region totems are enamelled a deep shade of violet blue with white lettering. It is commonly believed that this blue was based on Great Eastern Railway colours. We have compared a totem from **Chadwell Heath**, the ex-GER station in Essex, with a GER Claud Hamilton class 4–4–0 loco tender.

The LNER perpetuated the use of dark blue enamel and was the first of the 'Big Four' companies to use Gill Sans lettering on enamel signs and engine nameplates.

When it came to the Southern Region, we have three quite distinct shades of green to consider (dark, mid- and light green). The first half-flanged totems were of the darker green variety. As manufacturing progressed fully flanged totems appeared with three different shades. We should therefore look at the first of these shades compared to the Malachite Green of the Southern Railway. Alongside the Cathedral City totem Salisbury from Wiltshire, we show a portion of a pre-war SR 4–4–0 Schools class loco to illustrate this comparison. This seems to bear out the theory.

The later totems were a much lighter shade of green. The Southern Railway used to paint some of their locomotives in a much lighter shade of green and we show one of 25 SR totems from the County of Devon, alongside a section of a Battle of Britain light Pacific of 1946 in 'sunshine livery'. Again the comparison is quite credible.

The mid-green shade is a subtle shade variation of the darker green, which only becomes apparent when all the three different colours are shown together, as we have attempted to depict with the collage of three SR totems that follows.

Even more curious than the three different greens was the choice of which green to use at each station. Was the decision made by the BR Board, a Regional Manager, the supplier involved or a third party? We feel after looking at all the evidence that the decision was purely random, bearing in mind that some stations had totems of all three shades along with differing flange types. Reference to any of the committee meetings may shed some light. We would be grateful for any extra information here.

If we thought the SR had a strange variation in colours, the choice of tangerine for the NER totems at first seems very strange. When the primary colours of red, blue and green are taken out, there is apparently not a great deal left. However, before the 1948 nationalisation some major ex-LNER stations were fitted with dark orange signs, so there was a precedent for this colour. BR lightened this a little, ending up with tangerine. The lighter coloured totems proved difficult to read in the inclement British weather, and almost impossible if the sun shone, so eventually the letters became black-edged. When fitted, they all brightened gloomy stations on dull days.

Certainly the choice of colour is a good one, from the collector's viewpoint. Only 125 stations were equipped with tangerine totems, with a very high percentage of these in Yorkshire. However, it would have been interesting to see a purple **York** or a pink **Beverley**! Even within the basic colour of tangerine there were distinct shades, and these are discussed in more detail in Chapter 5. We leave this short review of the regional colours with an NER totem and predecessor shown alongside each other from the joint LMS/LNER station of Leeds City – an LMS hawkseye in orange?

Station signing policy

The policy regarding the signing of stations is very complex and almost impossible to understand. As rules were made and issued, it is difficult to fathom why these were not adhered to. It is quite wrong to assume that all stations were fitted with totems. Some huge termini and major cities never had totems, while some of the smallest and most remote halts proudly displayed the regional signature. The Public Relations and Publicity Departments of the individual regions may have taken the decisions, so it is not surprising that there were inconsistencies.

One of the major factors in the decision-making process was almost certainly money. The cost of fitting mainline stations such as Crewe or Edinburgh Waverley with totems would have been considerable, so they may not have been made for this reason alone. But to counter this argument, other large stations (**Birmingham Snow Hill**, **Preston** and **Carlisle**) were signed, so the mystery deepens. Evidence shows 36 signs were made for **Bournemouth West** alone! It is curious that many of the major railway centres were never fitted with totems. This was the ideal place to cement the corporate image with so many people passing through. The list below of the major stations where current evidence indicates no totems is therefore quite surprising.

Aberdeen	Ashford (Kent)	Banbury
Blackfriars	Bournemouth Central	Bridlington
Chichester	Crewe	Doncaster
Dover Marine	Durham	Edinburgh Princes Street
Edinburgh Waverley	Euston	Fenchurch Street
Glasgow Central	Glasgow Queen Street	Glasgow St Enoch
Great Yarmouth	Hull Paragon	Inverness
Liverpool Central	Liverpool Exchange	Liverpool Lime Street
Liverpool Street	Manchester Piccadilly	Marylebone
Middlesborough	Newcastle Central	Norwich Thorpe
Nottingham Victoria	Plymouth	St Pancras
Sheffield Midland	Sheffield Victoria	Southampton Central
Victoria		

It is interesting that all of the four larger stations in Liverpool were not fitted, nor the two main Glasgow and Sheffield stations. What price today for a light blue Edinburgh Waverley, an orange Newcastle, or a dark blue Doncaster (probably the most desirable of all for the LNER aficionados)? However, our computers have allowed us to imagine how they might have appeared:

Other desirable items *may* have been Norwich Thorpe, Durham or Crewe. Obviously there were many smaller stations never re-signed, far too many to list here. However reference to *Jowett's Atlas*, or the *Dictionary of Railway Stations* will show that less than half of the network stations ever had totems. Reference to any of the RCH handbooks of stations would show that at the railway's zenith there were almost 7,000 stations and halts in Great Britain. Fewer than 3,000 of these were ever fitted with totems. We merely refer the reader to the appropriate regional chapter and corresponding database to see if your beloved signs were fitted, and if they were, whether they have survived.

From our list of stations without totems, the most surprising city is probably London. Of the major stations, **Cannon Street**, **Charing Cross**, **Kings Cross**, **Paddington**, **Broad Street** and **Waterloo** had totems, but the other 50 per cent did not. Of the four Manchester stations, **Central**, **Exchange** and **Victoria** were fitted but Piccadilly missed out. We *did* say the policy was confusing!

Technology was advancing during the 1950s, and the development of the fluorescent tube was destined to play a part in station signing policy. These were installed at many stations in the '50s, and this may explain the absence of totems at these locations. The station name could be embossed or printed on the light cover so that it could be easily read by day or night. Fortunately, owing to rewiring costs, these did not have a huge impact on the demise of the totem until after most of the totems had been installed. In most cases the fluorescent tube was a larger item, as shown below.

Totem and gas lamp about to be removed, October 1977! (Alan Young)

However, at some stations totems hung for a very short period (particularly on the East Coast Main Line at **Potters Bar**, **Hatfield**, **Hitchin**, **Essendine**, **Grantham**, **Newark**, **Retford** and **Northallerton**). From our research it seems that all these were removed in the late '50s, to be replaced by electric monsters. Rumour has it that the updating crews lifted lamps and totems together, and buried the whole lot in new station car parks and in dumps nearby. Are they still buried within earshot of today's tracks we wonder? All we can say now is dream on for a **Grantham** or a **Newark Northgate**, or start digging! The old gas lamps hold such evocative memories and were a familiar sight for many years at most stations. You simply cannot replace the scene that follows with black and white signs and modern electric lighting.

Sky and scrapman threaten in April 1975. (J. Wenham)

You only have to go to auctions, swapmeets or some of the wonderful collections around the country to appreciate the intrinsic beauty of a totem collection. When all the colours are together the effect can be breathtaking, as in the photo that follows, showing one from each region.

Having looked here at the design, layout, colours and manufacturing, the next chapter looks at the early days of collecting, when a few pioneers had the foresight to start putting collections together. Even BR did not really appreciate the true historic value of the thousands of artefacts they had until well into the totem-collecting era.

CHAPTER 3

The Collecting Pioneers

Introduction

Let us transport ourselves back to the late 1950s. You have just gone on to the platform at **Newark Northgate** and calmly asked the Station Master if you could buy a totem from him. All you receive in return is a quizzical look and the question, 'What on earth do you want that rubbish for, sonny?' The totems had only been up a few years and now lighting strips had arrived. Totems in 1958 were worthless scrap, but in today's market a **Northgate** would be a real collector's piece.

Nowadays that quizzical look would turn to utter disbelief if you asked the same question of today's railway official. The railways themselves are now on the bandwagon of 'controlled disposal' through their own sales and marketing channels. This chapter explores the early years of the hobby, looks at the first auctions and the treasures that were on offer for next to nothing (or even nothing if you had the cheek to ask!).

The start of collecting

Fortunately there were some far-sighted individuals who were impervious to the mockery, the quizzical looks and the disbelief. They have saved some real treasures for us and future generations to enjoy. It would have been easy to scrap everything from each station, because of the large number of staff employed at that time. The 1955 Modernisation Plan, with a gradual move away from the regional colours, precipitated the wholesale removal of much of the railway's local identity and the disposal of many thousands of totems. The final nail in the 'totem coffin' came with the Corporate Identity Programme in 1965. Even then, despite grand ideas, the actual implementation took almost twenty years to complete.

It would seem that removal began in the east, particularly the East Coast Main Line and in Cambridgeshire, Essex and Suffolk. It is also not widely known that a few major West Coast Main Line stations had modernisation carried out in the early 60s. This included the refurbishment of waiting rooms, the provision of modern heating, better lighting and of course the removal of colourful signs. Black and white was the order of the day, so these new clinical alloy signs and bits of 'bent aluminium' were soon to be seen all over the stations. Some examples of WCML stations suffering this early fate included **Watford Junction**, **Wembley Central**, **Rugby Midland**, **Coventry**, **Birmingham New Street**, **Wolverhampton High Level**, **Stafford** and **Carlisle**. Any of these today are 'rare birds' indeed. Just two of these rare birds follow.

At the same time on the Western Region early re-signing took place at **Bath Spa**, **Bristol Temple Meads** and **Cardiff General**. Again these are much sought-

after today and almost impossible to obtain. It has been commonly assumed that only roundels existed at **Temple Meads**, but our photographic evidence confirms the existence of conventional totems at the ends of the main platforms. Conversely, totems lasted for another 20+ years at some other locations. We have much photographic evidence of totems in place in the late '70s with the regional colours still showing proud. Two of these (ScR and MR) are represented below.

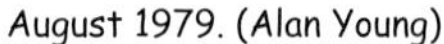
August 1979. (Alan Young)

April 1974. (Alan Young)

While we will never know who the first totem collector was, he was almost certainly not alone. There are several signs that were removed from stations all over the country in the mid-1950s that have been saved; just one person could not have saved them all. Organised sales did not start until about 1964, so literally walking off with them or handing a few shillings to a porter or scrapman probably liberated any totems before that date. On the small stations it would have taken workmen less than an hour to remove all the regional signs, so during the late '50s and early '60s hundreds (possibly thousands) were scrapped and buried with other rubble and earth during the rebuilding. If you are lucky enough to unearth a totem that may have been in somebody's shed for 40+ years, the condition will undoubtedly be rather sad. That totem may also be the only survivor from that station. Examples here include **Brightside** (near Sheffield) that suddenly came to light in 2000 (below), and of course the **Burton-on-Trent** (of two skips fame) described in Chapter 5.

You then face the dilemma of leaving the totem as found, or trying to restore it to its former glory. This is very much a personal decision, but you may be amazed at the transformation that a quality restoration can achieve. We have to say that after seeing many attempts at restoration over the years, the results of a good piece of work are very pleasing to the eye, as the two examples below testify.

Restoration by Dave Brennand

Restoration by Peter Allibone

The reasons behind this strange habit of preserving old enamel signs are many and varied, but there is no doubt that these evocative little signs are masterpieces in their own right. They encapsulate an era that many people loved. Enamels of all sizes and types are perfect mementoes of the great days of railways. Even people with no interest in this form of transport know they represent a bygone age. When you watch *Antiques Roadshow* on BBC1, you may be astounded each week by the obscure objects some people have chosen to collect. Why they have saved these treasures is nowhere near as important as the fact they have done so. We really do owe a huge debt of thanks to those early railwayana pioneers. Their efforts saved some of our heritage that went largely unnoticed until 1964.

The Beeching influence and the first auctions

In collecting terms, 1964 was a momentous year. The influence of economic measures under the direction of Dr Richard Beeching was creating mountains of redundant station artefacts (lamps, furniture, tickets, wood, brass, etc.) and the wholesale scrapping of locomotives gave rise to nameplates, worksplates, and smokebox numbers in abundance. Fortunately there was a man who decided that collectors would pay higher prices than the scrap merchant for these treasures.

Mr George Dow was then the PR&PO Manager at Stoke-on-Trent. He was a man with railways in his blood, and the disposal orders received from Railway Headquarters must have gone against the grain. Here was a person who had witnessed first hand the huge changes that were needed to build a better railway, but he also knew that the price to be paid in historical terms was high. Many of the locomotives going for scrap could have worked on for at least another decade, as some had been built only a few years previously. The station signs he was ordered to remove had been up for less than 10 years in some cases. There was nothing wrong with them, but they had to go. They no longer conformed to the sleek image that the railway managers wanted to portray. George's decision to hold auctions was prompted by his wife Doris, who had also previously worked for the LNER. She reaffirmed there would be greater profit in selling to collectors, and so the first auctions were born. They were organised on Mr Dow's behalf by Charles Butler and Sons, and were held in the Old Road Motor Depot in Stoke-on-Trent. The first totems were not sold individually, but in lots of four or five! In 1964 for just £1 10*s* 0*d*, you could have bought five fully flanged MR **Newcastle** totems! One went through the Romsey Auction in 2000 and a princely sum was paid for the item shown below!

Those first auctions saw totems mainly local to Mr Dow's office going under the hammer. These included **Fenton**, **Kidsgrove Liverpool Road**, **Newchapel & Goldenhill**, **Normacot**, **Pitts Hill**, **Stafford**, **Stoke on Trent** and **Trentham**. These rarely surface today and would be sought after if they did. Documentation then was not as good as today, but some of the original catalogues with the prices made are known to exist. Two of today's gems from those early sales are shown below.

News of George Dow's success must have spread through to Railway Headquarters, especially regarding the profitability of the first Stoke sales. Soon instructions were sent out to all Divisional Managers that certain items were not regarded as scrap. Totems were included in this list. All managers were instructed to achieve the highest prices for all redundant assets, and once the word was out, interested parties put in their bids for their local totems. We suspect many 'under-the-table' deals were struck at this time!

Just as today, there were winners and losers, but to avoid disappointment alternative choices were sometimes offered. We would guess that there were a few dozen far-sighted people in about 1960 who started their collections, and by the mid-'60s this had grown to a couple of hundred. Today this figure may be a thousand or more, and not all are within these noble shores! The original 1991 book found many collectors, active and dormant alike, so a real stimulus to totem collecting was achieved. This new work has involved us in many hundreds of hours of work just to produce a new framework and enhanced databases. We know not everybody will find all the signs they are looking for, but the reader will get many hours of pleasure hunting those 'rare birds'!

The growth of totem collecting

After the Stoke-on-Trent sales, the next area to take up the idea was Derby. Sales took place throughout the '60s at one of the old goods sheds. Literally hundreds of totems from the Derby/Notts area were disposed of here. If you want an elusive sign from any one of the following locations, rest assured it will turn up one day, as they were all apparently saved. Those totems known to have gone through Derby include **Basford North**, **Basford Vernon**, **Bulwell Common**, **Bulwell Market**, **Coalville Town**, **Daybrook**, **Great Longstone**, **Gresley**, **Hucknall Byron**, **Hucknall Central**, **Ilkeston Junction**, **Ilkeston North**, **Linby**, **Mansfield Town**, **Mansfield Woodhouse**, **Moira**, **Newstead**, **Radford**, **Rolleston Junction**, **Stretton** and **Sutton Junction**.

We are fortunate to have the original records to confirm such sales. One of the earliest was organised by the same Charles Butler and Sons who had worked with Mr Dow at Stoke. Note the number of signs from **Derby Friargate** there are around! No fewer than six, but even more astounding please note a dozen from **Ashby-de-la-Zouch**! The first one of these to reappear in 2001 at auction made a considerable sum, but the next eleven may not! Other classics on this list include **Bakewell**, **Broughton Astley**, and the delightfully named **Kirby Muxloe**.

BRITISH RAILWAYS RIVERSIDE SIDINGS AUCTION DERBY
SATURDAY 7TH NOVEMBER 1964
Auctioneers:- CHARLES BUTLER & SONS

The totem list includes how many of each name came under the hammer.

12 Ashby-de-la-Zouch	8 Coalville Town	1 Kirkby Bentinck
3 Awsworth	2 Countesthorpe	7 New Basford
9 Bagworth	6 Derby Friargate	6 Rushcliffe Halt
1 Bakewell	8 Desford	1 Ullesthorpe
8 Basford North	6 Hucknall Central	7 Wellingborough Midland
1 Broughton Astley	2 Ilkeston North	
8 Bulwell Common	4 Kirby Muxloe	

Smokeboxes.

42221 44248 44663 45564 46122 90205
43888 44332 44514 45620 46125 90408
43917 44362 44552 45641 46156
43951 44379 44572 45738 46165 44381 broken
44191 44380 44577
44213 46163 broken

Locomotive Nameplates

45535 Sir Herbert Walker K.C.B. £35
45561 Saskatchawén (both sides) £30 & £31
45564 New South Wales (both sides) £25 & £33
45577 New Brunswick (both sides) £27 & £27
45618 New Hebrides £28
45622 Nyasaland (both sides) £29 & £31
45611 Hong Kong £27

(Data from *Totem Exchange*)

Sales continued at these two locations for the next few years, but the frequency gradually increased. Between 5 June and 1 July 1967 five sales were held at Derby. One of these is reproduced below. Literally hundreds of items were sold, but the following is a list of totems at 5*s* each! Makes you sick, doesn't it?

Sudbury	Sandbach	Bagillt	Rugeley Town	Mostyn
Meir	Oswestry	Congleton	Connahs Quay	Queensferry
Tunstall	Radway Green	Machynlleth	Newtown	
Rugeley T.V.	Etruria	Kidsgrove Central	Hanley	
Oakamoor	Penkridge	Beeston Castle	Whitchurch (S)	
Holywell Jnc	Newport (s)	Nuneaton	Chilvers Coton	

(Data from *Totem Exchange*)

A similar sale held a year later showed a different list and some real inflation! This was held in Calvert Street Derby (Old BR Research Department) on 29 June 1968. In the list that follows are some real classics, **Rugby Central**, **Derby Nottingham Road** and **Repton & Willington**. Note the sign 'Trent' appears in this list. This is the rectangular sign referred to in Chapter 5. Note also the price for all of these items was 10*s*, double that of the year before! They are certainly around, but what price a Derby or Rugby today!

Station Name Signs.

Vitreous enamelled Station Lamp Totems in regional colours for the following stations:-

Alfreton	Hathern	Pye Bridge.	Trowell	
Ambergate	Humberston Rd.	Derby, Nottm Rd	Tutbury	
Ashwell	Ilkeston Jcn.	Repton & W.	Wigston Glen	
Blaby	Kibworth.	Rowsley.	Parva.	
Codnor Pk. & I.	Langley Mill & E.	Rugby Central.	Wigston Magna	10. 0. each.
Corby.	Luffenham.	Seaton.	Wingfield	
Desborough & R.	Manton.	Stanton Gate.	Westhouses	
East Langton.	Matlock Bath.	Stapleford.	Morcott	
Gretton.	Old Dalby.	Trent.	Nottingham.	
	Pear Tree & N.			

(Data from *Totem Exchange*)

By now the sales through BR were gathering speed and the regional offices became more active – Norwich, Stratford, Swindon, Eastleigh, Crewe, Glasgow St Enoch and Doncaster to name but seven. There were also auctions at other locations up and down the country: one example is shown below from Pickering, North Yorkshire.

Pickering Auction at Pickering Memorial Hall. Friday 30th July 1976.

LOT	No.	TOTEMS
36	NER.	South Milford no price
37	NER.	Goole no price
38	ER.	Eccles Road no price
39	ER.	Wrabness no price
40	MR.	St.Helens Junction £6.50p
41	ER.	Mistley £6.50p
42	ER.	Wood Green £8
43	ER.	Wood Green £8
44	ER.	New Southgate £8.50p
45	ER.	New Southgate £9
46	MR.	Meols £8
127	NER.	Seamer (double sided back to back) £7
128	NER.	Seamer £5
129	NER.	Stockton £5.50p
130	NER.	Stockton (ex cond) £10
131	NER.	Wakefield Kirkgate £6
132	NER.	Wakefield Kirkgate £6
133	NER.	Malton (double sided back to back) £13
134	NER.	Malton £8
135	NER.	Bempton £8
136	NER.	Thirsk £5.50p
137	NER.	Thirsk £5.50p
138	NER.	Thirsk £5.50p
139	NER.	Scarborough Central £9.50p
140	NER.	Thornaby £8
141	NER.	Huddersfield (double sided (back to back) £10.50p
142	NER.	Goole £5

Many doorplates were also on offer mostly ER. at £2 to £2.50p

(Data from *Totem Exchange*)

Sales from BR Regional centres were still going apace at some stations, as evidenced by a sales docket for Worcester Shrub Hill, kindly sent to us by John Lancelot.

British Rail

British Rail (Western)
Western Tower
18 Station Hill
Reading RG1 1NQ
Telephone Reading 55977 (STD 0734)
Telex 848461 Extn : 2588

STORES CONTROLLER

N.H. Attwood Esq
The Willows
32 Cherry Orchard
PERSHORE
Worcester

26/E/3/2

Date 21 August 1980

Dear Sir

REDUNDANT AND SURPLUS SIGNS – WORCESTER SHRUB HILL STATION

With reference to your letter of 24 July, I am pleased to advise you that your offer of £45.00 for the purchase of a Worcester Shrub Hill Totem sign, is accepted subject to the payment of purchase tax at the ruling rate 15%.

Upon receipt of your remittance to the value of £51.75 (£45.00 purchase price £6.75 VAT) arrangements will be put in hand for the issue of a letter authorising collection of the signs in question.

Yours faithfully

for Stores Controller

The rise and fall of Collectors Corner

One of the places that became a mecca for many of us started life as a regional centre for disposal. The outlet for the LMR was located just outside London's Euston station, and took the name Collectors Corner (CC). Before the formation of CC, Controllers in each region ran the sales, and before that it was the Divisional PR&PO Managers (as at Stoke). However, as the LMR was the largest of the 'big six', the number of items coming through their hands must have been considerable.

We believe CC started LMR artefact sales in late 1969, but it was not until well into the '70s that items from other regions started to appear there. During that time it became *the* place to acquire all types of railway 'stuff'. All the staff, particularly Bob Ballard, were extremely helpful and very knowledgeable. One of us (DB) spent a good deal of time finding out just which signs had passed through this location and the full list appeared in Issue 41 (October 1997) of *Totem Exchange*. In a 14-year period (1969–83) an array of totems from all regions was seen at Euston. It is because of these and other records that we have been able to confirm the survival of many totems. The numbers of different station names sold through CC by region were:

Eastern	10	Scottish	64
Midland	247	Southern	132
North Eastern	3	Western	49
Southern Targets	25	LMS Hawkseyes	5
4ft totems	5		

The 4ft totems were those from **Broad Street**, **Brondesbury**, **Queens Park** (LMR), **South Kenton** and **Weymouth**. The condition of some of the totems did however leave a lot to be desired – an example below of vandalism at its worst!

Collectors Corner was a nostalgic place to pass a few hours and had a unique atmosphere. The photograph below was taken about 1980.

As well as selling memorabilia from the railways, they began to make commission sales for those lucky individuals who had started their collections early. In effect CC became the first swapmeet location!

TOTEMS ON SALE AT COLLECTORS CORNER EUSTON, LONDON. JUNE 30th 1979.

ALL SR	ALL MR	OTHER INTERESTING TOTEMS (MOSTLY SALE ON COMMISSION)		
Banstead	Earlstown			
Berwick	East Didsbury	WR. Didcot	£ 75	1980
Brentford Central	PRICES £6 each	ER. Plaistow	£ 75	1981
Carshalton	(both damaged)	SR. Brighton	£ 60	1981
Carshalton Beeches		ScR.Nairn	£ 70	1981
East Dulwich	ScR	ScR.Dingwall	£155	1982
East Putney	Stirling £16	ScR.Wick	£172	1982
Elmstead Woods		ScR.Lairg	£172	1982
Ewell East	ALL WR	ScR.Tain	£172	1982
Folkestone West	Gerrards Cross £21	SR. Sidcup	£ 55	1983
Hackbridge	Seer Green & Jordans £30	ScR.Montrose	£100	1983
Hurst Green	(both overpainted	WR. Sea Mills	£150	1983
Putney	black & white)	NER.Harrogate	£200	1983
Smitham		MR. St.Annes	£ 75	1984
Stoneleigh				
Wandsworth Town		SR.TARGETS		
West Sutton	SR. TOTEM PRICES	Topsham	£ 30	1981
West Wickham	£11.50p to £15 except	East Croydon	£ 34	1983
Whitstable & Tankerton	East Dulwich £6.50p (damaged)			

By 1985 supplies of totems through Collectors Corner were limited and the bonanza period of collecting from there had passed. However, they still had totems passing through for another decade but nothing like the quantity enjoyed during the period of major station refurbishment. With the demise of BR and the formation of Railtrack, CC moved from London up to York but to the purists it was just not the same as the old CC. It was also a long way to trek for the southern collectors, of whom there are many. The York CC closed in January 2001. We wonder whether the name will eventually be bought and trading may start for a third time.

We close this short tribute to the Euston operation by showing some of the many items to pass through their hands over the years. We have chosen one for each region as a fitting tribute to the work they did for our hobby. These images do not appear elsewhere in this work.

The auction scene in the '80s

In the late '70s and early '80s auctions were held in several places. These included Malton, Loughborough, Bath, Malvern, Temple Meads Bristol and Bitton. (Malton is still a current venue for auctions, but all the others have fallen by the wayside.) During this time specialist newsletters had been appearing as the railwayana movement slowly gathered speed. Below is a section of an advert from *Railway Collectors Newsletter*, No. 74 (December 1979) in which some real gems were on offer. The mention of Newark and Yarmouth South Town should be taken with a pinch of salt, as our information shows no Newark survivors and that neither station in Yarmouth was fitted with totems.

FOR EXCHANGE

TOTEMS: NEWTONMORE - EXCELLENT CONDITION. COUPAR ANGUS - PURE MINT.
CARRON - EXCELLENT CONDITION. ROXBOROUGH - PURE MINT.
OXFORD - VERY GOOD. FORFAR - EXCELLENT CONDITION.
FORRES - VERY GOOD. ELGIN - VERY GOOD.
DINGWALL - EXCELLENT CONDITION. SILVERTOWN - VERY GOOD.
NEWARK - VERY GOOD. BOURNEMOUTH WEST - MINT CONDITION.
(2 TOTEMS AND/OR CASH FOR B/WEST)
YARMOUTH SOUTH TOWN - VERY GOOD.

These early auctions did not have the attendance of some of today's, but nevertheless they produced some fine items at bargain prices. Below is an extract from the Bitton auction of September 1980 where six totems were on offer, three of these being in the first nine lots.

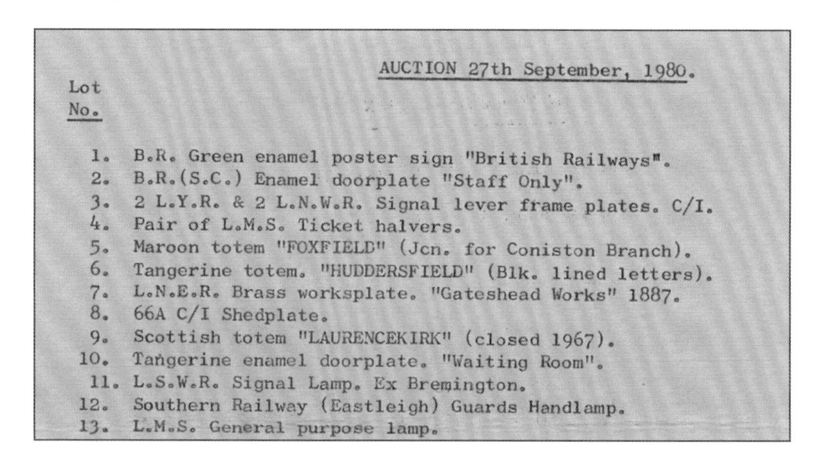

AUCTION 27th September, 1980.

Lot No.	
1.	B.R. Green enamel poster sign "British Railways".
2.	B.R.(S.C.) Enamel doorplate "Staff Only".
3.	2 L.Y.R. & 2 L.N.W.R. Signal lever frame plates. C/I.
4.	Pair of L.M.S. Ticket halvers.
5.	Maroon totem "FOXFIELD" (Jcn. for Coniston Branch).
6.	Tangerine totem. "HUDDERSFIELD" (Blk. lined letters).
7.	L.N.E.R. Brass worksplate. "Gateshead Works" 1887.
8.	66A C/I Shedplate.
9.	Scottish totem "LAURENCEKIRK" (closed 1967).
10.	Tangerine enamel doorplate. "Waiting Room".
11.	L.S.W.R. Signal Lamp. Ex Bremington.
12.	Southern Railway (Eastleigh) Guards Handlamp.
13.	L.M.S. General purpose lamp.

All the auctions had anywhere between 200 and 450 lots and part of the fun we have had in researching this book was to review just what was on offer in this 15-year period. This has enabled us to build as complete a picture of survivors as possible for each of the database sections. At Loughborough University an auction on 15 August 1987 had no fewer than 40 items, including two Hawkseyes, a Snow Hill roundel and one of the Durham enamels we show in Chapter 5. The totems included **Elm Park** (ER), **Kidsgrove Liverpool Road** (MR), **Marske** (NER), **Blantyre** (ScR), **Budleigh Salterton** (SR) and **Reading General** (WR): one auction and a superb set!

Today some of the real gems are appearing, items that all of us had long thought disappeared, so we hope this book stimulates further 'finds'. Interest and prices rose steadily through the '80s but the auction scene (and the desire for totems) was not as buoyant as it is today. Following is a section of the price lists for the Temple Meads auction in October 1988.

Totems				
	SR	Ilfracombe £240	Ash Vale £66	Vauxhall £65
	WR	Perranporth £270	Clarbeston Rd. £65	
	LMR	Tamworth £52		
	ScR	Newtownmore NS £90		

By the late 1980s swapmeets were being held all over England, the most notable being Quorn, Dinting and Newbury. Premier Auctions was 'top dog' at this time, with events at Nottingham, Kidlington, Malvern, Loughborough and Bath. However there were other auctions held in Solihull and Buxton, with Wells Cundall in Watford and Malton. Then a newcomer came on to the scene, Sheffield Railwayana Auctions at Myers Grove. This eventually grew into the leading event for railwayana today. Interest really started to take off towards the end of the 1980s, and in the decade that followed totems took their rightful place in the railway scene.

There are those who think that just because they were only used for a very short period in the whole lifetime of railways, totems are still the poor relation. Should you go to one of today's auctions, you will see for yourself the real interest in this branch of collecting. We close this short review with a few images of items purchased for 'peanuts' during the real growth time of totems.

Collecting today

So how does the new collector make a start now? Like it or not, today's railwayana scene is dominated by auctions, but there are collectors' newsletters, with many adverts from private individuals who sometimes have spare totems. You can also make contacts with collectors all over the country through swapmeets, or just by phoning any of the ads you see in a variety of publications. The best method is to follow up each lead that looks interesting. This may include talking with retired railwaymen or advertising in the local paper for the area where you think the totem could be. Occasional totems still surface at toy fairs or model railway exhibitions. Many of the auction houses today provide colour catalogues and some good information to enable bids to be made, either in person or by phone. There are always people there with good knowledge, so do not be afraid to ask. Below is part of a page from an auction catalogue to illustrate one of these sources.

If you are in Canada, there is a railway shop in the Grand Central Station in Toronto, Ontario, that often has British Railways signs of all types. They have even turned up in Australia, where one of us (RF) spotted a **Hough Green** in a collectors' shop in Sydney. Needless to say, this was repatriated without any hesitation and now proudly resides in a northern collection close to its original home. Many totems found their way to the USA (see Appendix) and can be seen in a variety of locations.

One of the greatest advances in totem collecting came along in 1994, when collectors Alf Miles and Oliver Neal from the Derby area formed a newsletter called *Totem Exchange*. This simple idea has given hundreds of collectors a means to improve their collections. Today well over 120 subscribers from all over the UK (and a few from abroad) regularly communicate through this network. To everyone's sorrow Oliver Neal unexpectedly died in 1999. Fellow 'totem buffs' decided to recognise his friendship and contribution. Through family and many friends, collectors have placed seven totems and one Southern target in the NRM at York. This memorial, unveiled in April 2000 (and shown on page 23), has filled gaps in the National Collection and is a fitting tribute to his memory. *Totem Exchange* still lives on and is a useful contact base for readers wanting to possess a few of these treasures.

There is no doubt that collecting interest is much higher now than at any time since totems were taken down and placed into collections. We close this section on the early days with another image of Collectors Corner in its heyday in 1974. The pile of totems on the floor in the left-hand side of this shot appear to be all from the Penrith to Keswick section in the Lake District. We can see two totems from **Penruddock**, part of one from **Blencow** and of course **Keswick** at the front. Who knows what else is buried in the pile! On the right-hand wall we find **Blackburn**, **Bushey & Oxhey**, **Chorley**, **Elstree & Borehamwood**, **Godley Junction**, **Hartford & Greenbank**, **Leyland** and **Reedham**. We will refrain from disclosing their prices, as the pain could be unbearable!

(Photo from *Totem Exchange*)

The National Collection

A small collection of totems forms part of the National Collection, at the NRM in York. Considering the absolutely wonderful display of nameplates in the NRM, the totem collection is extremely modest by comparison. Up until two years ago there were very few totems on public display, but the opening of 'The Works' has allowed the full collection to be brought out of store and displayed (though not so prominently) in the large hall, along with some wonderful nameplates. The totems are mounted on three large boards high up, so they are difficult to see. The Collection consists of:

Board 1	Board 2	Board 3
Goudhurst (SR)	Cheam (Target)	St. Margarets (Target)
Brighouse (NER)	Cardington (MR)	Crews Chill (ER)
Chesterfield Central (ER)	Market Weighton (NER)	Henlow Camp (MR)
Pulborough (SR)	Shefford (MR)	Charing Cross (SR)
Chatburn (MR)	Shrewsbury (WR)	Bradford Exchange (NER)
Sanquhar (ScR)	Allanfearn (ScR)	Swindon (WR)
Leeds Central (NER)	Elmesthorpe (MR)	Fleetwood (MR)
Shefford (MR)	Swindon (WR)	Hatch End (MR)
Flamborough (NER)	Henlow Camp (MR)	Huddersfield (NER)
	Wokingham (Target)	

Many of these are quite common but **Chatburn**, **Chesterfield Central**, **Crews Hill**, **Market Weighton**, **Leeds Central** and the superb **Brighouse** and **Huddersfield** totems would grace many a collection.

(Author's collection – courtesy NRM)

The recent Neal Memorial has added a further eight items to this list and these are shown left, together with the half-size gunmetal dedication totem at the bottom (beautifully hand-made by fellow collector Barry Hayward).

Totems on public display

In addition to the National Collection there are displays of totems up and down the country and in some weird and wonderful places. The Severn Valley Railway (SVR) (Bridgnorth to Kidderminster) probably has one of the largest, with more than 20 around the station bar at Bridgnorth station and over three dozen at the Kidderminster Railway Museum, as shown below.

(Author's collection – courtesy Severn Valley Museum)

The number of totems at Bridgnorth changes as members swap some items for others in their collections, but the number at Kidderminster is fairly constant. It includes the late Brian Edge's West Midlands collection, and is a wonderful collection of WR totems, probably the best currently on public display. Some of these have never appeared in public auction and are quite rare. It is a display worth visiting.

The other major display to visit is at Brookside Garden Centre, Poynton, Cheshire. The railwayana collection here is very large and includes some 100+ totems and 5 Southern targets. Just as the SVR has a fine Great Western selection, Brookside has a quite superb LMR collection, focusing mainly on the North Wales Coast line and around the Manchester area. There are also some WR and NER totems, SR targets, some wonderful headboards and station running in boards. For the railwayana collector, a visit to Brookside is a must. The owner Chris Halsall has very kindly sent us the following shots to whet the appetite!

(Photos by and courtesy of Chris Halsall)

At Huddersfield and Euston stations there are the 'Heads of Steam' bars and restaurants where items of railwayana (including totems) may be seen and sometimes purchased. At some of the smaller preserved railways there are displays of totems local to that region. We would suggest looking in *Steam Railway* magazine for a complete listing of all the preserved railways and their local contact details, to ask what is on display before you visit.

The railway museum at **Darlington** is also well worth a visit. This has a small but fine collection of tangerine totems, along with a few other railwayana treasures from that part of the world. The picture below is in the main hall and shows a superb quartet of NER items. The totems from **Etherley** and **Heighington** are not at all common, and would sit well in any NER collection. Contrast the light tangerine of **Cargo Fleet** with the dark **Etherley** below it. Tangerine might be an unusual colour for station signs but it is certainly eye-catching!

(Author's collection – courtesy Darlington Railway Museum)

Every so often special public displays are put on that include totems and other valued items of railwayana. A couple of totem shows were organised in the mid-'90s by Brian Amos in the East Midlands, and we have included shots of the 1994 display alongside. In the top photo we find such rarities as **Wednesbury Central**, **Rugeley Town**, **Law Junction**, **Deepcar**, **Kimberley** and **Heswall Hills**. In the middle picture we would pick **Derby Friargate**, **Darlington**, **Aberdare**, **Besses o' th' Barn**, **Kings Cross**, **Melton Constable**, **Starcross** and **Brundall Gardens Halt**. Finally, in the lower picture, the treasures are **Barry Island**, **Bodmin North**, **Tavistock North**, **Leeds City**, **Ilkeston North**, **Keith Town** and **St Budeaux Victoria Road**.

Sheffield Railwayana Auctions staged a couple of displays, one a few years ago that featured totems from around the Sheffield area. This enabled some wonderfully rare dark blue, maroon and tangerine items to be seen in public together for the first time. These included **Bolton on Dearne**, **Chesterfield Midland**, **Chesterfield Central**, **Cromford**, **Dore & Totley**, **Edale**, **Great Longstone**, **Millers Dale** and **Wath Central**.

In July 2001 a quite superb exhibition of Western totems was brought together for display at Sir William McAlpine's private museum in Oxfordshire. Below are some photos depicting the event. Over 100 WR totems were on display!

(All pictures courtesy www.railsale.net, Paul Arnold)

The first photo shows the treasures from **Porthcawl**, **Wootton Bassett**, **Westbury (Wilts)** and **Staines West**. In the second shot we might choose **St Erth**, **Small Heath & Sparkbrook**, the unique **Penychain**, **Harlech** and **Clynderwen**. And from the final picture, we would suggest **Bicester North**, **St Annes Park**, **Ellesmere**, **Montgomery** and **Kingswear** for your shopping list.

CHAPTER

4 Collecting Themes

Introduction

This chapter is, in some ways, one of the more interesting we have researched. Naturally, everybody would love to own **Kings Cross**, **York**, **Kyle of Lochalsh**, **Paddington**, **Besses o' th' Barn**, **Darlington** or **Waterloo** totems, but there are just not enough to go round. It is really down to personal preference as to what should be the basis for any collection. We hope to stimulate a few ideas through our own brief review of some collecting themes.

Major stations

One of the very basic themes, especially for collectors in the south, could be suburban London or major stations in London. If we list just some of these, many evocative and desirable names emerge, including **Broad Street**, **Cannon Street**, **Charing Cross**, Euston, **Kings Cross**, Liverpool Street, **London Bridge**, Marylebone, **Paddington**, St Pancras and **Waterloo**. It would have been wonderful to have Euston or St Pancras in the collection, but the signing policy (whatever that was) clearly passed them by. Of those London termini where totems did exist, the sheer rarity of such items makes almost any of them desirable. Just look at the super quartet below.

Our research has shown that even where stations were fitted with totems, it was impossible to work out the logic. Taking **Kings Cross** for example, the majority of rail travellers never saw the famous KX totems. This is because only platform 16 was fitted with them (the one you arrived at if you had travelled via Hotel Curve from Moorgate). A few others bore the appendage 'York Road' at the suburban station, just before that line disappeared into the murky depths towards Moorgate. We show these two very elusive totems side by side.

Not every platform had totems at **Paddington** or **Waterloo**, so the number surviving in proportion to the size of these stations is small. In addition of course, Waterloo had Southern targets, so if a **Waterloo** totem proves elusive, a target is just as collectable. **Broad Street** had both conventional and 4ft totems, neither of which is common. Other major stations include Britain's second largest city, Birmingham. Here the collector has a choice of three, **Snow Hill** and **Moor Street** (WR), plus **New Street** (MR). Of the trio, **Birmingham New Street** is the rarest, due to almost all of the totems being lost during the major rebuilding in the early '60s. Two of these are shown below.

Three Manchester stations carried totems, but we have four variants. The odd man out of this quartet is the two-line **Manchester Central**, which is actually a 4ft long totem, whereas the other three are the standard 3ft in length.

Glasgow fared quite badly, with both Central and St Enoch being devoid of totems. **Queen Street** only had them on the Low Level platforms. The word Glasgow did appear on two totems, **Glasgow Cross** (in the heart of the city) and

Port Glasgow (along the River Clyde near Greenock). **Glasgow Cross** totems are not known to have survived, but at least we can include the other, one of only four with the word 'Port'.

The next largest city, Liverpool, was also almost devoid of totems bearing the city name, the exception being **Liverpool Central Low Level** (4ft totem). Collectors may have to be content with the suburban signs, such as **Aintree Sefton Arms**, **Blundellsands and Crosby**, **Seaforth and Litherland** or **Bootle Oriel Road**.

Bristol, Sheffield and Edinburgh fared no better and the collector is again going to be disappointed. We have no totems containing the words Sheffield or Edinburgh, but Bristol did better with totems at both **Temple Meads** and **Stapleton Road**. How many of us would love either a Glasgow Central or a Sheffield Victoria totem in our collections? Well, dream we must – for there are none!

Basic collecting themes

Outside the major cities, we feel the most interesting (and difficult) themes to collect are sections of main lines (ECML, WCML, WR to Bristol, Birmingham to Wolverhampton, etc.). This is a very high standard to aim for, because sooner or later there will be one or two stations that no amount of advertising or the waving of wads of money can succeed in prising loose, as none have survived. Even the real heavyweights in our collecting fraternity probably cannot complete a major line from London to anywhere, but that does not deter anybody from trying!

Just look at the two main routes to the north. The WCML was electrified much earlier than the ECML, but totems from the ECML are more elusive. Both routes have stations steeped in railway history with some great totem names. Just consider **Watford Junction**, **Rugby Midland**, **Nuneaton**, **Stafford**, **Warrington**, **Preston**, **Lancaster**, **Carlisle**, **Carstairs** and **Motherwell**. The LMR route is much more tortuous than their long-time bitter rivals on the ECML. During the late nineteenth century there was fierce competition between the two protagonists, resulting in the famous 'Race to the North'. At that time a great deal of effort was expended to ensure that these routes maximised passenger carrying on the lines north to Scotland.

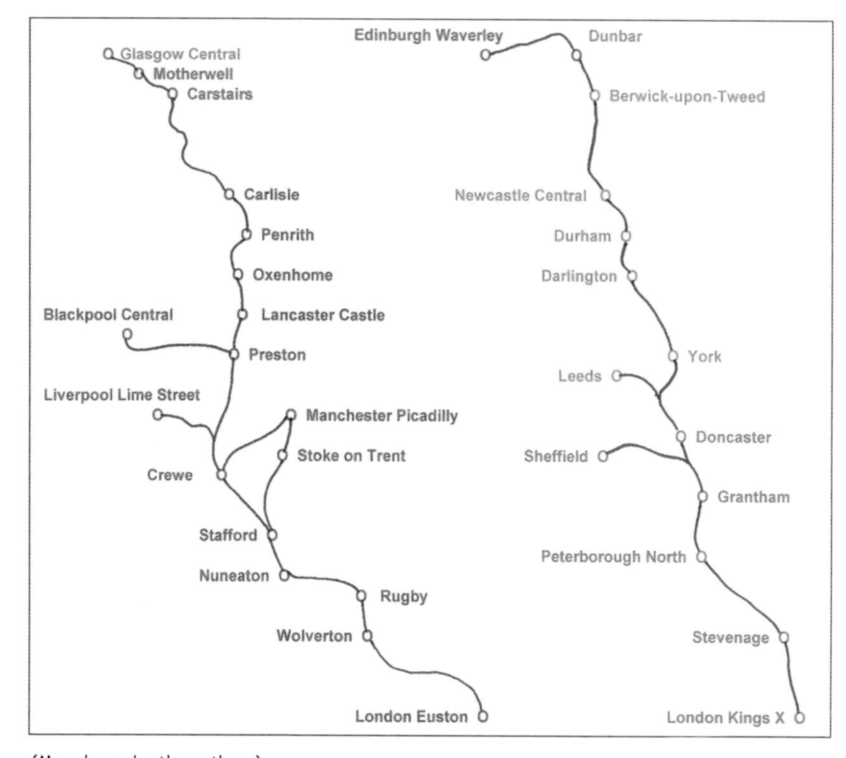

(Map drawn by the authors)

If we thought the WCML had some good totem names, just look at the ECML, on the right above. **Kings Cross**, **Peterborough North**, **Grantham**, **Newark Northgate**, **York**, **Darlington**, and **Berwick upon Tweed** is an incredible set, and we dare to suggest, impossible to obtain! If you travel further north out of Edinburgh, you could add **Inverkeithing**, **Dundee Tay Bridge** and **Montrose**. The WCML would be maroon to light blue but the ECML is dark blue to tangerine to light blue.

The two maps above reflect the totem colour changes you would have seen as you moved north out of London on these respective routes. Of course there are major branches from each of the main routes serving large cities. On the WCML all lines seem to join at Crewe, with routes from Chester, Derby, Shrewsbury and Manchester all branching off the main south to north route. On the ECML Lincoln, Sheffield, Leeds and Bradford all branch from this main artery. We have put three totems from each route together in the small collage that follows.

Just this set of six would grace any wall! (And we have included the real classics elsewhere in this book.)

The WR mainline out of **Paddington** also contained some wonderful names. The southern lines split at **Reading** and rejoin at **Taunton**, while the South Wales arm runs north from Bristol. The map below is just the southern portion of the WR, and almost any of the names on this map are desirable to WR fans.

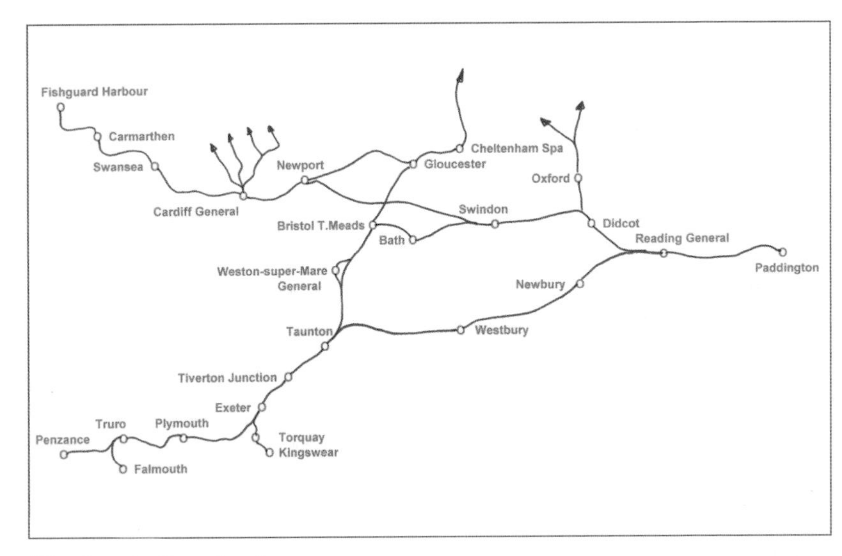

(Map drawn by the authors)

A superb western quartet is shown below:

You may decide that a mainline collection is not for you and that a cross-country route or the local branch is a more personal alternative. Ideally, try to collect a line that nobody else is working on. We appreciate that this is difficult to do, unless you are in contact with many other collectors and you swap information (and sometimes totems). Here, we have found *Totem Exchange* of some benefit in recent years. Just reading a list of wanted items gives a good pointer as to the theme of somebody's collection. We know of several people trying for the North Wales route, Cambrian routes, the S&D from Bath to Bournemouth and the Waverley route from Carlisle to Edinburgh, to name just four. Knowing the history of these routes and the names involved, we can understand why these are desirable. If we took just one totem from these four routes, we would have yet another stunning quartet, so maybe aiming a bit lower and going for one of each from the classic routes is an idea?

Another possible theme may be the local stations from your own county, real or adopted – because it may be the county of your youth, a former trainspotting centre or where you now live. It is surprising how many of us are now living miles away from where we were born and grew up. The real seeds of collecting are sown where we spent (or mis-spent) our youth. Within our fraternity there is a concentration of collectors in London, the West Midlands, Derby/Nottingham, Lancashire and Yorkshire. We could take this theme a stage further and extend it to a whole county (this is the reason we have included the old county against each of the stations listed in the appropriate chapters). The basis for the county data is the 1958–60 era, when most of the totems were in place. We have cross-checked the county for every station against old OS maps. Collecting counties is actually quite popular. In England, for example, Rutland had only five stations with totems and these are shown below along with **Gretton** (Northants). Deviating slightly, how about collecting town names in different colours? For **Newport** fans a great quartet is also shown alongside! Either of the Scottish **Newport-on-Tay** totems would complete this set, as Newport (Tees-side) did not have totems. Shame!

(Mike Harris)

In some of the Scottish counties only a few towns and villages had railway access. Roxburghshire is a case in point: with the quartet shown below plus **Melrose** and **Rutherford** totems you would have the set!

We know of collectors looking at Cornwall, Derbyshire, Devon, Gloucestershire, Leicestershire, Lincolnshire, Norfolk, Nottinghamshire, Oxfordshire, Shropshire and Suffolk. Anybody trying for Kent, Lanarkshire, Lancashire, Renfrewshire, Surrey or Yorkshire is going to have a mighty big collection! Even those collecting the smaller counties such as Berkshire, Herefordshire or Northamptonshire have a very difficult task to complete the whole set.

Popular themes

Possibly one of the most popular themes of today is seaside towns. Many of these lie on the south coast, so here we may choose **Penzance**, **Torquay**, **Budleigh Salterton**, **Weymouth**, **Bournemouth West**, **Brighton**, or **Eastbourne**. As we progress up the east coast we could include **Clacton**, **Frinton**, **Lowestoft**, **Hunstanton**, **Scarborough**, **Whitby**, and **St Andrews**. Coming down the west coast, we could name **Blackpool**, **Colwyn Bay**, **Criccieth**, **Portmadoc**, **Aberystwyth** and **Tenby**. And moving further south into Somerset, Devon and Cornwall is the fantastic quintet of **Weston-Super-Mare**, **Ilfracombe**, **Bude**, **St Ives** and **Carbis Bay**.

We know of at least one eminent collector going through the locomotives works and engine sheds. Here you could have **Brighton**, **Darlington**, **Haymarket**, **Stratford**, **Swindon**, and **Willesden Junction** (note again, one from each region). Christian names are another popular theme and here we have a large number to choose from (though not many with our own names on). Such totems, in alphabetical order, include: **St Andrews**, **St Annes**, **Alexandra Parade**, **Allanfearn**, **Ashley**, **Barry**, **Ben Rhydding**, **Beverley**, **Bradley Fold**, **Burton Joyce**, **Castle Douglas**, **Chester Road**, **Clare**, **Craigendoran**, **Davenport**, **Exeter St Davids**, **Dean Lane**, **Douglas West**, **Dudley**, **Exeter St Thomas**, **ort William**, **Glen** (appears on several Scottish totems), **Harrietsham**, **Hazel Grove**, **Helensburgh**, **Johnston** (WR), **Johnstone** (ScR), **Jordanhill**, **Keith Junction** (or **Town**), 15 totems begin with **Ken**, **Kimberley**, **Kings Lynn**, **Kirkby Stephen East**, there are several **Kirks**, **Lampeter**, **Lawrence Hill**, **Lee**, **Lenham**, **Lincoln St Marks**, **Manuel**, **Markinch**, **Marks Tey**, **Martin Mill**, **Mary** (on four totems), **Maxton**, **Maxwell Park**, **Micklefield**, **Moira**, **Normanton**, **Old Kilpatrick**, **Patricroft**, **Percy Main**, **Peter** (four totems), **Rose Grove**, **Rose Hill**, **Roy Bridge**, **St Helens**, **St Budeaux Victoria Road**, **St James Street**, **St Johns**, **St Lukes**, **St Margarets**, **St Michaels**, **Scotstoun**, **Shirley**, **Sidcup**, **Stanlow & Thornton**, **Stevenage**, **Swansea Victoria**, **West St Leonards**, **Whitecraigs**, **Williamwood**. We have included a set of six selected from this large list, including two ladies' names.

If trying to find your surname on a totem gives you a thrill, then there are many to choose from (including the colours Green, White, Brown, Black, etc.). Fortunately for us there are two with our surname on, but unfortunately neither is Brennand. So we are left with **Furness Vale** and **Kirkby in Furness**.

Sport can be interpreted several ways – this may be the location where the game is played (**Old Trafford**, **Ibrox** and **Hampden Park**), or something more 'off the wall' such as **Badminton**, **Bat & Ball**, **Denham Golf Club**, or **Wembley Stadium**. Then there are the famous horse racing courses for the punters among us, such as **Epsom Downs**, **Aintree**, **Chepstow** and **Lingfield**. (The story of wooden totems at **Gatwick Racecourse** is given in Chapter 5.) Golf courses appear as **St Andrews**, **Hoylake**, **Birkdale**, **Sandwich**, **Carnoustie** and **Gleneagles**, to name but a few. This sextet is really quite elusive, but not impossible. Finally, trees, plants, and even types of wood are known to have been the basic themes of some collections. Millions enjoy gardening, and thousands of people are employed in this and the forestry industry, so this is a more popular theme than many of us would realise. Remember, however, that certain totems carry some of the most delightful names, often belying the fact that the actual town or city suburb is much less salubrious!

Other suggested themes

Here you are only limited by your imagination. You may choose just sheer rarity, or pick from a variety of ideas such as only those with lower panel wording, junctions, cathedral cities, or words on the totem such as City, Town or Village. We know of several people who have based their own collections on such themes; indeed both of us use one from this list. Take cathedral cities for example. Here travelling from south to north we can include **Truro**, **Exeter**, **Salisbury**, **Winchester**, **Portsmouth**, **Guildford**, **Canterbury**, **Rochester**, **St Albans**, **Chelmsford**, **Ely**, **Bury St Edmunds**, **Cambridge**, **Oxford**, **Bristol**, **Cardiff** (actually **Llandaff for Whitchurch**), **Gloucester**, **Hereford**, **Worcester**, **Birmingham**, **Coventry**, **Derby**, **Southwell**, **Nottingham**, **Leicester**, **Peterborough**, Sheffield, **Lincoln**, **Manchester**, Liverpool, **Blackburn**, **Wakefield**, **Bradford**, **Leeds**, **Ripon**, **York**, **Carlisle**, Durham, Glasgow, Edinburgh, **Dunblane**, **St Andrews** and **Elgin**. It would have been wonderful if those not in bold had been fitted, so one of us will never complete the collection!

Another really popular theme could simply be items from the same region. Below is a small Southern collection. Another common theme is collecting lower panelled items, and this could also be combined with a regional theme as shown in the second picture below. This Western octet is from a private collector in the Midlands.

We mentioned totems and posters earlier. Some very evocative seaside posters were produced to advertise the holiday camps so popular in the '50s. These were the heydays of 'Hi-de-hi' at Butlins and Pontins. This would actually form an interesting collection, with **Minehead**, **Filey**, **Bognor Regis**, **Clacton**, **Skegness**, **Morecambe**, and **Penychain** among the set. If we then put the totem with the poster we have a wonderful sight, such as this **Clacton** pair below.

(Courtesy National Railway Museum/Science & Society Picture Library)

One collector is looking at birds and animals as a theme, again so that totems from all regions can be put together. In this list we can include **Blackhorse Road** (ER), **Catford Bridge** (SR), **Rathen** (ScR – two in one here!), **Hawkesbury Lane**

(MR), **Batley** (NER) and **Fishguard Harbour** (WR). It is therefore possible to have one of each colour with almost any theme you choose. Most people, however, stay local, and we close this chapter with three photos from other private collections.

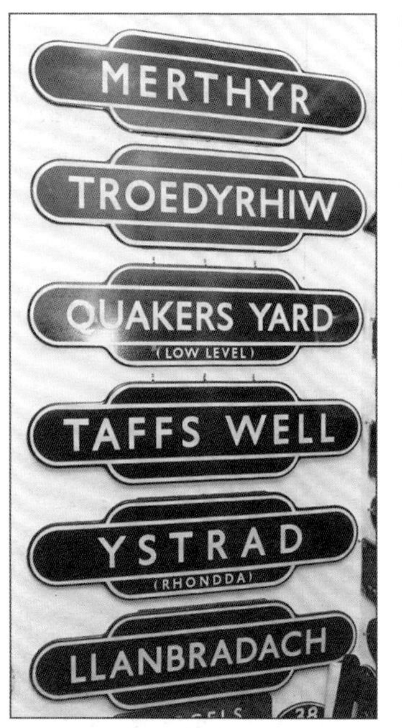

CHAPTER

5 The Rare and Unusual

Introduction

Although the design of totems was supposed to be standardised, there are many examples of items not conforming to the standard. The variations include letter layout, letter size, totem shape, colour and even basic materials. Nearly all totems were enamelled metal, but we have instances of wooden and plastic totems being used. There were variations in the colours used and some of the North Eastern region totems had their lettering edged in black. Also, in later years the Western Region experimented with black and white totems at a few selected stations. The purpose of this chapter is to discuss and document just some of the large number of variants we have come across in our research. Some of these are quite rare and others not so rare. We would stress, however, that our comments should not be taken as a statement on rarity value. We are probably in the same situation as everybody else with regard to correctly estimating totem values in today's market – that is, hit and miss!

The Western Region oddities and rarities

Some of the very first Western Region totems were flangeless, with a variation in the curvature in the upper and lower sections of the sign. As far as we are aware, these were only found at **Little Kimble**, **Moreton-in-Marsh** and **Radstock West**. We show a **Radstock West** totem below, with the face drillings clearly visible. It was common to have weathering around these holes.

There were two other early signs, considerably longer and narrower than the conventional totem. These had a flattened, almost 'squashed' totem shape on an enamelled sheet. They were only found at **Helston** in Cornwall and **Kings Nympton** in Devon. Quite why these locations were chosen is a mystery, but the signs are certainly most unusual as shown by **Helston**, following.

The Western Region also used large circular signs at two important locations: **Birmingham Snow Hill** and **Bristol Temple Meads**. These signs, termed 'roundels', were fully flanged and just over 34in in diameter. The totem in the centre was almost full size, at 32in long by 9.5in wide. These items were carried on the building walls inside the main roof area. Conventional totems were also used at the ends of the main platforms at both stations.

Conventional **Birmingham Snow Hill** totems appear on the railwayana scene from time to time, but those from **Bristol Temple Meads** have yet to surface. We suspect that these two stations were regarded as key locations on the WR network (outside **Paddington**), and it was just possible that the management wanted to show this importance. We therefore wonder why **Swindon** was not selected as well, being the 'home' of the former GWR with the major locomotive works. We can only speculate about the true reason why just two stations were chosen, but there is no denying how unusual they are. (As an added bonus, 'roundels' make excellent coffee tables!).

The WR also had one totem quite different to any other, at the Butlins holiday camp station **Penychain** in Caernarvonshire, where blue and yellow signs were fitted. Clearly there must have been an agreement between the BR Board and Butlins. There were Butlins camps in other parts of the UK, including **Minehead** and **Blackpool**. As branch termini they could also have been blue and yellow. However, this was not to be, as these stations were not dedicated purely to the holiday camps. Heads of Ayr was another Butlins location, but the station did not have totems. Below is the unique sign from **Penychain**.

The WR also experimented in the '60s with black and white signs. These were specially ordered, and below we have included two particularly superb examples from **Hayes & Harlington** and **Langley (Bucks)** on the WR main line out of **Paddington**.

Similar signs could also to be found at **Bourne End**, **Devonport**, and **Torquay**. The sign at **Torquay** (Gill Sans lettering) was doubly unusual, as this was the only plastic item on the entire WR. The 'chunky' lettering at **Bourne End** and **Langley (Bucks)** was distinctly non-standard!

Overpainting occurred in a few instances that we have been able to determine for this region. Strangely, some **Kensington Olympia** totems ended up with 'reverse colours'. Upon closure of the main line platforms at **Willesden Junction** in 1962, some of the surplus totems were then re-used at **Kensington Olympia**. They are unusual (looking like a bad negative) and not so appealing as the standard chocolate and cream sign (note the red of the original totem underneath). In the photographs that follow, compare this variant with other conventional signs from the same station. It is possible that some **Willesden Junction** totems only survive owing to their re-use.

Other instances of overpainting were on the former GWR/GCR joint main line through **High Wycombe** and **Princes Risborough**. The following stations were overpainted black and white: **Paddington**, **Denham**, **Denham Golf Club**, **Gerrards Cross**, **Sear Green & Jordans**, **Beaconsfield**, **High Wycombe** and **Princes Risborough**. It is suspected this was the first attempt at a corporate image. Two black and white totems from **Malvern Link** were discovered some years ago. When one of these was cleaned with paint stripper a perfect chocolate and cream sign was revealed – a blessing in disguise we could say! We have included a shot of the totem as found in the database – a most unusual item, for which Simon Turner deserves our thanks.

The totems from **Highbridge for Burnham-on-Sea** were available in two designs. In Chapter 7 we have included one variant in the database (the FF version). Below is the second type with the '&' on the top line of the totem (the HF version).

The same also applies to **Seer Green & Jordans**. Totems are available with either 'and' or '&' in the main body of the sign, but here all the signs were fully flanged. Some of the half-flanged WR totems were produced with enamelled brown flanges. These included those at **Borth**, **Exeter (St Thomas)**, **Instow** and **Stroud**. There are rumours that the first station to be fitted with totems was **West Ealing** on the main line from **Paddington**. If this is true we suspect these may have been up for more than 20 years.

The final area we want to address in this region is the wide variation in colour. This ranges from a real dark chocolate brown to almost a mid-brown. There were also variations because of weathering, but these are clearly detectable. There is no denying there were real differences between the later full-flanged totems and those first made. Contrast a dark brown from **Leominster** with the mid-brown of **Great Malvern**. Of course colour depends very much on environment and totem age.

Finally, no matter how much research and work we may have done, the unexpected still happens. This was the case a few years ago when a totem from **Carbis Bay**, a small Cornish station on the branch to **St Ives**, suddenly appeared. Needless to say it caused a real buzz throughout the totem-collecting world and was quickly sold through Sheffield Railwayana Auctions.

The Eastern Region oddities and rarities

The Eastern Region had some totems that are unique. There were fewer colour variations than on any of the other five regions, because it was difficult to move away from the basic colour; nevertheless there are some 'oddballs'. The first of these variations was lettering size, which was both larger and smaller than the prescribed height. Large letters appeared at **Beccles**, **Diss**, **Elm Park**, **Holmes**, **Rayleigh**, **Skegness**, **Thetford**, **Wickford** and **Witham**. The letters on these totems were 3.5in high instead of the standard 3in. (These are spread across the region, so this policy was not local.) We show examples from Thetford in Norfolk and Holmes (closed 1955) in Yorkshire. The large letters seem out of scale when compared with conventional totems.

There were also two unusual totems where small lettering appeared in the middle of the name. These were **Hopton on Sea** and **Saxham and Risby**. The **Saxham and Risby** totem is shown below.

Some early ER totems were made the standard 36in long, but were narrower, being only 9.5in wide compared to the usual 10in standard. These curiosities appeared at **Halesworth**, **Heath**, **Pitsea**, **Roydon**, **Shoeburyness**, **Thorpe Bay**, **Tilbury Town** and **Upminster Bridge**. They tended to suffer from fading more than the later totems.

The final oddity in this region is the totem from Torksey in Lincolnshire (or should that be **Torkesey**). The town, between **Lincoln** and **Retford**, has the spelling without the first 'e'. The reason for the totem being spelt with the additional 'e' is baffling. **Whittlesea** in Cambridgeshire is a similar curiosity – as the town is actually called Whittlesey.

The region has some rare items and totems eagerly sought by collectors from stations that were 'sanitised' early on. All the stations at **Southend-on-Sea** (**Central**, **East** and **Victoria**) had their totems removed early in the '60s. They all had a life-span of less than 10 years – what a waste! The stations were large, so the number of items involved was considerable. A similar fate was in store for the totems at **Grantham**, **Retford**, **Cambridge**, and **Ely**. In 2000 a **Retford** totem turned up unexpectedly at a Malton auction.

All the totems from **Southend-on-Sea** were lower panel and none have been seen since they were removed. Just to prove the Southend stations had totems, we have included a lovely black and white image below showing **Southend Central** in the mid-1950s. The totems are clearly in place! (In Chapter 8 there are also official BR shots of **Southend-on-Sea Victoria** *in situ* in 1956).

(British Rail)

Other major rarities from this region include **Barnsley Exchange**, **Cambridge**, **Colchester**, **Hatfield**, **Newark Castle**, **Newark Northgate**, **Newmarket**, **Stamford Town** and **Westcliff on Sea**. There are many totems still to be accounted for from Essex and from what is now the county of South Yorkshire. We truly hope several of these have been squirrelled away to reappear at sometime in the future!

The Southern Region oddities and rarities

This region has many variations, including lettering, colours and basic material. These are the use of non-Gill Sans letters (see Chapter 6), three shades of green for the basic totem, flanges that were produced in black or white and quite a few 'home-made' totems using wood. Other variations include all green totems, 4ft totems, and the only totem where the complete city name appears in lower case letters in the lower panel. The early totems produced were all half flanged and were of the dark green variety.

We believe that as fully flanged totems were introduced there was random colour and flange selection, but lighter green gradually became more predominant. To support this belief, notice how many lighter green totems you now find that are in very good or mint condition.

Next, we look at the white and black flange variants. Most Southern stations had the conventional white lettering, white lines and white flanges. However, some stations were fitted with both white and black flanged totems alongside each other, while some stations had black flanges only. The database contains details of the style installed at each station. We have listed almost sixty different stations with this black flange variation (about 12 per cent of the total) in Chapter 6. The black flange seems to frame the totem nicely, as shown by comparing **Whitstable & Tankerton** (black flange) to **Portsmouth & Southsea** (white flange).

Totems that were all green (with no white lines) were installed at six Southern stations: **Appledore**, some **Clapham Junction**, some **Wraysbury**, some **Margate**, some **Bromley South** and **Exeter Central**. They all look curiously unfinished as evidenced by the 4ft **Clapham Junction** totem below. Somehow, the white lines across the body really complete the look of the totem.

The totem from **London Road (Guildford)** is unique. It is the only one where a city name appears in the lower panel in lower case lettering. The only explanation we can find for this layout is to distinguish it from either **London Road High Level** (a *Midland* totem some 100 miles away in Nottingham!) or more likely from London Road (Brighton), which only had targets anyway! Whatever the reason, it is an oddity, but still desirable.

Wooden totems appeared at several locations. We have been able to determine that these included **Appledore** (Kent, not Devon), **Axminster**, **Clandon**, **Gatwick Racecourse**, **Holborn Viaduct**, and some at **London Bridge**. The Appledore signs are believed to have been used at **Bromley South** and then repainted.

(Colin Tyson)

The signs from **Gatwick Racecourse** are a real curiosity. They were apparently only used on race days, and were hand made by station staff. While totems were 'unofficial' at some locations, the one shown above appears to be official. The top layer is printed paper pasted to a wooden board with evidence of another pasted version underneath. Notice also that the curved sections are much steeper than on conventional design, like the early signs from **Radstock West**.

Totems 4ft in length were found at **Clapham Junction**, **Exeter Central** and at **Weymouth**. Both **Clapham** and **Weymouth** also had conventional 3ft totems. The **Clapham** and **Exeter** 4ft items were all green but the **Weymouth** 4ft totems had the conventional white lines.

Overpainting occurred at **Folkestone Junction** (some overpainted on **Kenley**) and at **Maiden Newton** (black and white, same name over the green and white totem). Some **Buxted** signs were painted over former all green **Wraysbury** signs. **Bere Ferres** totems were painted over totems formerly used at **Bingham Road**. Some **Ifield** totems were painted over **St Helier** signs. Totems from **Twickenham** are a curious shade of lime green, quite unlike any other in the region. There are some very desirable items in Southern territory; including anything from the old S&D line into Bath, Cornish and some Devon 'greens', i.e. **Barnstaple Town**, **Bridestowe**, **Bude**, **Callington**, **Combpyne**, **Okehampton**, **Seaton**, **Wadebridge** and **Yeoford**. For a time a **Bude** totem held the record price at £850 per letter!

There are also many rarities that have yet to see the light of day. These include **Alton**, **Bexhill Central**, **Crayford**, **Gravesend West**, **Lancing**, **Northfleet**, **Ottery St Mary**, **Reading South**, **Staines Central** and **Whitchurch North**. The station at **Reading South** was renamed **Reading (Southern)** in 1961 and several of these later items have appeared at auction. The elusive Reading South is shown *in situ* below.

The North Eastern Region oddities and rarities

This region had the smallest number of different stations carrying totems (125) and many of these are real collectable items. Uniquely the region had black-edged lettering (BEL) on some of the later produced items. It has been speculated that this was to help the traveller read the station name as he passed through, or to make them easier to read in those rare periods of bright sunlight! Whatever the reason, all the later batches had the black-edged letters added during the manufacturing process. A superb example from **Saltburn** is shown below:

The NER totems were either a bright tangerine or a darker shade of orange. Both colours appeared on the full flange types, but only the dark orange was used on the earlier half flanged designs. BEL was used on both colours. Below are examples of the two distinct shades, both with and without BEL

Certain NER totems carried wide 1in flanges: this design was unique to the NER. We would speculate that they came from a different manufacturer. They were almost impossible to bend – therefore durable and almost vandal proof! Some totems from **Burton Salmon**, **Ferrybridge**, **Scarborough Central**, **Wakefield Kirkgate** and **Whitby Town** carried examples of this design.

Other curious NER totems were those with tangerine flanges. These were quite distinctive in appearance and did not have black edged lettering. Examples of this style came from **Garforth**, **Pontefract**, **Prudhoe** and **Redcar East**. It seems strange to see tangerine outside the white lines, as shown in the side-on shot of **Garforth** and the superb **Redcar East**.

Two totems are uniquely enamelled with tangerine on the reverse. These came from **Darlington** and **Wakefield Kirkgate**. Some of the early **South Shields** totems were also very unusual: they were enamelled with the station name on both sides. A few years ago we had not heard of such a beast, but first-hand inspection has confirmed a genuine article.

The region has some wonderfully desirable items. Top of most collectors' lists might be a **York**, closely followed by **Scarborough Central**, **Whitby Town**, **Whitby West Cliff** or a host of other examples. In 2000 the fully flanged **York** totem was returned to its former intended location, as it appears this item was made as a spare but never used. The photo below compares the old with the new – we know which we prefer!

The great stations of Newcastle Central and Durham did not carry totems, but at Durham lovely rectangular lamp tablets around 18in in length were used. These dark orange signs were installed during the LNER administration, and survived for many years into BR ownership. This is where the unusual choice of tangerine for the NER totems probably came from. An example is shown below.

The area saw the first commercial railway in the world, which opened between **Stockton** and **Darlington** in 1825. Following is the pair of NER totems from this most famous British railway line. Note the difference the black-edged lettering makes on the **Stockton** totem.

The London Midland Region oddities and rarities

The Midland Region has its share of oddities and curiosities. Totems were supposed to be lettered in Gill Sans, with the height dependent on the number of letters in the name. Therefore we are not sure where the layout and design for **Besses o' th' Barn** comes from. This station is north of Manchester and closed in 1991 while the Tramlink was built, then reopened a year later by the Greater Manchester Passenger Transport Executive (GMPTE).

This region carried more of the 4ft variety totems than any other. These could be found at **Broad Street**, **Brondesbury**, **Harrow and Wealdstone**, **Liverpool Central Low Level**, **Manchester Central**, **Queens Park**, **Sandhills**, **South Kenton** and **Watford High Street**. Of these, only **Liverpool Central** (LL) and **Queens Park** did not have standard totems as well. The Liverpool Central totem (the only one where the actual city name appears) follows.

The **Manchester Central** 4ft totem (two-line version) had a completely different layout to the conventional 3ft sign shown alongside it below.

A very large totem, about 6ft long, was used at Liverpool James Street on the station wall, and a photo of this appeared in the July 1957 edition of *The Railway Magazine*. It was not possible to ascertain whether this was enamel or not. Roundels were used at James Street and Hamilton Square on the opposite sides of the Mersey. These were very similar to the GWR items described earlier but half the size. They did not carry the totem image or shape.

Quite a few totems were face drilled and these are identified in the database pages. Overpainting also featured on some totems. We have examples noted from **Wembley Stadium** (over **Watford Junction**), **Dent** (over **Burnley Central**), **Bletchley** (over **Berkhamsted**) and a few items from **Leicester Central** and **Rugby Central**, which had previously been used elsewhere. Some **Fleetwood** signs actually ended up being re-used in Scotland! The photograph below shows such a sign after first cleaning, with the light blue paint clearly evident. It would have been interesting to note in which location they were re-used north of the border.

A dilemma arises if you acquired a painted totem – do you leave it as purchased or return it to its former identity? Would you want **Watford Junction** or **Wembley Stadium** for example? The unusually painted **Wembley Stadium** follows.

As with the other regions there were distinct differences in the colours of some totems. The normal shade is exemplified with **Mansfield Woodhouse**, but alongside it is a much darker totem from **Penkridge** in Staffordshire.

The town of Bettws-y-Coed in North Wales had the station signs spelt **Betws-y-Coed** for some reason. **Town Green & Aughton** signs had peculiar small letters.

Horton-in-Ribblesdale had totems made in wood by the station staff, allegedly. Other curiosities from this region were the rectangular signs (as shown below) that hung on the station at Trent in Nottinghamshire. We are unsure whether this was meant to be a totem derivative, but it is certainly enamel, certainly made for BR and station-used. Does this make it a totem? We think not. Alongside it is the usual design of direction sign that pointed to the station.

The region has some real classic totems. We could name **Bassenthwaite Lake**, **Carlisle**, **Settle**, **Shap**, **Derby Friargate**, or **Besses o' th' Barn** as the regional classics, but this is only our opinion. Some of these are quite rare and the full list of rarities can be found by consulting our database pages in Chapter 9.

Finally we would like to finish this short review of the LMR oddities and rarities with the story of the **Burton-on-Trent** totem. This passed through auction at Sheffield in 2000 and is the only known survivor from this location. It was actually rescued from not one but two disposal skips – a rare distinction indeed! The battered condition is a testament to its history, but we are glad an example has lived on.

The Scottish Region oddities and rarities

This was a very large area with the second highest number of totems (517). When this number is combined with those from the LMR (the enlarged LMS region) the result is almost half the total number of different totems made. Considering just Scotland, there were surprisingly few oddities associated with this region. Wooden totems appeared at **Balmossie Halt**, **Barry Links** and **Golf Street Halt**. Some plastic totems were used at **Portobello**, east of Edinburgh and **Girvan** in Ayrshire. As with other regions, there were differences in the basic shade, as illustrated by the darker blue of **Alexandria** and the light blue from **Dumbarton Central** (both in the county of Dunbartonshire).

When it comes to classic names and rarities, Scotland has them in abundance! There are just too many to list, so we refer the reader to the database tables in Chapter 11. From the possibilities, we have selected just one of the true classics. However, we would point out that **Kyle of Lochalsh** carried at least 12 totems in 1974 – so be patient!

July 1978. (Alan Young)

Totems were still *in situ* at many locations in Scotland well into the late '70s and early '80s. The photo above is pure ScR – wonderful Scottish stone, evocative Caledonian Railway clock, the old lamp and totem, all untouched. For a short period totems were used alongside the new 'corporate image' signs, as at **Crianlarich Upper** in Perthshire.

August 1970. (Alan Young)

Stations renamed

A number of stations were renamed during the totem era. The totems with the old name were removed and replaced by signs carrying the new name. The survival of the older totem depends critically on the date of the renaming. Prior to 1964 there were no co-ordinated totem sales and the only interest came from a few far-sighted people. Consequently many totems bearing the older names were scrapped. The following are known to have had totems with both names:

Old name	Renamed	Date of renaming
Barmouth Junction	**Morfa Mawddach**	June 1960
Dolgelley	**Dolgellau**	September 1960
Folkestone Junction	**Folkestone East**	September 1962
Halifax Town	**Halifax**	June 1961
Harringay West	**Harringay**	May 1971
Hyde Junction	**Hyde North**	September 1951
Moorthorpe & South Kirkby	**Moorthorpe**	June 1961
Partick Central	**Kelvin Hall**	June 1959
Reading South	**Reading (Southern)**	September 1961
Sawley Junction	**Long Eaton**	May 1968
Waldron & Horam	**Horam**	September 1953
West Weybridge	**Byfleet & New Haw**	June 1962

A rare survivor here is the battered sign from **Waldron & Horam** – see Chapter 6.

Factors in rarity assessment

We have titled this chapter 'The Rare and Unusual', but what makes a totem rare? There are many factors, including:

1. How many were on the station?
2. How many have survived?
3. When was the station re-signed, or when were the totems removed?
4. Is the colour or layout unusual?
5. Are there unusual words on the totem (Platform, Tunnel, Viaduct, etc.)?

We would hasten to add that the prices made by totems at auction do not always relate to their rarity. Some common totems have made high prices simply because two people wanted them badly enough. The next time they appear in auction the price is often lower, simply because the competitive edge has gone. In this respect totems are really nicer versions of stocks and shares. Their value may (and does) fluctuate and there is no guarantee that purchases made for investment turn out to be so. We, and many of our fellow collectors, just want them because of their intrinsic qualities – real collecting!

We have commented on factors 1 to 4 throughout this chapter, for each of the six regions, and close with comments on some of the more unusual wording that can be found on a few totems. Below, we list a few guidance notes on the appendages used in each region:

ER: The word 'Junction' appears only three times (only once in the lower panel)
'Halt' appears only twice (once in the lower panel)
'Castle' appears twice
'Beach' appears once
'Garden' appears twice

MR: 'Junction' appears many times, but only once in the lower panel
'Halt' appears several times, but never in the lower panel
'Lake' and 'Port' appear only twice each
'Promenade' appears once
'Stadium' appears once (painted version)
'Castle' appears three times

NER: 'Junction' and 'Halt' do not appear in this region
'Colliery' and 'Square' appear once each

ScR: 'Junction' appears several times, but only once in the lower panel
'Halt' rarely appears in Scotland (curious given the size of some stations)
'Ferry' appears four times
'Pier' and 'Port' appear once each
'Platform' appears once
'Stadium' appears once

SR/WR: 'Halt' and 'Junction' are common for these regions

SR: 'Viaduct' appears once
'Beach' appears once
'Colliery' appears once

WR: 'Tunnel' appears only once
'Platform' and 'Port' appear once each

A most unusual combination of names is shown below.

There were also totem signs at Bowness Pier on Lake Windermere and we wonder if anybody can confirm if Ambleside Pier at the northern end of the lake also had totems? We have purposely not included this in the database, as it is not a railway station – as you can see!

Bowness Pier on Lake Windermere with two totems *in situ*. (Author's collection)

The perfect match for the picture above!

The only enamelled Scottish Halt totem.

DORCHESTER WEST
BATTERSEA PARK
FARNBOROUGH NORTH
HARRIETSHAM
NEWHAVEN HARBOUR
BIRCHINGTON-ON-SEA
WEST ST. LEONARDS

OCKLEY & CAPEL
UCKFIELD

BRIDESTOWE
WORTHING CENTRAL
LOUGHBOROUGH JUNCTION
QUEENBOROUGH
BOURNEMOUTH WEST
WOOLWICH DOCKYARD
ROCHESTER

SOUTHERN REGION TOTEMS

CHAPTER

6

The Southern Region

Introduction

Lush green pasture and fertile soils blend with gentle contours as the railway weaves an intricate web of lines across southern England. Hardly surprising is the fact that so many millions of people choose this area to live and work in. Perfectly situated between the capital and the coastal resorts are hundreds of timeless villages, where a short train ride can provide business or pleasure. For the totem collector, we have a marvellous concentration to choose from (138 in Kent alone!). Whether you require a reminder of your daily commute or a perfect bygone holiday, there is something for all tastes here.

(Courtesy National Railway Museum/Science & Industry)

History of the Southern Region

The Southern Railway, the smallest of the 'Big Four' at the 1923 grouping, owed its origins to three companies formed in the second quarter of the nineteenth century. These three, in order of size, were the London & South Western Railway (LSWR), the London, Brighton & South Coast Railway (LBSCR) and the South Eastern & Chatham Railway (SECR). One of the very first railways – the **Canterbury** and **Whitstable**, which opened in May 1830 – is located in the region. There were also early lines between London and **Greenwich** (1836), Nine Elms to Woking (1838), and London to Croydon (1839).

The LSWR started life as the London and Southampton Railway, before the absorption of the L&S in 1839. Nine Elms was the London terminus before the extension into **Waterloo** in 1848. Southampton to Winchester opened in 1839 and the lines into the naval area at **Portsmouth** were completed in 1841. Developments to the west came thick and fast with, first Southampton through Dorchester to **Salisbury** in 1847, then Andover in 1854 (from **Basingstoke**), and **Exeter** in 1860. Once in the West Country, the LSWR expanded rapidly, with **Okehampton**, Lydford, **Barnstaple** and **Ilfracombe** all being tied to the rail network. Plymouth Friary, however, was not reached until 1891, and **Bude** and Padstow a further seven years later. Little further construction occurred after the turn of the century and the network of just over 1,000 miles contributed almost half of the Southern Railway's 2,200 miles at the Grouping in 1923.

Portsmouth Harbour with dark green enamels adorning the station. (R. Blencowe)

The LBSCR formed through an amalgamation of the London & Brighton Railway with the London & Croydon in 1846. During the same year the Brighton, Hastings and Lewes Railway joined, and these lines were then extended west to Chichester, Havant and **Portsmouth**.

Further construction to **Wivelsfield**, Horsham, **Three Bridges** and **Eastbourne** occurred before the main terminus at Victoria was opened in 1860. Lines throughout Sussex and Kent were built from 1860 until 1880, including stations at **Shoreham**, **Guildford**, **Pulborough**, **Littlehampton**, **Tunbridge Wells**, **Leatherhead** and **Uckfield**. Although the second oldest member of the Southern companies, LBSCR building was not as prolific as the other two main members, so that some 450 miles of lines became the property of the Southern Railway in 1923.

The third member was the SECR, which owned around 460 miles of railway by 1923. It was formed relatively late in 1899, when the South Eastern Railway and the London, Dover & Chatham Railway pooled their resources and skills. The SER main line running from London to Dover was progressively opened from 1842 until 1844. Lines were also opened to **Paddock Wood** (1844), **Tonbridge** (1845), **Reading**, **Guildford** and Reigate (all 1849), **Strood** (1852), **Ramsgate** (1856) **Margate** (1856), **Lewisham** (1857) and Beckenham (1857). The SECR opened **Charing Cross** in 1864 and **Cannon Street** two years later. The LDCR had its roots in the East Kent Railway, beginning with the line from **Faversham** to **Strood** in 1858, extending to Dover in 1861. Further expansion saw lines open to Crystal Palace and **Herne Bay** in 1861, then **Margate** in 1863.

The Isle of Wight had an equally complex history with three companies operating different routes, namely **Newport** to Cowes in 1862, Ryde St John's to Shanklin in 1864 and Shanklin to Ventnor in 1866. There was also the short LSWR/LBSCR route from St John's Road to Ryde Pierhead via Esplanade, opening in 1880.

The Southern Railway was, in some respects, more far-sighted than the other three of the 'Big Four', through the use of electric traction before the First World War (in 1905). It was amazing to think that while Stanier was designing Pacific locomotives for the LMS, the SR was undertaking widespread electrification in Hampshire and Sussex. This may explain why their steam locomotives appear to be less charismatic than the Kings, Castles, A3s, A4s, Princesses and Duchesses of the other three companies (though most SR purists would certainly object to this observation!). At the same time as building railway lines in Devon and Cornwall (around Torrington, for example), they were closing others. By far the most famous of these was the narrow gauge Lynton and Barnstaple, which closed in 1936. Hopefully this may re-appear in the not-too-distant future!

Geography of the region

The physical geography of this region was relatively easy for the railway engineer to work with, as there were few major obstacles on their numerous routes. The system stretched as far as genteel Padstow in Cornwall, which is some 260 miles from **Waterloo**. The high concentration of people residing in Kent and Surrey resulted in some of the most complicated junctions ever seen, along with hundreds of miles of viaducts to carry large numbers of trains into London each day. The region's geography is characterised by three distinctive areas: (1) the many popular seaside towns of the '20s and '30s along the south-east coast, (2) the North and South Downs in the central part of the region, and (3) the rolling hills of Dorset and Devon in the west. The terrain of Devon meant railway building was the most difficult in the entire region, with some very steep inclines. These routes ran through some of the most picturesque countryside to seaside towns such as **Ilfracombe**. The same was also true of Dorset, which has a rich tapestry of scenic lines and some beautiful unspoilt resorts for those requiring some escape from everyday life. The best known are Lyme Regis (a tortuous route through unusually named **Combpyne**), **Weymouth**, Swanage and **Bournemouth**.

(Both posters courtesy of the South Devon Railway – Tindale Collection)

The famous Somerset & Dorset Railway also plied its trade through the county and must rate as one of the most collectable lines in totem terms. Anybody fortunate enough to have travelled over the S&D (or 'Slow & Dirty' as it was known by more frequent users) will remember the delights of **Blandford Forum**, **Shillingstone** and **Stalbridge**. Beyond **Templecombe** came that 'Holy Grail' of any S&D collector – the wonderfully named **Evercreech Junction** in WR colours. We have been fortunate in finding photos of all these for our readers to drool over. Many of the nicer names in Dorset only appear in 'target' form, such as Corfe Castle, Swanage and Bridport.

Further east, the counties of Hampshire and Wiltshire are crossed by rivers draining into the English Channel. The rolling hills around **Salisbury** and east of **Winchester** contrast with the mainly flat countryside surrounding the New Forest and Solent areas. Here are some very desirable names, such as **Brockenhurst**, **Hinton Admiral**, and **New Milton**. The range of hills known as the South Downs runs from **Fareham** along to **Eastbourne**. These hills are crossed by three main lines, namely those to **Littlehampton**, **Brighton** and **Newhaven**. Numerous routes also cross the North Downs in Surrey and Kent, the most notable being those to Dorking, Reigate and **Sevenoaks**. In between these ranges of hills the Ashdown Forest and Rolling Ridge around **Crowborough** are the only hilly terrain that separates the Vale of Sussex and the Weald of Kent.

An incredible Somerset & Dorset collection.

To the north, the sprawl that is suburban London sees a large number of lines carrying financiers, civil servants and office workers on their daily commute. If you are collecting totems from South London you have more choice than any other area in the country! If we take for example, **Barnes Bridge**, **Cannon Street**, **Charing Cross**, **Honor Oak Park**, **Loughborough Junction**, **New Cross**, **Peckham Rye**, **Vauxhall** and **Waterloo** (all in the county of London), this would make quite a set! Below are two more of Alan's shots of SR totems *in situ* for us to enjoy, the first from Sussex and the second from Kent.

(Alan Young)

(Alan Young)

The Southern Region database, guidance notes and general database comments

Each regional database draws upon the knowledge of many totem experts from all over the country, who generously provided us with a wealth of basic data. The pages that follow are the result of hours of painstaking research, phone calls and visits. We have adopted the same format for all the databases, so these comments will apply in this and the subsequent five chapters. As previously stated, station names in **bold** indicate that totems were fitted.

The first column alphabetically lists all the stations known to have been fitted with totems. A few of the signs have variations, so where necessary you will find symbols and explanations. In the case of Southern Region totems they may be found with black flanges 'BF', white flanges 'FF', or in some cases both. In the case of NER totems we find 1in wide large flange totems, denoted by 'LF'. A few Midland, Western and North Eastern signs were totally flangeless or flat. Half-flanged totems are denoted as 'HF'.

The old county names of the mid-1950s were chosen as the basis for the data in the second column. We have cross-checked these against Ordnance Survey maps (series seven), and to be on the safe side RCH books have also been studied. (We have included this column as the basis for those trying to complete entire counties.) The third column is the layout of the wording on the totem where known. If nothing is shown, then the wording is in one line. If '2 line' is shown, this denotes that the wording occupies two lines within the central panel. If 'LP' is shown, this denotes that some wording occupies the lower panel. There are a handful of totems where wording covers two lines of the centre panel and the lower panel, so these are shown as '3 line'.

The fourth column is the flange data (if known). Although we have made great strides in amassing information since the first book on totems was published, there are still gaps in our knowledge. The fifth column relates to station closure. Where no date is shown, the station is still in operation. The sixth and seventh columns on the right-hand side will probably give the greatest stimulus to the uncovering of the real 'gems'. These relate to whether the totem has appeared at a public auction and whether one or more is known to have survived. We expect all these columns to change with time, and have designed them so that the reader can amend as new information comes to light (hence the formation of the Totem Study Group).

We now propose to make a few short comments on some of the stations found in the Southern database, to aid the collector in his quest for the more elusive signs. Clearly space will not permit us to look at every entry, so we have restricted our comments to the more unusual and rare locations, or those with an interesting history.

A: **Addiscombe** is located near Croydon, South London, and it has yet to appear in auction. Another totem yet to appear in public is **Alresford** in Hampshire (closed 1973 but reopened by the Mid-Hants Railway in 1977). Similarly we do not know of the survival of **Alton**, junction for the 'Watercress Line'. **Appledore** in Kent was opened by the South Eastern Railway in 1851 and became one of the few stations where wooden totems were hung. Wooden totems were also used at **Axminster** in Devon, which was opened by the L&SWR in 1860 and was the junction for the former Lyme Regis branch. **Aylesford** is a rare Kent totem, for a station that the SER opened in 1856.

B: **Basingstoke** is an important mainline station that opened in 1839 and surprisingly a totem has yet to appear in a public auction. The majority of signs here were targets. Rare **Belmont** is located between **Sutton** and **Banstead** in Surrey. It was renamed from the more romantic California in 1875. We have also to confirm the survival of a **Bexhill Central**. Photographs show that the station definitely had totems. **Bramber** in Sussex (located on the closed line from Shoreham-by-Sea to Christ's Hospital) was opened in 1861 and closed in 1966. This is one of the more elusive Sussex items yet to emerge in public. **Bude** has appeared in auction, and once held the distinction of being one of the most expensive of all Southern totems. The station was a late development (opened 1898, closed 1966) when most of that part of Cornwall lost its railway connections.

C: **Callington** is one of only a handful of SR totems in Cornwall, and to date only one has been seen at auction. It was opened by the Plymouth, Devonport & South Western Junction Railway in 1909, as Callington Road. The SE&CR opened London's **Cannon Street** terminus on the north side of the Thames in 1866. It closed briefly in 1926 and 1974 for track and building alterations. The East Kent Railway opened **Chatham** in 1858, but despite its size there do not appear to be many surviving totems. This old Medway town was once home to England's largest naval base. Established in the reign of Henry VIII, it is now an important heritage site. **Chestfield & Swalecliffe Halt** was a latecomer on the scene – not opening until 1930, it is situated on the North Kent line. It had three versions. These are a two-line full-flange totem, and a lower panel version with both full and half flanges. The last of these is the most commonly found.

Clapham Junction evokes memories of endless train activity and trainspotting at Britain's busiest station. It opened in 1863 to replace Clapham Common – opened in 1846. Two types of totem were hung here, with 3ft and 4ft variants. The 4ft version did not have white lines and we have included a photo of this rare version in the database. There were arguably more totems at **Clapham Junction** than at any other station. The superbly named **Cobham & Stoke D'Abernon**, which the L&SWR opened as Cobham in 1885, gained its current title in 1951. There are two versions of the totem, of which the full-flanged two-line version is much rarer.

Collington Halt opened as Collington Wood Halt in 1905, only to close the following year. It reopened in 1911 as West Bexhill Halt, and gained its current name in 1929. It is a rare totem, with only one appearance at auction so far. In the section discussing the geography of the region, we mentioned **Combpyne**. This former L&SWR halt on the picturesque Lyme Regis branch, was opened in 1903 and finally closed in 1965, when the cuts really started to bite. It is one of the few Devon green totems yet to appear at auction. There were only one or two totems on the station, so we are not surprised.

Cowden is in Kent, south of **Edenbridge** on the line to **Uckfield**. The station opened in 1888 and this elusive totem has not appeared in auction to date. The delightful Kent village of **Cranbrook** lost its railway in 1961, upon the closure of the Hawkhurst branch (nicknamed 'The Hop Pickers' Line'). All the intermediate stations had full flanged totems fitted, albeit briefly. The Cranbrook & Paddock Wood Railway originally opened this station in 1893 and Hawkhurst retained targets until closure. A rare Hawkhurst branch set is shown below.

The survival of a **Crayford** has yet to be confirmed. The station is a former SE&CR structure, opened in 1866 on the North Kent main line between Bexley and **Dartford**. There were only totems on the platform extensions. Totems from **Crowborough and Jarvis Brook** are a little unusual because of the length of wording in the lower panel. This gives a very full appearance to the totem. The station, on the line from **Eridge** to Lewes, opened as Crowborough in 1888 and became Crowborough again in 1980.

D: **Dean** is a former L&SW station opening in 1847 and still in use today. We have been unable to locate a survivor. **Deepdene** has undergone a few name changes. The LB&SC station opened as Box Hill in 1851 and closed in 1917. It reopened in 1919 and was renamed Deepdene in 1923 before being renamed again as Dorking (Deepdene) in 1987. It appeared for the first time at auction in 2000. **Dilton Marsh Halt**, just south of Westbury in Wiltshire, is one of the few former GWR stations with SR totems. It opened in 1937, and closed in 1994 only to be reopened a month later. The number of totems on the station was only two to four.

Dover Priory is much rarer as a totem than in target form. In Hampshire the station at **Dunbridge** released its first totem at the March 2002 SRA. An L&SWR station that opened in 1847, it acquired the name Mottisfont Dunbridge in 1988, because of the closure of **Mottisfont** in 1964, a decision that only took 24 years to accomplish!

E: **Edenbridge** in Kent is where the main east-west line from Ashford to Guildford crosses the main line running south from London to Eastbourne. It is a former SE&C station opening in 1842. In 1888 Edenbridge (LB&SC) was opened, but owing to confusion with the SE&C station of the same name it was renamed **Edenbridge Town** in 1896. Both totems are known to survive. **Elmers End** is another of those delightful black-edged totems, which has only appeared once in auction to date. The SE&CR opened the station in 1864. **Elmstead Woods** has appeared more often than any other in auction and was probably the totem that many people started their collections with, including one of us! For the record, Elmstead was a former SE&CR station that opened in 1904. It was renamed **Elmstead Woods** in 1908 and is a relatively large station for such a small place. **Emsworth** in Hampshire is a rare totem. The station is located on the South Coast line between Chichester and Southampton. It was an early LB&SC station opening in 1847.

An even more elusive totem is **Evershot**. This is another GWR station with green totems, opening in 1857 and closing in 1966 as part of the Beeching cuts. The station was on the main line from **Castle Cary** down to **Weymouth**. At **Exeter Central** we find the unusual 4ft all green no white line totems. The station opened as Exeter Queen Street in 1860 but took its present name in 1933. Although one or two are in private hands, one has yet to appear in a public auction.

F: **Farnham** (opened by the L&SWR in 1848) has not been seen at auction yet, and we have not managed to track down a photo either. **Folkestone** has three stations, at least nine names and an unbelievably complicated naming history. The first (temporary) station opened in June 1843, but closed in the same year when the line was extended to the town. In 1849 the new station was renamed Folkestone Old, and again in 1852 to **Folkestone Junction**, then Folkestone Junction (Shorncliffe) in 1858. Just to confuse matters, it then became **Folkestone East** in 1962, which only lasted three years, as the station closed in 1965. **Folkestone Harbour** opened in 1849 but closed in 1856 when the new SE&C station opened nearby. This station closed in 1915, reopened in 1919 (after the First World War) closed again in 1939 and reopened in 1945 (after the Second World War), only to be closed and re-opened a third time in 1960. This is quite a history, and interestingly the totem is known but has not appeared in auction. Finally there is **Folkestone West**, which was renamed from the old Shorncliffe station in 1962. We haven't finished yet! Folkestone Central was renamed from Radnor Park in 1895, Folkestone Pier opened in 1876 and closed in 1883, and last but not least Folkestone Warren Halt was opened in 1886, and closed and reopened three times before being finally closed in 1971. The last three stations were not fitted with totems. If all that confuses you, then spare a thought for the poor passengers! **Ford** in Sussex was renamed in 1863 from the first station at Arundel. **Fulwell** is one of the few southern totems located in Middlesex. It was built by the Thames Valley Railway in 1864, then became Fulwell & New Hampton in 1874, Fulwell & Hampton Hill in 1887, Fulwell for Hampton Hill in 1913 and finally Fulwell in 1948.

G: **Gatwick Racecourse** is probably one of the most interesting totems in the entire SR. These were wooden of construction with a paper overlay (see Chapter 5). **Gillingham** totems had both black and white flanges. Gillingham in Dorset did not have totems. In the past it has been assumed that the different colours meant different locations, and auction houses have wrongly attributed them to Dorset to increase their value. **Goudhurst** is a former SE&C station that closed in 1961. It has appeared in auction, but is sought after because only three are known.

Grange Road in Sussex, just west of East Grinstead, is much sought after. **Gravesend West** is one of the scarcest totems in the region and is not believed to have survived, because of very early closure in 1953. Totems from **Greatstone-on-Sea**, a late SR station opened in 1937, are rare. (The suffix 'Halt' was added in 1954, but not to the totem).

An NBL D84XX Type 1 stops for a crew change at Hither Green. (A.C. Ingram)

H: The Southern Railway opened **Hamble Halt** in 1942; BR officially dropped the suffix in 1969. The existence of a survivor from here has not yet been confirmed. The renaming of **Ham Street & Orlestone** took place in 1897, as it was known as Ham Street until that date. It reverted to Ham Street in 1976. It is a rare totem. **Hartfield** and **Heathfield** have both yet to appear in auction. The former was open for exactly 99 years, closing in 1967. The latter was completed by the LB&SCR in 1880 and closed in 1965.

Holborn Viaduct had enamel and wooden totems. The High Level terminus opened in 1874 and closed in 1990, upon the completion of the Thameslink line, which uses the former Low Level trackbed. We know of a wooden survivor (shown above), but not the enamel version. Other notable totems in this part of the database are the wonderfully named **Honor Oak Park**, elusive **Horam** (formerly Waldron & Horam in Sussex), **Holmwood** (Surrey), plus **Hook** and **Horsebridge** (both Hampshire). Another of that elusive trio from the Hawkhurst branch line is **Horsmonden**, which closed in 1961.

I: **Idmiston Halt** (north-east of **Salisbury** in Wiltshire) had a short life, opening in 1943 only to close just over 25 years later. There were very few totems here.

Some **Ifield** (Sussex) totems were overpainted on former **St Helier** (Surrey) totems. The old North Devon terminus of **Ilfracombe** was rather hastily wiped from the railway map in 1970, but fortunately most of the totems were saved and future generations will have some reminder of the one-time glory days of train travel to this popular resort.

Itchen Abbas is a former L&SWR station, and a real rarity, with very few totems known to survive. The station opened in 1965 and was closed by BR in 1973. It lies just beyond the current terminus of the Mid-Hants Railway at **Alresford**.

K: **Kemsley Halt** on the Sheerness branch in Kent has only made one appearance at auction, while **Kidbrooke** – an SECR station just south-east of Blackheath – has not been seen in auction so far.

L: Totems from **Lancing** in Sussex are not known to have survived at this time. The station was opened by the LB&SCR in 1845, closed two years later and was reopened again in 1849. Similarly we have yet to find a **Lee** totem that has survived, as these were only fitted to the platform extensions. In some timetables this station, which opened in 1866, is called Lee for Burnt Ash.

One of the most superb light green totems is **Longfield for Fawkham & Hartley**. This has an interesting naming history, opening in 1872 as Fawkham, being renamed Fawkham for Hartley and Longfield in 1910, then to the name on the totem in 1961 and finally to the present name of Longfield in 1968. The totems were therefore only up for less than a decade, which accounts for their usually good condition. We have yet to confirm the flange type for **London Bridge**, but we have found that this station also had some wooden totems. **Loughborough Junction** had both two line and lower panel type lettering, the latter being the much rarer species.

M: **Marchwood** closed in 1966, an early victim of Dr Beeching's pruning. **Mayfield** in Sussex closed the year before. Neither has appeared in auction. **Marston Magna** is a rare green totem in the Western Region, appearing in auction at Sheffield for the first time in 2000. The station opened as Marston in 1865 and was renamed **Marston Magna** in 1895, closing in 1966. **Merstone** on the Isle of Wight is very rare. We know of only one survivor, remarkable for a 1956 closure. **Milborne Port Halt** and **Minster (Thanet)** are desirable lower panelled totems, as is the other Isle of Wight rarity of **Mill Hill** (opened 1862 and closed in 1966).

N: **New Beckenham**, **New Eltham** and **New Malden** – all commuter stations – have yet to appear publicly, but are known to exist. **New Romney & Littlestone-on-Sea** has one of the longest names and is the only one with hyphens in the second line. This former SE&C station opened as Lydd in 1884 and was also named New Romney and Littlestone before the full name was added in 1888. It closed in 1967. A photo of **Normans Bay Halt** with totems is known, but a survivor is not – yet! The survival of a totem from the ex-SE&CR station at **Northfleet** (opened 1849) has yet to be confirmed.

O: **Okehampton** was opened by the LSWR in 1871 and closed in 1972. The totems are a wonderful light green with full flanges. The equally superb name of **Ottery St Mary** is not known to have survived as a totem. The station opened as Sidmouth (before the line was driven nearer to the coast) in 1875 and closed in 1967. Other rarities are **Overton** (west of Basingstoke) and **Oxshott** near Epsom in Surrey.

P: **Partridge Green** is sought after because of the name, even though a couple have appeared in auction. **Portslade & West Hove** is not common. The station opened as Portslade in 1840 and closed seven years later. It reopened in 1857 and was renamed to include West Hove in 1927. It became Portslade again in 1980.

R: The first **Rainham** (Kent) totem appeared at auction in March 2002 at Sheffield. Before that we did not know of any survivors. The station opened as Rainham & Newington in 1858 and was renamed Rainham in 1862. It was again renamed Rainham (Kent) by BR in the late 1960s to avoid confusion with Rainham in Essex, which is only a few miles away as the crow flies. However, a train journey between the two would take about two hours owing to the lack of any Thames rail crossing. Although the CTRL is being built, this will not benefit local travellers.

Reading (Southern) (former SE&CR) has an interesting history. It was opened as Reading in 1855 and was renamed **Reading South** by BR in 1949. In 1849, the earliest station was opened by the Reading Guildford & Reigate Railway east of that location. This station closed in 1855 when the SE&CR station opened. **Reading South** became **Reading (Southern)** in 1961 and closed in 1965. This is the totem often seen in auction. An original half-flanged **Reading South** totem would be a find indeed!

Ropley is another curious totem, not easy to find. It is now part of the 'Watercress Line' of the Mid Hants Railway that re-opened in 1977. The station (L&SWR) opened in 1865 and was closed in 1973. Few totems are known to have survived. **Rotherfield & Mark Cross** is found in both one and two line versions. The station opened in 1868 as Rotherfield and was renamed Crowborough in 1880. It became **Rotherfield & Mark Cross** in 1901, and closed in 1965. **Rudgwick** is a very difficult totem to find. It is one of several stations on the former Guildford to Christ's Hospital line that closed in 1965, at a time when Dr Beeching was pruning railways from the English countryside.

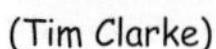
(Tim Clarke)

(Alan Young)

S: **St Budeaux Victoria Road** is a sought-after totem, being a super name and a lower panel example to boot! The station first opened in 1890 as St Budeaux for Saltash by the L&SWR, until 1949 when BR added the Victoria Road. BR also added the word Halt in 1965, but the totems never carried this. **St James Park Halt**, which has not yet been confirmed as a survivor, was opened as Lion's Holt Halt (L&SWR) in 1906. It was renamed in 1946. **Seaton** in Devon opened in 1868 as Seaton & Beer (what a name!), and is much sought after – rarely appearing in auction.

Shillingstone on the former S&D will always be collectable, and first opened in 1863. **Sittingbourne and Milton Regis** is desirable as 'Milton Regis' appears in the lower panel giving a full appearance to the totem. Both **Snodland** and **Southbourne Halt** are not common, but these pale into insignificance compared with **Sparkford** and **Staines Central**. **Sparkford** is another WR station that carried SR totems, and is located just into Somerset, south of Castle Cary. It opened in 1856 and closed in 1966. Staines opened in 1855 and was again renamed Staines by BR in 1966. We believe that the totems were installed for less than 10 years. **Southwick**, **Staplehurst** and **Steyning** are not common, nor is **Streatham Hill** in South London.

There are very few stations with a different layout and different flange colours. One such example is **Swanscombe Halt** (see below) on the North Kent line between **Dartford** and **Gravesend**. **Sunnymeads** is interesting because it is one of the few SR totems in Buckinghamshire. **Sway** appeared in auction for the first time in 2000. The station opened in 1888 and is located in the lovely New Forest in Hampshire.

T: **Tavistock North** is one of those few 'Devon greens' that has always been desirable and is quite rare. The L&SWR station opened late in 1890 as Tavistock and BR gave it the title **Tavistock North** in 1949. **Templecombe** has appeared in auction several times, but being partially an S&D station is always desirable. The wonderfully named **Three Oaks & Guestling Halt** is one of the few three-line SR totems. Originally Three Oaks Bridge Halt it opened in 1907 and was named Three Oaks Halt two years later by the SE&CR. The name on the totem was given in the mid-'50s and in 1969 the Halt was dropped. It is now known as Three Oaks and is located just north of **Hastings**.

Tunbridge Wells Central (SE&CR) opened in 1846 as Tunbridge Wells. The 'Central' was added in 1923 to distinguish it from **Tunbridge Wells West** (LB&SCR) which opened in 1866, also as Tunbridge Wells (imagine the confusion: two stations in the same town with the same name!). When the West closed in 1985, Central became the only station and the confusion finally ceased. **Twickenham** is the only SR station that had light green half-flanged totems. The station was one of the first in the region to have totems installed in 1954 with the opening of the rebuilt station. The colour is a lime green shade and was not adopted elsewhere.

U: **Upper Halliford Halt** appeared in auction for the first time in 2000. Halliford Halt, north of Shepperton in Middlesex, opened in 1944 and the 'Upper' was added after just three months. The Halt was dropped in 1969. A rare two-line version of **Upper Warlingham** is shown here. The standard style is one line.

You may notice that the two signs above have slightly different lettering than normal. This closely resembles Helvetica lettering, and could only be found on certain SR totems for some unknown reason. This style had no geographic location, as the stations carrying them were spread across the region. It may have been a last ditch attempt at a 'corporate image' totem by a renegade manager.

W: **Wadebridge** is a rare 'Cornish green' and much sought after! There were in fact two stations in the town, but not at the same time. The first was opened as early as 1834 by the Bodmin & Wadebridge Railway and closed in 1886. Two years later the L&SWR opened the second station, which finally closed in 1967. **Waldron and Horam** is just as desirable because of a very early renaming in 1953 to **Horam**. The station opened as Waldron and Horam Road in 1900 and the Road was dropped in 1935. The original totems were up for only three or four years. The photo in our database is of one that had been dug up! **Waterloo** would be a desirable totem in any collection and we have explained the development of this station at the start of this chapter. Contrary to popular belief, most Waterloo totems came from Waterloo East station – a fact that does not make them any less desirable however. **Weymouth** had both 3ft and 4ft totems with only the former appearing so far in auction. **West Moors** is a rare bird, as only three totems are believed to have existed. It was also known as West Moors for Ferndown.

Whitchurch North in Hampshire is rumoured to have survived, but this needs confirmation. It was first opened by the L&WSR in 1854 and was renamed Whitchurch (Hants) by BR in 1972. **Winchester City** opened early in 1839 as Winchester. It became **Winchester City** in 1949 to distinguish it from the GW station known as Chesil or Cheesehill. The wonderfully named **Woodmansterne** (located just north of Chipstead in Surrey) was opened in 1932. The totem has not appeared in auction thus far. **Wraysbury** is one of the most unusual totems. Two variants exist – one shown below and one in the database. The more unusual has to be the version with no white lines, also found on some **Margate** totems. Interestingly, two stations have been built at Wraysbury, but this has no connection with the two variants! The first station opened in 1848 and closed in 1861 when a larger station was completed.

Y: There are so few SR stations beginning with 'Y' that all those listed are desirable. **Yalding** was an early station, opening in 1844. The station is south-east of Maidstone in Kent. Both totems from Yeovil would grace any collection and we have included pictures of both. **Yeovil Pen Mill** (GWR) opened first in 1854, followed by **Yeovil Town** (joint GW/L&SW) seven years later. The last train departed **Yeovil Town** in 1966.

Totems from the Southern region have been considered by some to be of lower value than the other regions, because of the large numbers available in a small area. Aside from the common suburban names, however, there are some very desirable classic names, and the largest number of Halts – only three or four of which have never appeared in public. Who cannot be moved with names like **Bere Alston**, **Blandford Forum**, **Budleigh Salterton**, **Chislet Colliery Halt**, **Crowborough and Jarvis Brook**, **Devonport Kings Road**, **Itchen Abbas**, **Littlehaven Halt**, **New Romney & Littlestone-on-Sea**, **St Budeaux Victoria Road**, **Waterloo** and **Yeovil Pen Mill** to choose from? They are all out there somewhere! Just to prove this point, here are some further pictures that we have not used elsewhere in this tribute to the Southern Region.

Earlier in this chapter we mentioned the totems at **Combpyne**, or should this be totem, as this picture clearly shows only one totem, which does not appear to be located anywhere near the platform! This early 1960s picture was taken shortly before the closure of the Lyme Regis branch.

(R. Blencowe)

It was widely recognised that the Southern Region liked to retain its former identity. We illustrate this with two examples. First we show this delightful Feltham direction sign. Feltham only had targets, and once had a large marshalling yard and locoshed (70B). The second example alongside is an early tinplate type sign and would have been used on a station frontage. It measures approximately 5ft long.

(Dawlish Museum)

To finish this chapter, and to complement the **Combpyne** picture, we show the Lyme Regis junction station at **Axminster** complete with 'barley-twist' lamp-posts and wooden totems *in situ*. In BR timetables this station was shown as Axminster for Lyme.

Chapter 6 Totem Listing

BF = black full flange: **FF** = white full flange

Place name		County	Southern Region			Totem in	Totem
			Layout	Flange	Closed	Auction	Survived
ABBEY WOOD		London		HF/FF		✓	✓
ADDISCOMBE		Surrey		**BF**	1997		✓
ADDLESTONE		Surrey		HF		✓	✓
ADISHAM		Kent		FF		✓	✓
ALBANY PARK		Kent		HF/FF		✓	✓
ALDRINGTON HALT		Sussex	LP	FF		✓	✓
ALRESFORD	re-opened 1977	Hampshire		HF	1973		✓
ALTON		Hampshire		FF			
AMBERLEY		Sussex		FF		✓	✓
ANDOVER JUNCTION		Hampshire		HF		✓	✓
ANGMERING		Sussex		**BF**/FF		✓	✓
APPLEDORE	wood only	Kent					✓
ARDINGLY		Sussex		FF	1963		✓
ARUNDEL		Sussex		FF		✓	✓
ASH		Surrey		HF/FF		✓	✓
ASHURST		Kent		FF			✓
ASH VALE		Surrey		FF		✓	✓
AXMINSTER	wood only	Devon					✓
AYLESFORD		Kent		FF			
AYLESHAM HALT		Kent	LP	FF		✓	✓
BAGSHOT		Surrey		FF		✓	✓
BALCOMBE		Sussex		FF		✓	✓
BALHAM		London		**BF**		✓	✓
BANSTEAD		Surrey		FF		✓	✓
BARCOMBE MILLS		Sussex		HF/FF	1969	✓	✓
BARMING	also **BF**	Kent		HF/FF		✓	✓
BARNEHURST		Kent		FF		✓	✓
BARNES		Surrey		HF		✓	✓
BARNES BRIDGE		Surrey		FF		✓	✓
BARNHAM		Sussex		**BF**		✓	✓

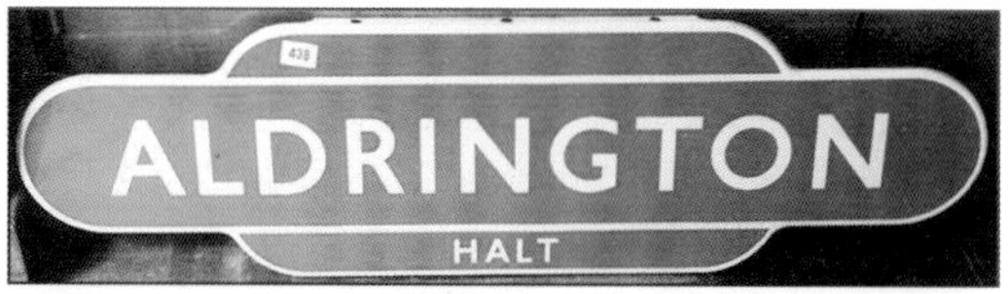

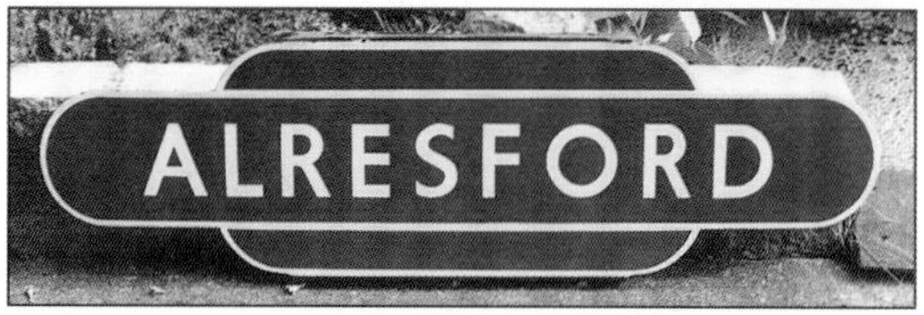

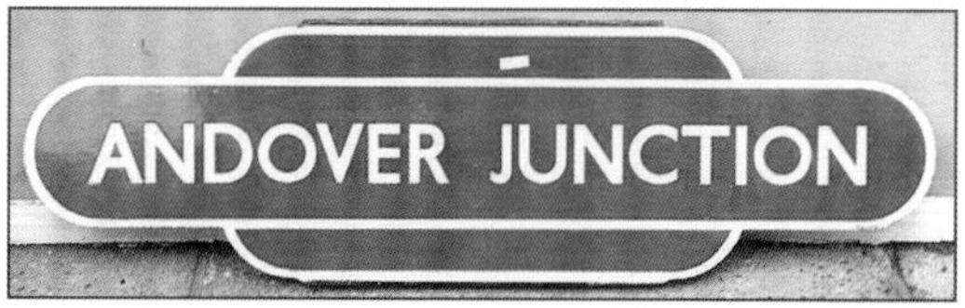

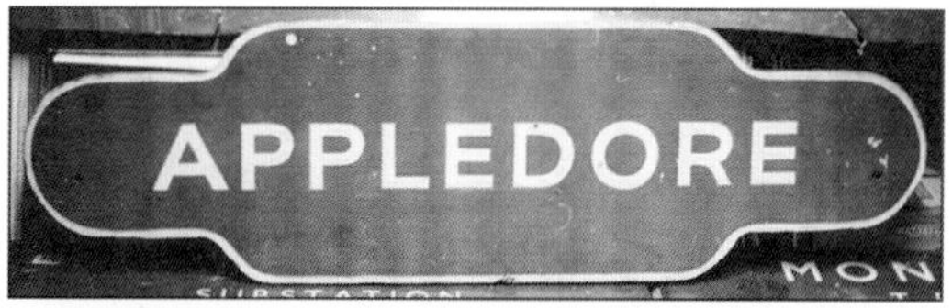

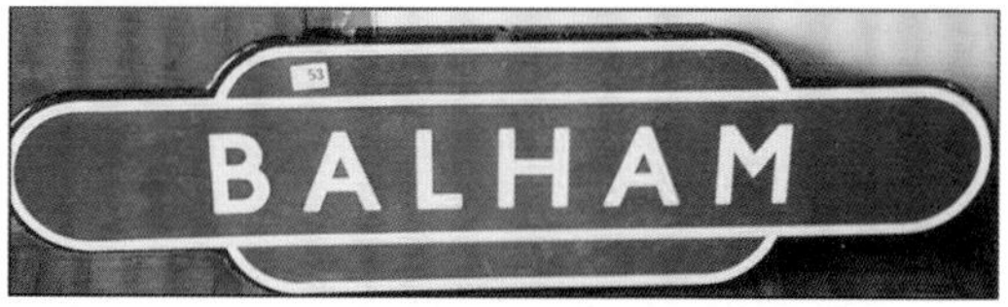

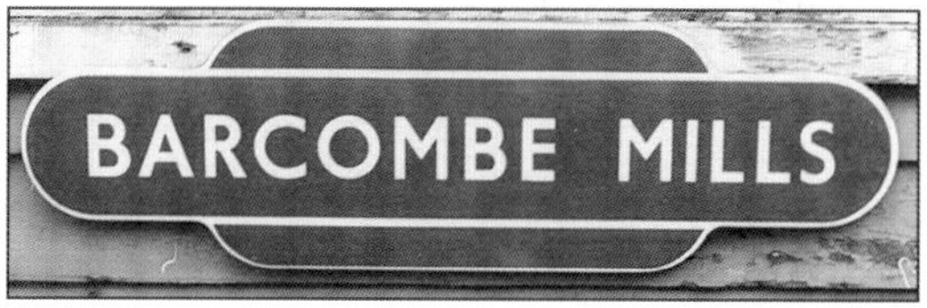

Place name		County	Layout	Flange	Closed	Auction	Survived
BARNSTAPLE TOWN		Devon		FF	1970	✓	✓
BASINGSTOKE		Hampshire		HF			✓
BAT AND BALL		Kent		HF			✓
BATTERSEA PARK		London		HF		✓	✓
BEARSTED AND THURNAM		Kent	2 line	FF		✓	✓
BECKENHAM HILL		London		FF		✓	✓
BEDDINGTON LANE HALT	re-opened 2000	Surrey	LP	FF	1997	✓	✓
BEKESBOURNE		Kent		FF		✓	✓
BELLINGHAM		London		FF		✓	✓
BELMONT		Surrey		FF			✓
BELTRING AND BRANBRIDGES HALT		Kent	2 line	FF		✓	✓
BELVEDERE		Kent		HF		✓	✓
BENTLEY		Hampshire		FF		✓	✓
BERE ALSTON		Devon		FF			✓
BERE FERRERS	Bingham Road overpaint	Devon		FF			✓
BERWICK		Sussex		FF		✓	✓
BEXHILL CENTRAL		Sussex		FF			
BEXHILL WEST		Sussex		FF	1964		✓
BEXLEYHEATH		Kent		HF/FF		✓	✓
BINGHAM ROAD	re-opened 2000	Surrey		**BF**/FF	1983	✓	✓
BIRCHINGTON-ON-SEA		Kent		FF		✓	✓
BISHOPSTONE		Sussex		FF		✓	✓
BLACKHEATH		London		**BF**			✓
BLACKWATER		Hampshire		FF		✓	✓
BLANDFORD FORUM		Dorset		HF	1966		✓
BODMIN NORTH		Devon		HF	1967	✓	✓
BOGNOR REGIS		Sussex		FF		✓	✓
BOROUGH GREEN AND WROTHAM		Kent	2 line	FF			✓
BOSCOMBE		Hampshire		HF	1965	✓	✓
BOSHAM		Sussex		FF		✓	✓
BOTLEY		Hampshire		**BF**/FF		✓	✓
BOURNEMOUTH WEST		Hampshire		FF	1965	✓	✓
BRACKNELL		Berkshire		FF			✓

Place name	County	Layout	Flange	Closed	Auction	Survived
BRAMBER	Sussex		FF	1966		✓
BRAMLEY (Bramley for Silchester)	Hampshire		FF		✓	✓
BRAMLEY & WONERSH	Surrey		**BF**	1965		✓
BRENTFORD CENTRAL	Middlesex		HF/FF		✓	✓
BRIDESTOWE	Devon		FF	1968		✓
BRIGHTON	Sussex		FF		✓	✓
BRIXTON	London		FF		✓	✓
BROADSTAIRS	Kent		FF		✓	✓
BROCKENHURST	Hampshire		FF		✓	✓
BROCKLEY	London		FF		✓	✓
BROMLEY NORTH	Kent		HF		✓	✓
BROMLEY SOUTH	Kent		FF		✓	✓
BROOKLAND HALT	Kent		HF	1967		✓
BUDE	Cornwall		FF	1966	✓	✓
BUDLEIGH SALTERTON	Devon		FF	1967	✓	✓
BURGESS HILL	Sussex		FF		✓	✓
BUXTED (some o/p on Wraysbury **BF**)	Sussex		FF		✓	✓
BYFLEET AND NEW HAW	Surrey	2 line	FF		✓	✓
CALLINGTON	Cornwall		FF	1966	✓	✓
CANNON STREET	London		FF		✓	✓
CANTERBURY EAST	Kent		FF		✓	✓
CANTERBURY WEST	Kent		FF		✓	✓
CARSHALTON	Surrey		**BF**		✓	✓
CARSHALTON BEECHES	Surrey		FF		✓	✓
CATERHAM	Surrey		**BF**		✓	✓
CATFORD BRIDGE	London		**BF**/FF		✓	✓
CHARING CROSS	London		**BF**		✓	✓
CHARLTON	London		HF		✓	✓
CHARTHAM	Kent		**BF**/FF		✓	✓
CHATHAM	Kent		**BF**/FF		✓	✓
CHEAM	Surrey		FF		✓	✓
CHELSFIELD	Kent		**BF**/FF		✓	✓

Place name	County	Layout	Flange	Closed	Auction	Survived
CHERTSEY	Surrey		HF		✓	✓
CHESTFIELD & SWALECLIFFE HALT	Kent	LP	HF/FF		✓	✓
CHESTFIELD & SWALECLIFFE HALT	Kent	2 line	FF		✓	✓
CHIPSTEAD	Surrey		**BF**		✓	✓
CHISLEHURST	Kent		FF		✓	✓
CHISLET COLLIERY HALT	Kent	LP	**BF**	1971		✓
CHRISTCHURCH	Hampshire		FF		✓	✓
CLANDON also wood	Surrey		HF/**BF**		✓	✓
CLAPHAM	London		FF		✓	✓
CLAPHAM JUNCTION + 4' totems FF	London		FF		✓	✓
CLOCK HOUSE	Kent		**BF**/FF		✓	✓
COBHAM & STOKE D'ABERNON	Surrey		HF		✓	✓
COBHAM & STOKE D'ABERNON	Surrey	2 line	FF		✓	✓
COLLINGTON HALT	Sussex		FF		✓	✓
COMBPYNE	Devon		FF	1965		✓
COODEN BEACH	Sussex		HF/FF		✓	✓
COOMBE ROAD	Surrey		**BF**/FF	1983	✓	✓
COULSDON NORTH	Surrey		FF	1983	✓	✓
COULSDON SOUTH	Surrey		FF		✓	✓
COWDEN	Kent		HF			✓
CRANBROOK	Kent		FF	1961		✓
CRANLEIGH	Surrey		**BF**	1965	✓	✓
CRAYFORD	Kent		FF			
CROWBOROUGH AND JARVIS BROOK	Sussex	LP	FF		✓	✓
CROWHURST	Sussex		FF		✓	✓
CUXTON	Kent		FF		✓	✓

Place name	County	Layout	Flange	Closed	Auction	Survived
DARTFORD	Kent		FF		✓	✓
DATCHET	Buckinghamshire		FF		✓	✓
DEAL	Kent		FF		✓	✓
DEAN	Wiltshire		**BF**			
DEEPDENE	Surrey		FF		✓	✓
DEPTFORD also HF	London		**BF**/FF		✓	✓

Place name	County	Layout	Flange	Closed	Auction	Survived
DEVONPORT KINGS ROAD	Devon	LP	HF	1964	✓	✓
DILTON MARSH HALT	Wiltshire	LP	FF			✓
DORCHESTER SOUTH	Dorset		HF/FF		✓	✓
DORCHESTER WEST	Dorset		FF		✓	✓
DORMANS	Surrey		FF		✓	✓
DOVER PRIORY	Kent		FF		✓	✓
DUMPTON PARK	Kent		FF		✓	✓
DUNBRIDGE	Hampshire		**BF**		✓	✓
DUNTON GREEN	Kent		**BF**/FF		✓	✓
DURRINGTON-ON-SEA	Sussex		FF		✓	✓
EARLEY	Berkshire		**BF**			✓
EARLSWOOD	Surrey		**BF**/FF		✓	✓
EASTBOURNE	Sussex		**BF**		✓	✓
EAST CROYDON	Surrey		FF		✓	✓
EAST DULWICH	London		FF		✓	✓
EAST FARLEIGH	Kent		FF		✓	✓
EASTLEIGH	Hampshire		HF		✓	✓
EAST MALLING HALT	Kent	1line/ LP	FF		✓	✓
EAST PUTNEY	London		FF		✓	✓
EAST WORTHING HALT	Sussex	LP	FF		✓	✓
EDENBRIDGE	Kent		FF		✓	✓
EDENBRIDGE TOWN	Kent		FF		✓	✓
EDEN PARK	Kent		HF/**BF**			✓
EFFINGHAM JUNCTION	Surrey		FF		✓	✓
ELMERS END	Kent		FF		✓	✓
ELMSTEAD WOODS	Kent		HF/FF		✓	✓
ELTHAM PARK	London		HF	1985	✓	✓
ELTHAM WELL HALL	London		FF	1985	✓	✓
EMSWORTH	Hampshire		FF			✓
EPSOM	Surrey		FF		✓	✓
EPSOM DOWNS	Surrey		FF		✓	✓
ERIDGE	Sussex		FF		✓	✓

Place name	County	Layout	Flange	Closed	Auction	Survived
ERITH	Kent		HF/FF		✓	✓
ESHER	Surrey		FF		✓	✓
EVERSHOT	Dorset		FF	1966		
EWELL EAST	Surrey		FF		✓	✓
EXETER CENTRAL 4'only all green	Devon		FF			✓
EXMOUTH	Devon		FF		✓	✓
EXTON	Devon		FF		✓	✓
FALCONWOOD	London		FF		✓	✓
FALMER	Sussex		FF		✓	✓
FARNBOROUGH NORTH	Hampshire		FF		✓	✓
FARNHAM	Surrey		FF			✓
FARNINGHAM ROAD	Kent		FF		✓	✓
FAVERSHAM	Kent		FF		✓	✓
FAYGATE	Sussex		HF		✓	✓
FISHBOURNE HALT	Sussex	LP	FF		✓	✓
FISHERSGATE HALT	Sussex	LP	FF		✓	✓
FOLKESTONE EAST	Kent		FF	1965	✓	✓
FOLKESTONE HARBOUR	Kent	2 line	FF			✓
FOLKESTONE JUNCTION renamed 1962	Kent	2 line	FF		✓	✓
FOLKESTONE WEST	Kent		FF		✓	✓
FORD	Sussex		FF		✓	✓
FRANT	Sussex		FF			✓
FRATTON	Hampshire		FF		✓	✓
FRIMLEY	Surrey		FF		✓	✓
FULWELL	Middlesex		FF			✓
GATWICK RACECOURSE wood only	Sussex					✓
GILLINGHAM	Kent		**BF**/FF		✓	✓
GIPSY HILL	Surrey		FF		✓	✓
GODSTONE	Surrey		FF		✓	✓
GORING-BY-SEA no hyphens FF	Sussex		HF/FF		✓	✓
GOUDHURST	Kent		FF	1961	✓	✓

Place name	County	Layout	Flange	Closed	Auction	Survived
GRANGE ROAD	Sussex		**BF**/FF	1967		✓
GRAVESEND CENTRAL	Kent	LP	**BF**		✓	✓
GRAVESEND WEST	Kent		HF	1953		
GREATSTONE-ON-SEA	Kent		FF	1967		✓
GREENWICH	London		HF			✓
GROOMBRIDGE	Sussex		FF	1985	✓	✓
GROVE FERRY AND UPSTREET	Kent	2 line	FF	1966	✓	✓
GROVE PARK	London		HF/FF		✓	✓
GUILDFORD	Surrey		FF		✓	✓
GUNNERSBURY	Middlesex		HF/FF		✓	✓
HACKBRIDGE	Surrey		FF		✓	✓
HAILSHAM	Sussex		FF	1968		✓
HALLING	Kent		FF		✓	✓
HAMBLE HALT	Hampshire		HF			
HAMPDEN PARK	Sussex		FF		✓	✓
HAMPTON	Middlesex		FF		✓	✓
HAM STREET AND ORLESTONE	Kent		HF			✓
HARRIETSHAM	Kent		FF		✓	✓
HARTFIELD	Sussex		FF	1967		✓
HASSOCKS	Sussex		FF		✓	✓
HASTINGS	Sussex		FF		✓	✓
HAVANT	Hampshire		FF		✓	✓
HAYDONS ROAD	Surrey		FF		✓	✓
HAYES	Kent		**BF**		✓	✓
HAYWARDS HEATH	Sussex		FF		✓	✓
HEADCORN	Kent		HF/FF		✓	✓
HEATHFIELD	Sussex		FF	1965		✓
HELLINGLY	Sussex		HF/FF	1965	✓	✓
HENFIELD	Sussex		FF	1966	✓	✓
HERNE BAY	Kent		FF		✓	✓
HERSHAM	Surrey		FF		✓	✓
HEVER	Kent		HF			✓

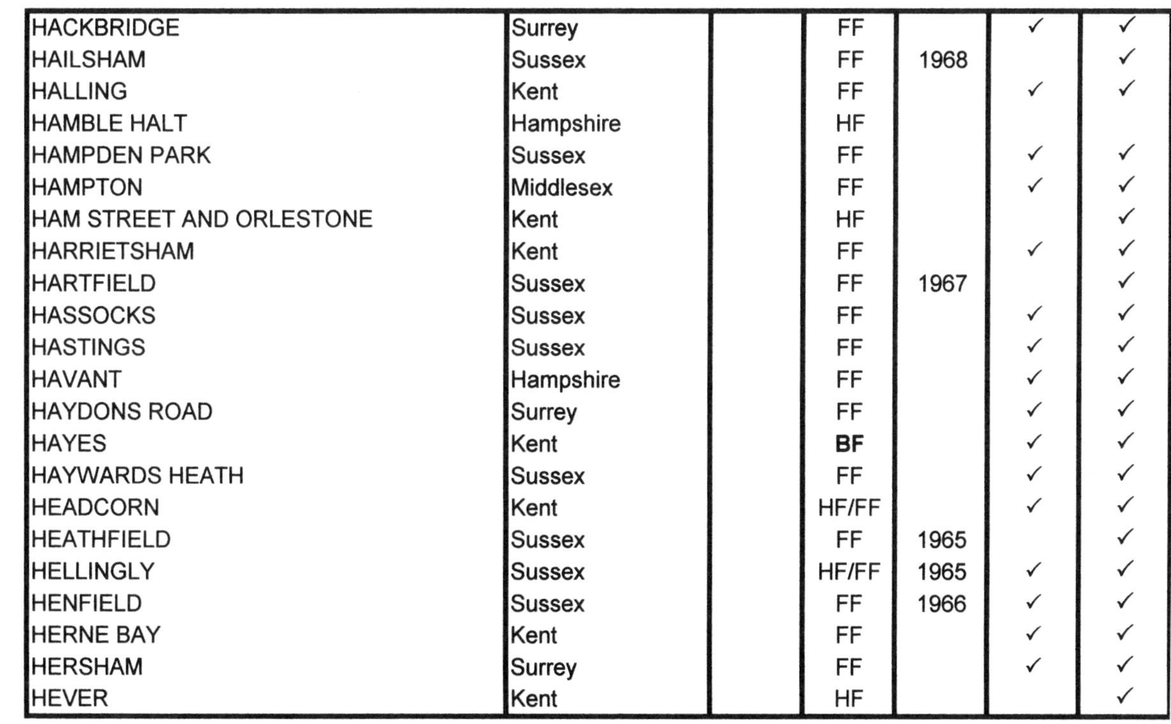

Place name	County	Layout	Flange	Closed	Auction	Survived
HIGHAM	Kent		HF/**BF**		✓	✓
HIGH BROOMS	Kent		HF			✓
HILDENBOROUGH	Kent		**BF**/FF		✓	✓
HINCHLEY WOOD	Surrey		FF			✓
HINTON ADMIRAL	Hampshire		**BF** ?			✓
HITHER GREEN	London		HF/FF		✓	✓
HOLBORN VIADUCT some wood	London		FF	1990		
HOLLINGBOURNE	Kent		FF		✓	✓
HOLMWOOD	Surrey		FF			✓
HONITON	Devon		FF		✓	✓
HONOR OAK PARK	London		FF			✓
HOOK	Hampshire		FF			✓
HORAM	Sussex		HF/FF	1965		✓
HORSEBRIDGE	Hampshire		FF	1964	✓	✓
HORSMONDEN	Kent		FF	1961		✓
HOVE	Sussex		FF		✓	✓
HURST GREEN	Surrey		FF		✓	✓
IDMISTON HALT	Wiltshire	LP	FF	1968		✓
IFIELD (some o/p on St. Helier)	Sussex		HF			✓
ILFRACOMBE	Devon		FF	1970	✓	✓
ISFIELD	Sussex		HF	1969	✓	✓
ITCHEN ABBAS	Hampshire		HF	1973		✓
KEARNSEY	Kent		FF		✓	✓
KEMSING	Kent		FF		✓	✓
KEMSLEY HALT	Kent		FF		✓	✓
KENLEY	Surrey		**BF**/FF		✓	✓
KENT HOUSE	Kent		HF/FF		✓	✓
KIDBROOKE	London		HF			✓
KINGSTON	Surrey		FF		✓	✓
KINGSWOOD	Surrey		**BF**/FF		✓	✓
KNOCKHOLT	Kent		**BF**/FF		✓	✓

Place name	County	Layout	Flange	Closed	Auction	Survived
LADYWELL	London		HF		✓	✓
LANCING	Sussex		FF			
LEATHERHEAD	Surrey		FF			✓
LEE	London		FF			
LEIGH HALT	Kent		FF		✓	✓
LENHAM	Kent		FF		✓	✓
LEWISHAM	London		HF/FF		✓	✓
LINGFIELD	Surrey		FF		✓	✓
LITTLEHAMPTON	Sussex		FF		✓	✓
LITTLEHAVEN HALT	Sussex		HF			✓
LONDON BRIDGE + wood which exist	London					
LONDON ROAD (Guildford)	Surrey	LP	FF		✓	✓
LONGFIELD FOR FAWKHAM &HARTLEY	Kent	2 line	FF		✓	✓
LOUGHBOROUGH JUNCTION	London	2 line	FF		✓	✓
LOUGHBOROUGH JUNCTION	London	LP	HF			✓
LOWER SYDENHAM	London		**BF**/FF		✓	✓
MAIDEN NEWTON	Dorset		FF		✓	✓
MAIDSTONE BARRACKS	Kent		FF		✓	✓
MAIDSTONE EAST	Kent		FF		✓	✓
MARCHWOOD	Hampshire		FF	1966		✓
MARDEN	Kent		HF/FF		✓	✓
MARGATE (some all green)	Kent		FF		✓	✓
MARSTON MAGNA	Somerset		FF	1966	✓	✓
MARTIN MILL	Kent		FF		✓	✓
MAYFIELD	Sussex		FF	1965		✓
MAZE HILL	London		FF		✓	✓
MEOPHAM	Kent		FF		✓	✓
MERSTHAM	Surrey		HF/FF		✓	✓
MERSTONE	Hampshire (IOW)		HF	1956		✓
MICHELDEVER	Hampshire		HF			✓
MILBORNE PORT HALT	Somerset	LP	FF	1966	✓	✓
MILLBROOK	Hampshire		FF		✓	✓

Place name	County	Layout	Flange	Closed	Auction	Survived
MILL HILL	Hampshire (IOW)		HF	1966		✓
MINSTER THANET	Kent	LP	FF		✓	✓
MITCHAM re-opened 2000	Surrey		FF	1997	✓	✓
MITCHAM JUNCTION	Surrey		FF		✓	✓
MORDEN ROAD HALT re-opened 2000	Surrey		HF	1997	✓	✓
MORDEN SOUTH	Surrey		FF		✓	✓
MORTIMER	Berkshire		FF		✓	✓
MORTLAKE	Surrey		FF		✓	✓
MOTTINGHAM	London		HF/FF		✓	✓
MOTTISFONT	Hampshire		FF	1964	✓	✓
MOUNTFIELD HALT	Sussex	LP	FF	1969		✓

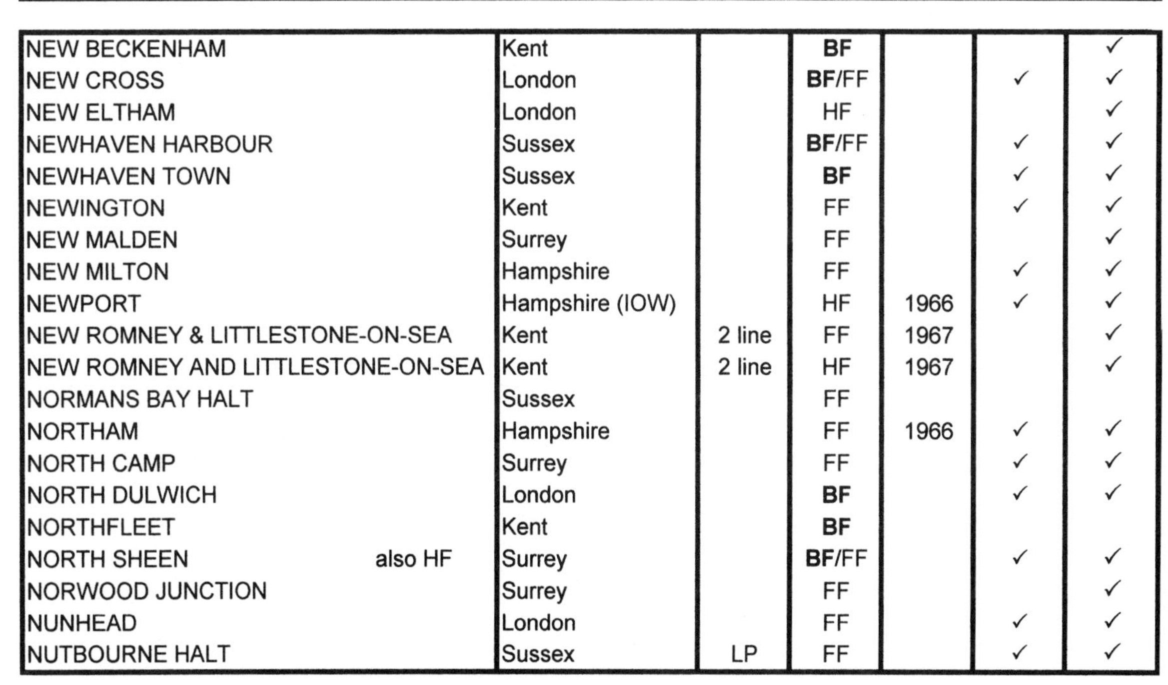

Place name	County	Layout	Flange	Closed	Auction	Survived
NEW BECKENHAM	Kent		**BF**			✓
NEW CROSS	London		**BF**/FF		✓	✓
NEW ELTHAM	London		HF			✓
NEWHAVEN HARBOUR	Sussex		**BF**/FF		✓	✓
NEWHAVEN TOWN	Sussex		**BF**		✓	✓
NEWINGTON	Kent		FF		✓	✓
NEW MALDEN	Surrey		FF			✓
NEW MILTON	Hampshire		FF		✓	✓
NEWPORT	Hampshire (IOW)		HF	1966	✓	✓
NEW ROMNEY & LITTLESTONE-ON-SEA	Kent	2 line	FF	1967		✓
NEW ROMNEY AND LITTLESTONE-ON-SEA	Kent	2 line	HF	1967		✓
NORMANS BAY HALT	Sussex		FF			
NORTHAM	Hampshire		FF	1966	✓	✓
NORTH CAMP	Surrey		FF		✓	✓
NORTH DULWICH	London		**BF**		✓	✓
NORTHFLEET	Kent		**BF**			
NORTH SHEEN also HF	Surrey		**BF**/FF		✓	✓
NORWOOD JUNCTION	Surrey		FF			✓
NUNHEAD	London		FF		✓	✓
NUTBOURNE HALT	Sussex	LP	FF		✓	✓

Place name	County	Layout	Flange	Closed	Auction	Survived
OAKLEY	Hampshire		FF	1963	✓	✓
OCKLEY & CAPEL	Surrey		HF		✓	✓
OKEHAMPTON	Devon		FF	1972	✓	✓
ORE	Sussex		FF		✓	✓
ORPINGTON	Kent		HF		✓	✓
OTTERY ST. MARY	Devon		FF	1967		
OVERTON	Hampshire		HF		✓	✓
OXSHOTT	Surrey		FF		✓	✓
OXTED	Surrey		FF		✓	✓
PADDOCK WOOD	Kent		FF		✓	✓
PARTRIDGE GREEN	Sussex		FF	1966	✓	✓
PECKHAM RYE	London		FF		✓	✓
PETTS WOOD	Kent		FF		✓	✓
PEVENSEY AND WESTHAM	Sussex	2 line	FF		✓	✓
PEVENSEY BAY HALT	Sussex	LP	FF		✓	✓
PINHOE re-opened 1983	Devon		FF	1966	✓	✓
PLUCKLEY	Kent		**BF**/FF		✓	✓
PLUMSTEAD	London		HF		✓	✓
POKESDOWN	Hampshire		HF		✓	✓
POLEGATE	Sussex		FF		✓	✓
PORTON	Wiltshire		HF	1968	✓	✓
PORTSLADE & WEST HOVE	Sussex	2 line	FF		✓	✓
PORTSMOUTH & SOUTHSEA	Hampshire		HF/FF		✓	✓
PORTSMOUTH HARBOUR	Hampshire		HF/FF		✓	✓
PRESTON PARK	Sussex		FF		✓	✓
PULBOROUGH	Sussex		FF		✓	✓
PUTNEY	London		HF		✓	✓
QUEENBOROUGH	Kent		FF		✓	✓
QUEENS ROAD BATTERSEA	London	2 line	FF		✓	✓

Place name	County	Layout	Flange	Closed	Auction	Survived
RAINHAM	Kent		HF		✓	✓
RAMSGATE	Kent		FF		✓	✓
RAVENSBOURNE	London		FF		✓	✓
READING SOUTH (renamed Southern 1961)	Berkshire		HF	1965		
READING (SOUTHERN)	Berkshire	2 line	FF	1965	✓	✓
REEDHAM	Surrey		**BF**		✓	✓
RIDDLESDOWN	Surrey		FF		✓	✓
ROCHESTER	Kent		**BF**		✓	✓
ROPLEY	Hampshire		FF	1973		✓
ROTHERFIELD & MARK CROSS	Sussex	2 line	FF	1965		✓
ROTHERFIELD & MARK CROSS	Sussex		**BF**	1965	✓	✓
ROWFANT	Sussex		**BF**/FF	1967	✓	✓
RUDGWICK	Sussex		HF	1965		✓
RYE	Sussex		FF		✓	✓
ST. BUDEAUX VICTORIA ROAD	Devon	LP	HF		✓	✓
ST. DENYS	Hampshire		FF		✓	✓
ST. HELIER	Surrey		FF		✓	✓
ST.JAMES PARK HALT	Devon		FF			
ST. JOHNS	London		HF/FF		✓	✓
SALISBURY	Wiltshire		HF		✓	✓
SANDERSTEAD	Surrey		**BF**		✓	✓
SANDHURST HALT	Berkshire	LP				
SANDLING FOR HYTHE	Kent	LP	HF		✓	✓
SANDWICH	Kent		FF		✓	✓
SEAFORD	Sussex		FF		✓	✓
SEATON	Devon		FF	1966		✓
SELHURST	Surrey		FF		✓	✓
SELLING	Kent		FF		✓	✓
SELSDON	Surrey		**BF**	1983	✓	✓
SEMLEY	Wiltshire		FF	1966	✓	✓
SEVENOAKS	Kent		FF		✓	✓
SHEERNESS-ON-SEA	Kent		FF		✓	✓

Place name	County	Layout	Flange	Closed	Auction	Survived
SHEPHERDS WELL	Kent		FF		✓	✓
SHERBORNE	Dorset		FF		✓	✓
SHILLINGSTONE	Dorset		**BF**	1966		✓
SHOLING	Hampshire		FF		✓	✓
SHOREHAM	Kent		FF		✓	✓
SHORTLANDS	Kent		FF		✓	✓
SIDCUP	Kent		HF			✓
SIDMOUTH JUNCTION re-opened 1971	Devon		FF	1967	✓	✓
SITTINGBOURNE	Kent		FF		✓	✓
SITTINGBOURNE AND MILTON REGIS	Kent	3 line	**BF**		✓	✓
SLADE GREEN	Kent		FF		✓	✓
SLINFOLD	Sussex		HF	1965		✓
SMITHAM	Surrey		FF		✓	✓
SNODLAND	Kent		FF			✓
SNOWDOWN AND NONINGTON HALT	Kent	LP	HF/**BF**		✓	✓
SOLE STREET	Kent		FF		✓	✓
SOUTHBOURNE HALT	Sussex	LP	FF			✓
SOUTHEASE & RODMELL HALT	Sussex	LP	FF		✓	✓
SOUTH MERTON	Surrey		FF		✓	✓
SOUTHWATER	Sussex		FF	1966	✓	✓
SOUTHWICK	Sussex		FF			✓
SPARKFORD	Somerset		FF	1966		
STAINES CENTRAL	Middlesex					
STALBRIDGE	Dorset		HF	1966	✓	✓
STAPLEHURST	Kent		HF/FF			✓
STEYNING	Sussex		FF	1966		✓
STONE CROSSING HALT	Kent	1 line/LP	**BF**		✓	✓
STONE CROSSING HALT	Kent	LP	FF			✓
STONEGATE	Sussex		HF		✓	✓
STONELEIGH	Surrey		FF		✓	✓
STREATHAM	Surrey		FF		✓	✓
STREATHAM COMMON	Surrey		FF			✓
STREATHAM HILL	Surrey		FF			✓

Place name	County	Layout	Flange	Closed	Auction	Survived
STROOD	Kent		FF		✓	✓
STURRY	Kent		HF		✓	✓
SUNBURY	Middlesex		HF		✓	✓
SUNDRIDGE PARK	Kent		FF		✓	✓
SUNNYMEADS	Buckinghamshire		FF		✓	✓
SURBITON	Surrey		FF		✓	✓
SUTTON	Surrey		FF		✓	✓
SUTTON COMMON	Surrey		FF		✓	✓
SWALE HALT	Kent		FF		✓	✓
SWANSCOMBE HALT	Kent		FF		✓	✓
SWANSCOMBE HALT	Kent	LP	**BF**		✓	✓
SWAY	Hampshire		FF		✓	✓
SYDENHAM HILL	London		**BF**		✓	✓
SYON LANE	Middlesex		FF		✓	✓
TADWORTH	Surrey		FF		✓	✓
TAVISTOCK NORTH	Devon		HF	1968	✓	✓
TEMPLECOMBE re-opened 1983	Somerset		FF	1966	✓	✓
TEYNHAM	Kent		FF		✓	✓
THORNTON HEATH	Surrey		FF		✓	✓
THREE BRIDGES	Sussex		HF/FF		✓	✓
THREE OAKS AND GUESTLING HALT	Sussex	3 line	FF			✓
TONBRIDGE	Kent		FF		✓	✓
TOOTING	London		FF		✓	✓
TUNBRIDGE WELLS CENTRAL	Kent	LP	FF		✓	✓
TUNBRIDGE WELLS WEST	Kent		FF	1985	✓	✓
TWICKENHAM (light green only)	Middlesex		HF		✓	✓
UCKFIELD	Sussex		FF		✓	✓
UPPER HALLIFORD HALT	Middlesex	LP	**BF**		✓	✓
UPPER WARLINGHAM	Surrey	1&2 line	FF		✓	✓
VAUXHALL	London		FF		✓	✓

Place name	County	Layout	Flange	Closed	Auction	Survived
WADDON	Surrey		FF		✓	✓
WADDON MARSH HALT re-opened 2000	Surrey		**BF**	1997	✓	✓
WADEBRIDGE	Cornwall		FF	1967		✓
WALDRON AND HORAM renamed 1953	Sussex		HF	1965		✓
WALMER	Kent		FF		✓	✓
WALTON ON THAMES	Surrey		**BF**		✓	✓
WANBOROUGH	Surrey		HF		✓	✓
WANDSWORTH COMMON	London	2 line	FF		✓	✓
WANDSWORTH ROAD	London		FF			✓
WANDSWORTH TOWN	London		FF		✓	✓
WARBLINGTON HALT	Hampshire	LP	FF		✓	✓
WARMINSTER	Wiltshire		HF/FF		✓	✓
WARNHAM	Sussex		FF			✓
WATERINGBURY	Kent		FF		✓	✓
WATERLOO	London		FF		✓	✓
WELLING	Kent		HF/FF		✓	✓
WEST BYFLEET	Surrey		HF		✓	✓
WESTCOMBE PARK	London		FF		✓	✓
WEST CROYDON	Surrey		HF/FF		✓	✓
WEST DULWICH	London		HF			✓
WESTENHANGER also **BF**	Kent		HF/FF		✓	✓
WESTGATE-ON-SEA	Kent		FF		✓	✓
WEST GRINSTEAD	Sussex		FF	1966	✓	✓
WEST MALLING	Kent		HF/FF		✓	✓
WEST MOORS	Dorset		FF	1964		✓
WEST NORWOOD	London		HF		✓	✓
WEST ST. LEONARDS	Sussex		FF		✓	✓
WEST SUTTON	Surrey		FF		✓	✓
WEST WEYBRIDGE (renamed)	Surrey		HF			✓
WEST WICKHAM also **BF**	Kent		HF/FF		✓	✓
WEYBRIDGE	Surrey		HF		✓	✓
WEYMOUTH (also 4' totems FF)	Dorset		HF		✓	✓
WHIMPLE	Devon		FF		✓	✓

Place name		County	Layout	Flange	Closed	Auction	Survived
WHITCHURCH NORTH		Hampshire					
WHITSTABLE & TANKERTON		Kent		**BF**/FF		✓	✓
WHITTON		Middlesex		FF		✓	✓
WHYTELEAFE		Surrey		FF		✓	✓
WHYTELEAFE SOUTH		Surrey		**BF**		✓	✓
WILTON SOUTH		Wiltshire		HF	1966	✓	✓
WIMBLEDON		Surrey		FF			✓
WIMBLEDON CHASE		Surrey		FF		✓	✓
WINCHELSEA		Sussex		**BF**			✓
WINCHESTER CITY		Hampshire		HF		✓	✓
WINCHFIELD		Hampshire		FF			✓
WINDSOR & ETON RIVERSIDE		Berkshire	LP	HF		✓	✓
WINNERSH HALT		Berkshire		FF			✓
WITHYHAM		Sussex		**BF**	1967		✓
WIVELSFIELD		Sussex		FF		✓	✓
WOLDINGHAM		Surrey		FF		✓	✓
WOODMANSTERNE		Surrey		FF			✓
WOODSIDE	re-opened 2000	Surrey		**BF**/FF	1997	✓	✓
WOOLWICH ARSENAL		London		HF/FF		✓	✓
WOOLWICH DOCKYARD		London		FF		✓	✓
WORPLESDON		Surrey		FF		✓	✓
WORTHING CENTRAL		Sussex		FF			✓
WRAYSBURY	+all green totems **BF**	Buckinghamshire		FF		✓	✓
WYE		Kent		FF		✓	✓
YALDING		Kent		FF			✓
YEOFORD		Devon		FF		✓	✓
YEOVIL PEN MILL		Somerset		HF		✓	✓
YEOVIL TOWN		Somerset		FF	1966	✓	✓

CHAPTER 7

The Western Region

Introduction

The Western Region, formed in the 1948 Nationalisation, was based totally on the boundaries of the former Great Western Railway. The GWR was arguably the most independent of all the railway companies, and even after the formation of BR it continued its freethinking policy. But history shows it was not just a railway. It had extensive shipping, lorry and even air subsidiaries. At its zenith, the GWR was an integrated transport company that we would love to see today. It developed its motive power based on a proven history of reliability and safety. The forerunner was Brunel, a quite brilliant engineer, who set the standard for 'God's Wonderful Railway', as the GWR was frequently called. This was the railway of broad gauge and passenger comfort. Eventually this led to crack expresses such as the 'Cheltenham Flyer' hauled by workhorse Castle-class engines. Before that, locomotives such as *City of Truro* and *Rover* had made names for themselves. This is the region of **Paddington**, **Bristol Temple Meads**, Swindon Works, trains to the West Country and the seaside towns of Devon and Cornwall. The poster images found on many stations in the heyday of the GWR and WR are real classics today. The two below are typical of superb GWR/WR marketing.

(South Devon Railway - Tindale Collection)

The history of the Western Region

The history of the Western Region is steeped in folklore. In March 1833 the young Isambard Kingdom Brunel was appointed chief engineer to the fledgling railway. His strategy was simple: build the fastest most comfortable railway from London to Bristol, a major port to the USA. At that time these were the two principal ports and Brunel saw the immense potential of railways. His vision was extraordinary for a man of his age, but it was not just the railway he designed. Just like Leonardo da Vinci some three hundred years before he turned his mind to many things. So were born bridges and viaducts (**Hanwell** and **Chippenham**), tunnels with classic portals (Box), and stations such as **Bristol Temple Meads**. This was later incorporated into the larger gothic-style Wyatt station, and both remain today as architectural masterpieces. The 'totem' below was recreated from a roundel (notice the aspect ratio is different to **Paddington** alongside it), but we have photographic evidence that **Bristol Temple Meads** did carry totems.

In some ways Brunel was too visionary. He conceived broad gauge (7ft ¼in) for his railway, so that greater speed, comfort and safety were available. One of the first consequences of broad gauge was the fact that GWR engines could not use Euston station (which was the original plan), and Brunel had to build his own station at **Paddington**. This was finally finished in 1853 and again later modified by Wyatt.

Swindon lies halfway between the two Brunel termini. The station was completed in 1835 and just over six years later the home of the GWR was established, following the decision to choose the growing town as the site for its locomotive works. This was completed in 1846. Daniel Gooch, who had worked with Stephenson in the north-east, was put in charge as superintendent at the age of 21! He worked for the GWR for a further 27 years. **Swindon**, being 80 miles from London, was the natural place for the junction to **Gloucester** and **Cheltenham Spa**. However, there it met the standard gauge of the Birmingham to Gloucester line; this being the first place where the gauges met, the initial operations proved chaotic! In 1844 the line from Bristol was extended west to Exeter, so within 12 years of its inception the outline of the GWR was in place.

The line north from **Didcot** developed at about the same time, with **Oxford** being reached in 1844 and Banbury in 1850. Several companies were building

WESTERN REGION TOTEMS

lines in the West Midlands. The area between **Wolverhampton** and **Birmingham** proved to be a legal battleground until 1854, when the GWR eventually reached **Wolverhampton** from their **Oxford** line. This was, however, a journey of 142 miles and shorter routes were examined, such as the 1887 line built through **High Wycombe**, **Princes Risborough**, Banbury and into **Warwick**. Thus was born the main **Paddington** to **Birmingham Snow Hill** line.

The area from **Shrewsbury** to **Chester** was another legal battleground, as rival companies tried to win the freight traffic from the West Midlands to the port of Liverpool. The Shrewsbury and Chester Railway (S&CR) formed in 1845, and the Birmingham and Shrewsbury Railway Bill was given Royal ascent a year later. By 1852 developments occurred in South Wales, and the line from **Gloucester** to **Swansea** (via **Cardiff**) was completed. Several Welsh valley artery routes were also constructed, to facilitate the movement of huge amounts of coal from a myriad of Welsh collieries to the ports around the Severn Estuary. Thus by the mid-1850s the nucleus of the GWR was complete. The demise of Brunel's broad gauge came in a single monumental weekend during 1892 (Railtrack's successors please note), when all lines were converted to standard gauge.

In 1923 the GWR consisted of 3,800 miles of track. The enlarged GWR was formed from seven companies, the GWR itself plus:

The Barry Railway (BR)	The Cambrian Railway (CamR)
The Cardiff Railway (CR)	The Newport &South Wales (N&SWR)
The Rhymney Railway (RR)	The Taff Vale Railway (TVR)

Some of these were really tiny. The Cardiff Railway for example had 11 route miles, and it was not the smallest – the N&SWR came in at only 10 miles! The GWR was the real heavyweight of the seven with 3,005 miles; it was more than 10 times bigger than the next largest, the Cambrian at 295 miles. The collage that follows represents just one totem from six of the constituent companies (the N&SWR was just too small). At its zenith the GWR used to advertise itself as the 'railway of a thousand stations', but our database shows that fewer than half their stations were equipped with totems.

Some stations closed before the Beeching Era. Many of those in the following list were in Wales, and included are some desirable names: **Aberbeeg**, **Abertillery**, **Builth Wells**, **Caerleon**, **Kingsbridge**, **Llandilo Bridge**, **Perranporth**, **Pontrilas**, **Porthcawl**, **St Fagans** and **Upper Pontnewydd**. The database at the end of this chapter shows all the stations that were early closures, and details of those known to survive.

The geography of the region

At its peak the GWR extended over a quarter of Great Britain. The final domain was London to Liverpool, London to Cardiff (and the harbours of West Wales), west to Penzance, the whole of mid-Wales and most of North Wales. With this large area, the railway engineers saw a tremendous diversity of geography, ranging from the fast running lines through the Thames Valley, to the Devon banks of Dainton and Rattray, contrasting with the picturesque lines hugging the Cambrian Coast.

Starting at the extremities of the region, Devon and Cornwall have hundreds of miles of varied and magnificent coastlines, from the rocky north shores around Tintagel to sandy bays of St Michaels Mount and **Torquay**. These two counties are very different, the almost treeless and wild centre of Cornwall contrasting with rolling scenery of farming Devon. Railways took the easy routes where they could, to link the cities of **Exeter** and Plymouth to elegant **Truro**, as well as to the once bustling ports of **Falmouth** and **Penzance**. A train journey east over Brunel's famous bridge at **Saltash**, along the seawall at **Dawlish** and into **Exeter**, is one of the great railway journeys of the world. The whole area is dotted with secluded coves and pretty fishing villages with, we are sure, a wonderful smuggling past! The exotic gardens of the Cornish and Devon Rivieras contrast with the wild moorland terrain just a few miles away. Totems from these two counties, in particular the coastal routes, are very popular with collectors.

Torquay main platform, June 1976. (Alan Young)

Moving north, the main line splits at **Taunton**, with the northern loop going up to **Weston-super-Mare** and **Bristol**, while the southern line goes through **Castle Cary**, **Reading** and into **Paddington**. The counties of Wiltshire, Somerset and Dorset are termed Wessex. It is an area characterised by rolling hills and charming villages full of thatched cottages. Wessex is a paradise for the study of history or architecture, with prehistoric Stonehenge and Georgian Bath not far from each other. Expansive hills enabled sheep to graze and a flourishing wool trade to develop, so that textile towns like **Bradford-on-Avon** could grow. This is an area where the WR and SR criss-cross each other, and here are some classic totem names: **Evercreech Junction**, **Bath Green Park**, **Templecombe** and **Yeovil Pen Mill** (SR).

To the north the Cotswold Hills also have magnificent scenery, but gave only headaches to the railway builders. The climb up through the Golden Valley east from **Stroud** towards **Swindon** over Sapperton Bank has resulted in some wonderful railway photos over the years. Going north-east we come to **Oxford**, the city of 'dreaming spires' and classical sandstone centres of learning that have been there since the mid-13th century. From here the lines split: to the north we find the industrial West Midlands, the fertile Warwickshire plains, Royal **Leamington Spa**, the magnificent castle at **Warwick** and Shakespeare's County. This whole area has many small country halts. It is real totem collecting country! Further west is the Vale of **Evesham**, and the cathedrals of **Gloucester**, **Hereford** and **Worcester**. These are closely linked through the Three Choirs Festival. This is 'Nimrod' and 'Pomp and Circumstance' Elgar country dominated by the Malvern Hills. The 16th-century black and white timbered buildings of **Ledbury** contrast with the 19th-century stonework of **Great Malvern**. Indeed one of us (RF) feels this is rural England at its absolute best, and what an area to collect WR totems from.

In South Wales the steepness of some of the valleys gave rise to interesting construction problems. The Rhymney, Taff and Rhondda valleys are three of the more famous, but are quieter today than in past times. The decimation of the coal industry caused most of the valley stations to close. Reference to page 16 of *Wignall's British Railways Gazetteer* shows the extent of the cuts. **Cardiff** used to be our biggest coal exporting port, but it is now the centre of 'high tech' Wales. To the north of the valleys we find the leafy Wye Valley, the expansive hills of the Black Mountains, the Brecon Beacons, Fforest Fawr and Black Mountain. Further west we reach the Gower Peninsula and the loveliest part of South Wales, Pembrokeshire. Here is St Davids, Britain's smallest city, but a long way from the nearest station at **Mathry Road**.

Brecon station, 1961. (R. Blencowe)

Rural mid-Wales brings us wonderfully named totems – **Brecon**, **Llandrindod Wells**, **Builth Wells**, **Llandovery** and **Llanwrtyd Wells**. This is actually LNWR country, the furthest west this company ventured. (The GWR countered by running their line through LMR territory into Birkenhead.)

The wide expanse of Cardigan Bay was once a tourist mecca for thousands of families from the industrial West Midlands. In the summertime, I (RF) vividly remember the old A5 was always clogged with cars going west. This is *Cambrian Coast Express* country. The line from **Shrewsbury** cuts through the heart of the Cambrian Mountain ridge before reaching **Dovey Junction**.

At **Dovey Junction** the line splits, with the southern section terminating at **Aberystwyth**. The northern section runs all the way to the terminus at **Pwllheli**. This section has a classic set – **Towyn**, **Barmouth Junction**, **Harlech**, **Portmadoc**, **Criccieth**, **Penychain** and **Pwllheli** itself.

Behind the bay are the Cambrian Mountains, then the Clywydian Hills before we drop back into England. Along the border, castles are found all the way from Chester down to South Wales. These were fortifications to keep the Welsh out, or should it be the totems in! More than any other region, the geography of the GWR breaks the area into very compact and discrete sections, each with distinctive cultures and ways of life.

The Western Region database

The pages that follow have taken hours of poring over documents, books and maps in order to put together a station history that is both succinct and informative. We were fortunate that we had some GWR experts to call upon and quite a few hours of phone time have also gone into this section. As with other chapters the right-hand column on each page shows the totem survivors, and we are amazed how much this changed in the three years we were working on this book!

A: **Aberbeeg** is one of the many valley stations that closed early (1962). It opened in 1850 but we are unaware of any totems preserved in collections. **Abingdon** (formerly in Berkshire, but now Oxfordshire) was opened by the GWR in 1856, when a short branch was completed into the town. The branch station Abingdon Junction was closed on 8 September 1963 and the following day **Abingdon** also closed. No totems are thought to have survived. **Afon Wen** is another ex-Cambrian station near **Criccieth** in North Wales. It was open for less than 100 years (1867–1964) and several eminent collectors would welcome this in their collections! In this part of the database there are also a few totems that have not appeared in auction. These include **Aberdovey**, **Aberthaw**, **Abertillery** and **Albrighton**. The West Midlands station **Acocks Green and South Yardley** had two derivatives, both '&' and 'and' being used. We know that all of the six **Ashchurch for Tewkesbury** totems fitted have survived. Of the 16 stations in this section, 50 per cent have been closed for 30 years or more.

B: **Barry Dock** is an uncommon totem, despite being a survivor from the savage cuts that took place in Glamorgan. We have listed **Barmouth Junction** twice in the database, because the flange type and layout make them individuals. We do not know of any half-flanged survivors. **Bath Spa** was an early victim of re-signing and our work shows the totems were only up for around six years. The station opened in 1840 and the 'Spa' was added in 1949. It is very desirable to Western buffs! The picture of **Bath Spa** station below was taken in about 1970, when the totems had long gone. It would be nice to think that one from this wonderful place has survived somewhere.

Bath Spa station, 1970. (R. Blencowe)

Bath Green Park is equally desirable for both S&D and WR fans alike. The station opened in 1870 and was given the full name by BR in 1951. It is today very tastefully restored as a supermarket. We have confirmed both roundels and totems at **Bristol Temple Meads**, but the totems have proved elusive thus far. Neither of the totems from Builth have appeared in auction. The town actually had two GWR stations (Builth Road and **Builth Wells**) and one ex-LNWR station (**Builth Road High Level**, which had chocolate and cream totems). Builth Road Low Level (also Cambrian) does not appear to have been fitted, but as it only held this name for 12 years it is not surprising. Bowbridge Crossing Halt in the Stroud valley did not have totems but the direction sign from this location is quite a rarity and we could not resist its inclusion!

C: **Caerleon** is a name to grace a Welsh set! The station was south of Abergavenny and only had totems in place for just over a decade. **Cardiff General** was opened by the GWR in 1850. The 'General' was added in 1924 and it was renamed Cardiff Central in 1973. Being a mainline flagship station, refurbishment occurred early. The totems therefore disappeared and are now as rare as those from **Cardiff Queen Street** are common. We have included below a lovely shot of the old Queen Street station before modernisation. **Cefn On** is an elusive totem with a complex naming history. It carried the names Coed Colliery Halt (1915–49), Cefn On Halt (1949–69), **Cefn On** (1969–80) and Cefn-Onn (1980–6). We have not been able to confirm when they were removed, but only two were fitted. Totems from **Cheltenham Spa Lansdown** are rare. We know of only a few of these survivors from a station that opened in 1840. The LMS added the full name in 1925, and BR called it simply Cheltenham Spa after Malvern Road closed in 1966.

Cardiff Queen Street awaiting modernisation, May 1973. (Alan Young)

Other desirable and elusive names in this section may include **Churchdown** near Gloucester (opened in 1862 and closed in 1964), **Corsham** in Wiltshire (1841–1965) and **Criccieth** (opened in 1867). All are known to be present in collections but only **Churchdown** has surfaced in public. **Crumlin High Level**, located north of Cardiff on the cross-country route from Pontypool, has not been confirmed as a survivor. It opened as Crumlin for Western Valley in 1857 but took the 'totem name' in 1881 and closed in 1964. A few of the choice but not so common items are found below.

D: **Daisy Bank and Bradley** was an early West Midlands closure (1962), when the whole line from **Priestfield** to **Dudley** was axed. Two very desirable West Country totems are **Dawlish** and **Dawlish Warren**. The first named is by far the older station (1846), with **Dawlish Warren** opening in 1905 as Warren Halt, and despite being closed for a few years during the First World War, it is still operational today. **Devonport** is a real WR obscurity as covered in Chapter 3. Quite why only this Devon station was chosen for a black and white sign is a mystery. **Dinas (Rhondda)** totems are not thought to have survived, even though the station is open today as Dinas (named by BR in 1980). **Dolgelly** opened in 1869 (renamed **Dolgelley** in 1896). BR changed the name again to **Dolgellau** in 1960, so totems with the old name would have only been hung for 10 years. It is not surprising none are known. I remember travelling through **Dunstall Park** on the GWR line from **Wolverhampton Low Level** to **Wellington (Salop)** in the late '50s. This was a small station with only a few totems towards the ends of the platforms.

E: **Ellesmere** in northern Shropshire is wanted by several of the collecting fraternity. The station was open for 102 years, closing in 1965. One of the most classic of all totems is **Evercreech Junction**, a place synonymous with the S&D and a number of famous railway paintings. It closed on an emotional day in March 1966 after being open for 104 years. Totems from either of the stations in Exeter are collectable today. **Exeter St Davids** opened in 1846, the same day as St Thomas Exeter, which became **Exeter (St Thomas)** in 1897. Like **Dawlish Warren** it closed for a few years during the First World War, reopening in 1919. **Exminster** station opened in 1852 and we have evidence that the totems were painted wood.

F: **Falmouth** is a rare Cornish totem that has not yet appeared in auction. The station opened in 1863, but closed to traffic in 1970. However, five years later BR decided it was useful for shipping traffic and fully reopened it. Today it is named Falmouth Docks. **Fishguard & Goodwick** is a comparative rarity (closed in 1964, opened in 1965 and closed again in 1972), as is **Fladbury**, a small Cotswold station on the route of the *Cathedrals Express*.

G: There are not too many rarities here, as most have appeared in auction. All WR totems beginning with 'G' have been confirmed to survive somewhere.

Gorseinon in West Wales is probably the least common, but totems from **Great Malvern** and **Grimes Hill & Wythall** (a small halt south of **Tyseley**) are also not common. Two collectable items are shown below.

H: **Ham Mill Halt** is a small station in the Golden Valley in Gloucestershire. It opened in 1903 but closed in 1964. Very few of these signs were made, so the picture in our database is quite a catch! **Harlech** totems appear on several 'wants' lists, so be patient, as they were *in situ* relatively late. **Hayes & Harlington** is one of the rare black and white signs – we believe it never carried chocolate and cream totems. The station opened as Hayes in 1864 and took the totem name some thirty years later. **Heath Halt Low Level** has not yet been confirmed as a survivor. It was renamed from Heath Halt Cardiff (opened in 1911) in 1924 and renamed again in 1969 as Heath Low Level. We have now confirmed **Hungerford** is a survivor, as one appeared in auction in 2001. The station was named Hungerford Halt between 1964 and 1969.

I: **Instow** on the southern bank of the River Taw in Devon is sought after. Opening in 1855, it closed in 1965 only to reopen three years later for a two-week period in January 1968! The station at **Iver** opened in 1924, but a totem from there has yet to surface in a public auction.

K: We covered the many guises of **Kensington Olympia** in Chapter 3, but the station naming history is equally as complicated (Kensington Addison Road was one of the names). **Keyham** (opened on the main line west of Plymouth in 1900) has not yet been confirmed as a survivor. There are also several desirable names from the same part of the country in this section of the database. The Devonshire trio of **Kingsbridge**, **Kingskerswell** and **Kingswear** would make a super display for WR collectors and Royalists alike!

We doubt whether **Knighton** in Radnorshire ever had totems. The data is conflicting, but we have left the name in the listing until good photographic evidence appears. The station opened in 1861 but was renamed Knighton Halt in 1965, reverting four years later. It appears as Knighton for Presteigne in some timetables.

L: Both **Leamington Spa General** (ex-GWR) and **Leamington Spa Milverton** (ex-LNWR), have yet to appear in auction. Both stations have a complex naming history. General has held four different names since 1852, but Milverton has the most incredible naming history of any station we have researched. It took this name in 1952 before being closed in 1965. The station opened as Leamington in 1844 and had seven different names in the next 110 years! **Little Kimble** had an unusual early flangeless sign as previously discussed in Chapter 5, and below is the sign *in situ*.

(Alan Young)

We now enter the area of those wonderful Welsh names, which on their own would grace any wall. Of the more unusual and desirable we should mention **Llandilo Bridge** (opened in 1865 and closed in 1963), **Llandovery** (opened in 1858), **Llanharan** (opened in 1850 and closed 1964 – survival not confirmed), and the superbly named **Llanwyrtyd Wells**. This is one of the very few totems in the old county of Brecknockshire (the station opened in 1867 and is now named Llanwyrtyd). Virtually any of the names in this part of the database would be welcome in either of our collections! **Lye** (opened in 1863) has not appeared yet in auction and is one of the two shortest names on the whole of the WR. This alone makes it desirable.

M: **Maerdy**, at the north end of the branch from **Porth**, closed in 1964 along with six other stations on that branch line. It has not yet been confirmed as a survivor. The existence of totems at **Milford Haven** is in doubt. Evidence suggests that this station did not have totems fitted, so the jury is out! In 1962 the line south from **Moat Lane Junction** down to **Builth Wells** was axed. In 1972 **Moat Lane Junction** itself finally succumbed and this rare totem has yet to appear in auction. A rare gem from north Devon is **Mortehoe & Woolacombe**. This opened as Morthoe in 1874, was renamed Mortehoe (in 1902) and finally took the totem name in 1950. It closed in 1970.

N: **Newquay** (opened in 1876) is quite desirable in any Cornish collection, as it is one of only five branch line termini in the county with totems, the others being **Bude** (SR), **Falmouth**, **Looe** and **St Ives**.

July 1973. (Alan Young)

Newton Abbot is a famous location in south Devon, but the totem is not that rare – the station opened as Newton in 1846, with Abbot being added in 1877. **Neyland** is another Pembrokeshire totem whose existence is in doubt. It opened in 1856 as 'Milford Haven', but was renamed New Milford in November of the same year, before becoming Neyland in 1906. (Today's **Milford Haven** opened in 1893 as Milford.)

O: **Oakengates** is a very rare totem from Shropshire. During its history (opened in 1849) it has been named **Oakengates West** (1851–1956) for most of its life. It is now Oakengates for Telford, because of the new town growth in the 1980s. **Oakle Street** on the line between **Gloucester** and **Newport** closed in 1964. Any totems from here would have been only 10 years old at closure, but none have so far been confirmed. The wonderfully named **Old Hill (High Street) Halt** is one of the real classics. It was open for 59 years between 1905 and 1964. **Oxford** opened in 1844 and has been named Oxford General during its history. Considering it was a large station, the totems are rarely seen.

P: **Paddington** is one of *the* classic totems. Opening in 1838, the site has seen two main stations, with the present station being completed in 1859. **Par** in Cornwall shares the distinction (with **Lye**) of the shortest name on the WR. The station opened there in 1859. Neither **Pembrey & Burry Port** nor **Pembroke** have appeared in auction but we have photos of both below. Pembury (west of Llanelli) opened in 1852 and became **Pembrey & Burry Port** in 1887. **Pembroke** was opened in 1863.

Totems from **Pencoed**, on the main line west from Cardiff, have not yet been confirmed to have survived. The station opened in 1850 and closed in 1964, but was reopened by BR in 1992. **Penychain** has been discussed in Chapter 4. It actually opened in 1933 as Penychain Halt but took its final name in 1947. **Penzance** is a most desirable totem. It is the western terminus of the WR, opening in 1852. We have not yet confirmed that a **Pewsey** totem has survived, nor totems from **Ponthir** and **Pontlottyn**. Two of the stations are still open, with **Pewsey** being completed in 1862, and **Pontlottyn** in 1860. Ponthir was completed in 1874 but closed to passengers in 1962. Totems from **Porthcawl**, another South Wales, station re-appeared for the first time at auction in 2001, nearly 40 years after closure. This gives us hope that a few more gems will surface! **Princes End & Coseley** was one of the many West Midlands stations closed in 1962. The station opened and closed three times during the period 1863–1962. Other desirable items from this part of the database include **Portmadoc** and **Pwllheli**, both on the northern section of the Cambrian route. **Priestfield** (closed 1972) was a four-platform junction station that was the first east from **Wolverhampton Low Level** in the West Midlands. Very few survive as many were vandalised.

Q: The only WR station beginning with this letter is another collectors' classic – **Quakers Yard (Low Level)**. The station is on the Merthyr valley line and opened as Quakers Yard in 1858. The '(Low Level)' lower panel was added in 1924 and was removed again in 1968.

R: **Radstock West** was discussed in Chapter 5, being a very early small cornered totem. The existence of totems from **Radyr**, to the north of Cardiff, was confirmed when one unexpectedly appeared in the February 2001 Birmingham Railway auction. The station originally opened as Penarth Junction in 1863. **Rhymney** is an evocative name steeped in Welsh railway history. The station is now a terminus at the northern end of its namesake valley and opened in 1858. The line to the north closed in 1958. We have included photographs of rare items from **Ross-on-Wye**, **Round Oak** and **Royal Oak** in our database, none of which have appeared yet in auction. What about the desirable Reading pair below?

S: Any of the names beginning with 'St' are quite sought after. The Cornish trio of **St Austell**, **St Erth** and **St Ives** would make a wonderful display just on their own. All three are still open and the last two were completed on the same day (1 June 1877). **St Austell** is much older being opened in 1859. Another Cornish totem, **Saltash** has not appeared in auction – it opened the same day as **St Austell**. **St Fagans** in South Wales is a rare totem. We have not been able to confirm the existence of totems from **Saundersfoot** in Pembrokeshire, due to lack of photographic evidence. This station, which is halfway along the branch from **Whitland** to **Pembroke**, opened in 1866. **Severn Tunnel Junction** is an interesting item and sought-after these days. The station is at the western end of the Severn Tunnel and opened late in 1886. **Shrewsbury** is an important junction and the county town of Shropshire, opening as Shrewsbury General in 1849 to replace the first station in the town, built in 1848. The full flange totem is far less common than the half flange.

Totems from both **Skewen** near Swansea and **South Molton** in North Devon have yet to be confirmed as having survived. **Stonehouse (Burdett Road)** is a small station on the line from **Gloucester** to **Swindon** that opened in 1845. (BR added the lower panel name in 1951.) We believe the station only had four totems. **Stroud** totems are unusual because of the brown flanges. We cannot leave this section without mentioning **Swindon**, the home of the GWR. Although several totems have appeared in auction, it is still considered to be one of the Western collector's items. The station opened on 17 December 1840 and was named Swindon Junction between 1865 and 1902. Considering the importance attached to it by the GWR, it was not the architectural masterpiece of **Temple Meads** or **Paddington**.

(Dawlish Museum)

(Barry Hayward)

Other collectable names in this part of the database are **Shipton for Burford** (where the town name appears in the lower panel), **Shirehampton** and **Starcross**. This latter station is situated in the picturesque lower Exe estuary, south of Exeter, and is desirable among the Devon collectors.

T: Here we find some classic names. A trio of elusive gems – **Teignmouth**, **Tir Phil** and **Treorchy** – have all yet to be confirmed as survivors. **Teignmouth** is very sought after by several Devon aficionados. The present station opened in 1884. When the main coastal railway was realigned this station replaced the first Teignmouth that opened in 1846. Many classic photos and paintings exist of this location. **Tir Phil** is located in the upper Rhymney Valley and **Treorchy** in the upper Rhondda Valley both in South Wales. Both stations are still open, but we have no indication where all the totems went! Classic names in this section may include **Tenby**, **The Lakes Halt** (in Warwickshire and not Cumbria!), **Tonypandy & Trealaw**, **Torre**, **Totnes**, and **Treherbert**. **Torquay** is a most unusual totem (but not particularly rare), as described in Chapter 5. The station opened in 1859.

U: **Upper Pontnewydd** is located just west of Cwmbran in Monmouthshire. It was an early closure in 1962 and no totems are known to have survived, yet. The station opened in 1852 as Pontnewydd. During its history it has also been named Upper Cwmbran for just a few weeks (September 1881 to November 1881). **Uxbridge Vine Street** has been a desirable item over the years, because of its early closure in 1962. The station opened in 1856, and the 'Vine Street' was added in 1907.

W: **Wargrave** has not yet appeared in auction, but is a known survivor and **Warwick** is a sought-after county town totem. **Wednesbury (Central)** and **West Bromwich** closed along with all the stations on the ex-GWR route between **Wolverhampton** and **Birmingham Snow Hill** in 1972. Neither is a common totem.

We cannot pass **Wellington (Salop)** without a mention. It was the place where one of us (RF) really became hooked on railways and stations! There are two distinct variants: the half-flanged totem has in the lower panel 'Salop', whereas the full-flanged version used '(Salop)'. The station opened in 1849 and became **Wellington (Salop)** in the early '50s. It is still open today as Wellington Telford West. The survival of neither a **Weston Milton** or a **Weston-Super-Mare Locking Road** from the same county has yet been confirmed. Photo evidence of **Weston Milton** totems exists and the station only took its name in 1969, from Weston Milton Halt that opened in 1933. **Locking Road** closed in 1964 and a quality photo would be helpful to confirm existence. **Weston-Super-Mare General** is another of those collectable lower panel stations. The first station in the town opened in 1866 and closed in 1884 when replaced by the present station. From our research, it seems likely that totems went up in 1956, only to be removed in favour of our 'fluorescent friend' about six years later. This may account for their rarity.

Whitlocks End Halt (on the line south from Birmingham to **Stratford-upon-Avon**) is another elusive item. Stations on the same line that are equally elusive are **Wood End** and **Wootton Wawen Platform**. These three stations were small country halts, close to each other, with very few totems on each. The same is true of **Windmill End Halt** in the old south Staffordshire – closed in 1964. This station took this name in 1952, so the totems were only 12 years old when the line closed. **Wootton Bassett** near **Swindon** opened early in 1841. Rather interestingly it was renamed Wootton Bassett Junction in 1903, but sadly the totem did not carry the word 'Junction'.

Y: **Yate** is an elusive totem for those Gloucestershire collectors. It opened in 1844, was closed in 1965, but then reopened by BR in 1989. **Ynyshir** is not yet confirmed as a survivor. The station opened in 1876 as Ynishir but was renamed by BR in the early '60s. All other totems in this section are confirmed survivors, though **Yardley Wood** is not so common.

We cannot leave the Western Region without a few extra shots of totems *in situ*. The first of these is of **Birmingham Moor Street** in late July 1973.

Birmingham enamels still in place, July 1973. (Alan Young)

The Great Western Railway opened Moor Street station in 1909, but BR closed it in September 1987, the same day as the adjacent new station opened. The old station carried quite a few totems and several have appeared in auction.

Just further south was the cathedral city of **Worcester** with two stations. **Shrub Hill** is considered by many to be the main station, purely because it is the first station where trains from **Oxford** and **Paddington** called. **Worcester Foregate Street** is west of **Shrub Hill** on the line to **Great Malvern** and **Hereford**. The small map of the main lines that follows is shown alongside a Shrub Hill totem that had probably just been removed. It epitomises the city station in the '70s. The hanging brackets are still in place, and maybe the proximity of the litter bin sums this whole scene up nicely!

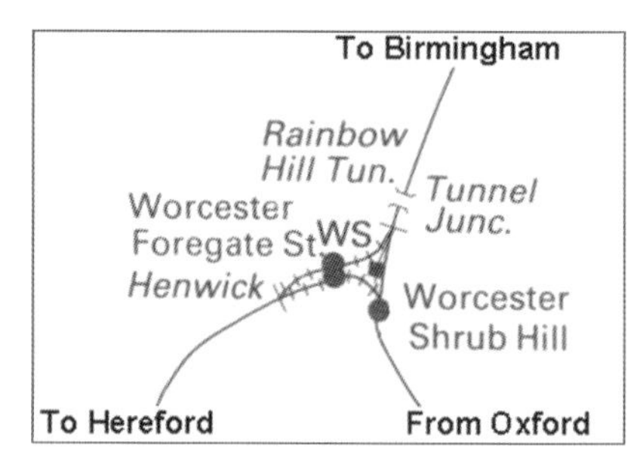

(Tim Clarke)

How much nicer it is to see the two Worcester totems alongside each other again and well cared for today.

Further south and west now, down to Cornwall and **Lostwithiel**, which opened in 1859. This lovely shot taken in the summer of 1977 shows unspoilt rural Cornwall at its best when 'flaking' chocolate and cream still reigned!

(Alan Young)

Next we go to the West Midlands and the closure of the old GWR main line across the region in 1972. GWR and LNWR lines crossed each other several times in this region, so when rationalisation occurred it was the GWR lines that closed after the LNWR lines were electrified and upgraded. **Wednesbury (Central)** was one of eleven stations to feel the axe in a single day.

Wednesbury Central the day after closure. (Mike Kilvington)

Finally we have included a 1960s shot of a rare Shropshire totem under its station lamp. **Albrighton** is located midway between **Wolverhampton** and **Wellington**. The station was opened by the Shrewsbury & Birmingham Railway in 1849.

(Dawlish Museum)

Chapter 7 Totem Listing

* = some brown flanges (throughout this database)

Place name	County	Western Region			Totem in	Totem
		Layout	Flange	Closed	Auction	Survived
ABERBEEG	Monmouthshire			1962		
ABERCYNON	Glamorgan		FF		✓	✓
ABERDARE HIGH LEVEL	Glamorgan	LP	HF	1964	✓	✓
ABERDOVEY	Merionethshire		FF			✓
ABERGAVENNY MONMOUTH ROAD	Monmouthshire	LP	HF/FF		✓	✓
ABERTHAW	Glamorgan		FF	1964		✓
ABERTILLERY	Monmouthshire		FF	1962		✓
ABERYSTWYTH	Cardiganshire		HF/FF		✓	✓
ABINGDON	Berkshire		HF	1963		
ACOCKS GREEN & SOUTH YARDLEY	Warwickshire		FF		✓	✓
ACOCKS GREEN & SOUTH YARDLEY	Warwickshire	2 line	FF		✓	✓
AFON WEN	Caernarvonshire			1964		
ALBRIGHTON	Shropshire		HF			✓
ASHCHURCH FOR TEWKESBURY	Gloucestershire	LP	FF	1971	✓	✓
ASHLEY HILL	Bristol		FF		✓	✓
AVONMOUTH DOCK	Somerset		FF		✓	✓
BADMINTON	Gloucestershire		HF	1968	✓	✓
BAPTIST END HALT	Worcestershire	LP	FF	1964		✓
BARGOED	Glamorgan		FF		✓	✓
BARMOUTH	Merionethshire		HF		✓	✓
BARMOUTH JUNCTION Renamed	Merionethshire		HF			
BARMOUTH JUNCTION Renamed	Merionethshire	LP	FF			✓
BARRY	Glamorgan		FF		✓	✓
BARRY DOCK	Glamorgan		FF		✓	✓
BARRY ISLAND	Glamorgan		FF		✓	✓
BARRYTOWN	Glamorgan		HF		✓	✓
BATHAMPTON	Somerset		FF	1966	✓	✓
BATH GREEN PARK	Somerset	LP	HF	1966	✓	✓
BATH SPA	Somerset		HF			
BEACONSFIELD	Buckinghamshire		FF			✓
BEARLEY	Warwickshire		FF			✓

Place name	County	Layout	Flange	Closed	Auction	Survived
BEDMINSTER	Bristol		FF		✓	✓
BEDWYN	Berkshire		FF			✓
BICESTER NORTH	Oxfordshire		HF		✓	✓
BILSTON CENTRAL	Staffordshire	LP	FF	1972	✓	✓
BILSTON WEST	Staffordshire		FF	1962		✓
BIRMINGHAM MOOR STREET new stn. 1987	Warwickshire	LP	FF	1987	✓	✓
BIRMINGHAM SNOW HILL re-opened 1987	Warwickshire	LP	FF	1972	✓	✓
BIRMINGHAM SNOW HILL	Warwickshire		Roundel	1972	✓	✓
BLACKWELL	Worcestershire		FF	1966		✓
BLAENRHONDDA	Glamorgan		FF	1968	✓	✓
BLAINA	Monmouthshire		FF	1962		✓
BLAKEDOWN	Worcestershire					✓
BLOWERS GREEN	Worcestershire		FF	1962		✓
BORDESLEY	Warwickshire		FF		✓	✓
BORTH brown flanges	Cardiganshire		HF		✓	✓
BOURNE END (B&W FF only)	Berkshire		HF/FF		✓	✓
BRADFORD-ON-AVON	Wiltshire		FF		✓	✓
BRECON	Brecknockshire		HF		✓	✓
BRENT	Devonshire		HF	1964		✓
BRETTEL LANE	Worcestershire		FF		✓	✓
BRIDGEND	Glamorgan		FF		✓	✓
BRIDGWATER	Somerset		FF		✓	✓
BRIERLEY HILL	Worcestershire					✓
BRISTOL STAPLETON ROAD	Bristol	LP	FF		✓	✓
BRISTOL TEMPLE MEADS	Bristol	LP	HF			
BRISTOL TEMPLE MEADS	Bristol		Roundel		✓	✓
BRITHDIR	Glamorgan		FF		✓	✓
BRITON FERRY	Glamorgan		FF	1964	✓	✓
BROMSGROVE	Worcestershire		FF		✓	✓
BUILDWAS	Shropshire		FF	1963	✓	✓
BUILTH ROAD HIGH LEVEL	Radnorshire	LP				✓
BUILTH WELLS	Radnorshire			1962		✓
BURNHAM (BUCKS)	Buckinghamshire		FF		✓	✓

Place name	County	Layout	Flange	Closed	Auction	Survived
CADOXTON	Glamorgan		FF		✓	✓
CAERLEON	Monmouthshire		FF	1962		✓
CAERPHILLY	Glamorgan		FF		✓	✓
CALNE	Wiltshire		FF	1965	✓	✓
CAMBORNE	Cornwall		FF		✓	✓
CARBIS BAY	Cornwall		FF		✓	✓
CARDIFF GENERAL	Glamorgan	LP	HF			
CARDIFF QUEEN STREET	Glamorgan	LP	HF		✓	✓
CARMARTHEN	Carmarthen		HF		✓	✓
CASTLE CARY	Wiltshire		FF		✓	✓
CEFN ON	Glamorgan		FF	1986		
CHACEWATER	Cornwall		FF	1964	✓	✓
CHARLBURY	Oxfordshire		FF		✓	✓
CHELTENHAM SPA LANSDOWN *	Gloucestershire	LP	HF			✓
CHELTENHAM SPA MALVERN ROAD	Gloucestershire	LP	HF	1966	✓	✓
CHEPSTOW	Monmouthshire		HF		✓	✓
CHIPPENHAM	Wiltshire		HF		✓	✓
CHIPPING CAMPDEN	Oxfordshire		FF	1966		✓
CHIRK	Denbighshire		FF		✓	✓
CHURCHDOWN	Gloucestershire		HF	1964		✓
CHURCH STRETTON	Shropshire		FF		✓	✓
CIRENCESTER TOWN	Gloucestershire		FF	1964	✓	✓
CLARBESTON ROAD	Pembrokeshire		HF		✓	✓
CLIFTON DOWN	Bristol		FF		✓	✓
CLYNDERWEN	Pembrokeshire		FF			✓
CODSALL	Staffordshire		FF		✓	✓
COGAN	Glamorgan		FF		✓	✓
COLNBROOK ESTATE HALT	Middlesex	LP	FF	1965	✓	✓
COLWALL	Worcestershire		FF		✓	✓
CORSHAM	Wiltshire			1965		✓
CORWEN	Merionethshire		FF			✓
COSFORD	Shropshire		HF		✓	✓
CRADLEY HEATH	Worcestershire		FF			✓

Place name	County	Layout	Flange	Closed	Auction	Survived
CRADLEY HEATH & CRADLEY	Worcestershire		FF		✓	✓
CRAVEN ARMS AND STOKESAY	Shropshire		FF		✓	✓
CRICCIETH	Caernarvonshire					✓
CRUMLIN (HIGH LEVEL)	Monmouthshire	LP	FF	1964		
CULLOMPTON	Devonshire		FF	1964		✓
DAISY BANK & BRADLEY	Staffordshire			1962		
DANZEY FOR TANWORTH	Warwickshire	LP	FF		✓	✓
DARBY END HALT	Worcestershire	LP	FF	1964		✓
DAUNTSEY	Wiltshire		FF	1965		✓
DAWLISH	Devonshire		FF		✓	✓
DAWLISH WARREN	Devonshire		FF		✓	✓
DENHAM	Buckinghamshire		HF		✓	✓
DENHAM GOLF CLUB	Buckinghamshire		FF		✓	✓
DEVIZES	Wiltshire		FF	1966	✓	✓
DEVONPORT black & white totem only	Devonshire		FF			✓
DIDCOT	Berkshire		FF		✓	✓
DINAS POWIS	Glamorgan		FF		✓	✓
DINAS (RHONDDA)	Glamorgan	?				
DOLGELLAU	Merionethshire		FF	1965	✓	✓
DOLGELLEY renamed 1960	Merionethshire		HF?			
DOVEY JUNCTION	Montgomeryshire		FF		✓	✓
DROITWICH SPA	Worcestershire		HF/FF		✓	✓
DUDLEY	Worcestershire		FF	1964	✓	✓
DUNSTALL PARK	Staffordshire		FF	1968		✓
EALING BROADWAY	Middlesex		HF		✓	✓
EARLSWOOD LAKES	Warwickshire		FF		✓	✓
ELLESMERE	Shropshire		FF	1965		✓
EVERCREECH JUNCTION	Somerset		FF	1966		✓
EVESHAM	Worcestershire		HF		✓	✓
EXETER ST. DAVIDS	Devonshire	LP	HF		✓	✓
EXETER (ST. THOMAS) some brown flanges	Devonshire		HF		✓	✓

Place name	County	Layout	Flange	Closed	Auction	Survived
EXMINSTER possibly painted wood	Devonshire			1964		✓
FALMOUTH *reopened 1975	Cornwall		HF	1970*		✓
FERNDALE	Glamorgan		FF	1964	✓	✓
FERRYSIDE	Carmarthenshire		FF		✓	✓
FILTON JUNCTION	Bristol		FF		✓	✓
FISHGUARD & GOODWICK	Pembrokeshire		HF	1964	✓	✓
FISHGUARD HARBOUR	Pembrokeshire		HF		✓	✓
FLADBURY	Worcestershire		FF	1966		✓
FRESHFORD	Wiltshire		FF		✓	✓
FROME	Somerset		HF		✓	✓
FURZE PLATT HALT	Berkshire	LP	FF		✓	✓
GERRARDS CROSS	Buckinghamshire		HF/FF		✓	✓
GLOUCESTER CENTRAL	Gloucestershire	LP	HF		✓	✓
GLOUCESTER EASTGATE *	Gloucestershire	LP	HF	1975	✓	✓
GLYN NEATH	Glamorgan		HF	1964	✓	✓
GOBOWEN	Shropshire		FF		✓	✓
GORING & STREATLY	Berkshire		HF		✓	✓
GORSEINON	Glamorgan			1964		✓
GOWERTON NORTH	Glamorgan		FF		✓	✓
GRANGETOWN	Glamorgan		FF		✓	✓
GREAT BRIDGE SOUTH	Worcestershire		FF	1964	✓	✓
GREAT MALVERN	Worcestershire		HF			✓
GRIMES HILL & WYTHALL	Warwickshire		FF			✓
GWERSYLLT	Denbighshire		FF		✓	✓
GWINEAR ROAD	Cornwall		HF	1964	✓	✓
HAGLEY	Worcestershire		FF		✓	✓
HALL GREEN	Warwickshire		FF		✓	✓
HAM MILL HALT	Gloucestershire		FF	1964		✓
HANDSWORTH & SMETHWICK	Warwickshire	1&2 line	FF	1972	✓	✓
HANWELL	Middlesex		FF		✓	✓

Place name		County	Layout	Flange	Closed	Auction	Survived
HARLECH		Merionethshire		FF		✓	✓
HATTON		Warwickshire		FF		✓	✓
HAVERFORDWEST		Pembrokeshire		HF		✓	✓
HAYES & HARLINGTON	black & white only	Middlesex		FF		✓	✓
HEATH HALT LOW LEVEL		Glamorgan	LP	FF			
HELSTON	early flat type sign	Cornwall		special	1962		✓
HENBURY		Gloucestershire			1964		✓
HENGOED (LOW LEVEL)		Glamorgan	LP	FF		✓	✓
HENLEY-IN-ARDEN		Warwickshire		FF		✓	✓
HENLEY-ON-THAMES		Oxfordshire		HF		✓	✓
HENWICK		Worcestershire		FF			✓
HEREFORD		Herefordshire		HF/FF		✓	✓
HIGHBRIDGE for (&) BURNHAM-ON-SEA		Somerset	2 line	HF/FF		✓	✓
HIGH WYCOMBE		Buckinghamshire		HF		✓	✓
HOCKLEY		Warwickshire		FF	1972	✓	✓
HONEYBOURNE		Worcestershire		HF	1969	✓	✓
HORFIELD		Gloucestershire		FF	1964	✓	✓
HUNGERFORD		Berkshire		FF		✓	✓
INSTOW	some brown flanges	Devonshire		HF	1965	✓	✓
IVER		Buckinghamshire		FF			✓
JOHNSTON (PEM)		Pembrokeshire		HF		✓	✓

= OLYMPIA can also be in brackets

Place name		County	Layout	Flange	Closed	Auction	Survived
KEMBLE		Gloucestershire		HF		✓	✓
KENSINGTON OLYMPIA #		London	LP	FF		✓	✓
KENSINGTON (OLYMPIA)	* painted	London	2line*	FF			✓
KEYHAM		Devonshire					
KEYNSHAM AND SOMERDALE		Somerset	2 line	FF		✓	✓
KIDDERMINSTER		Worcestershire		HF		✓	✓
KIDWELLY		Carmarthenshire		HF		✓	✓
KINGHAM		Oxfordshire		HF		✓	✓
KINGSBRIDGE	some brown flanges	Devonshire		HF	1963	✓	✓

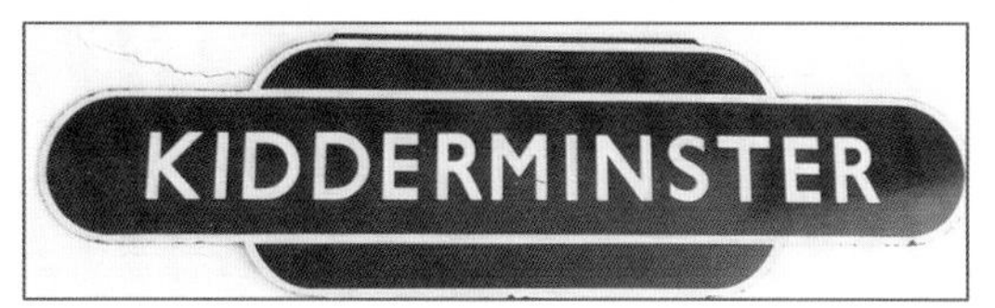

Place name	County	Layout	Flange	Closed	Auction	Survived
KINGSKERSWELL	Devonshire		FF		✓	✓
KINGS NYMPTON early flat sign	Devonshire		special		✓	✓
KINGSWEAR	Devonshire		FF	1971	✓	✓
KNIGHTON existence in doubt	Radnorshire					
KNOWLE & DORRIDGE	Warwickshire		FF		✓	✓
LAMPETER	Cardiganshire		FF	1965	✓	✓
LANDORE	Glamorgan		FF	1964	✓	✓
LANGLEY (BUCKS) black & white only	Buckinghamshire		FF		✓	✓
LAPWORTH	Warwickshire		FF		✓	✓
LAWRENCE HILL	Bristol		FF		✓	✓
LEAMINGTON SPA MILVERTON	Warwickshire	LP	HF	1965		✓
LEAMINGTON SPA GENERAL	Warwickshire	LP	HF			✓
LEDBURY	Herefordshire		HF		✓	✓
LEOMINSTER	Herefordshire		FF		✓	✓
LIMPLEY STOKE	Wiltshire		HF	1966	✓	✓
LISKEARD	Cornwall		HF		✓	✓
LITTLE KIMBLE early design	Buckinghamshire		Flat		✓	✓
LLANBRADACH	Glamorgan		FF			✓
LLANDAFF (FOR WHITCHURCH)	Glamorgan	LP	FF		✓	✓
LLANDILO BRIDGE	Carmarthenshire		FF	1963		✓
LLANDOVERY	Carmarthenshire		FF			✓
LLANDRINDOD WELLS	Radnorshire		HF		✓	✓
LLANELLY	Carmarthenshire		HF		✓	✓
LLANGOLLEN	Denbighshire		FF	1965		✓
LLANHARAN	Glamorgan			1964		
LLANIDLOES	Montgomeryshire		FF	1962	✓	✓
LLANTARNAM	Monmouthshire		FF	1962		✓
LLANTRISANT	Glamorgan		FF	1964	✓	✓
LLANWRTYD WELLS	Brecknockshire		FF			✓
LLANYMYNACH	Shropshire		FF	1967	✓	✓
LLWYNYPIA	Glamorgan		FF		✓	✓
LONG MARSTON	Warwickshire		HF	1966	✓	✓

Place name	County	Layout	Flange	Closed	Auction	Survived
LOOE	Cornwall		FF		✓	✓
LOSTWITHIEL	Cornwall		HF/FF		✓	✓
LUDLOW	Shropshire		HF		✓	✓
LYDNEY JUNCTION	Gloucestershire		FF		✓	✓
LYE	Worcestershire		FF			✓
MACHYNLLETH	Montgomeryshire		HF/FF		✓	✓
MAERDY	Glamorgan			1964		
MAIDENHEAD	Berkshire		HF/FF		✓	✓
MALVERN LINK some painted black on white	Worcestershire		HF		✓	✓
MALVERN WELLS	Worcestershire		HF	1965	✓	✓
MARSHFIELD	Monmouthshire		FF	1959		✓
MATHRY ROAD	Pembrokeshire		FF	1964	✓	✓
MELKSHAM	Wiltshire		FF	1966		✓
MERTHYR	Glamorgan		FF		✓	✓
METHYR VALE	Glamorgan		FF		✓	✓
MILFORD HAVEN existence in doubt	Pembrokeshire					
MINEHEAD	Somerset		HF/FF	1971	✓	✓
MOAT LANE JUNCTION	Montgomeryshire	LP	FF	1972		✓
MONTGOMERY	Montgomeryshire		FF		✓	✓
MONTPELIER	Bristol		FF		✓	✓
MORFA MAWDDACH	Merionethshire		FF		✓	✓
MORETON-IN-MARSH early design	Gloucestershire		Flat		✓	✓
MORTEHOE & WOOLACOMBE	Devon		HF	1970		✓
NAILSEA & BACKWELL	Somerset		FF		✓	✓
NEATH GENERAL	Glamorgan	1 line/LP	HF		✓	✓
NEWBURY	Berkshire		FF		✓	✓
NEWPORT HIGH STREET	Monmouthshire	LP	HF		✓	✓
NEWQUAY	Cornwall		HF		✓	✓
NEWTON ABBOT	Devonshire		FF		✓	✓
NEWTOWN	Montgomeryshire		HF		✓	✓
NEYLAND existence in doubt	Pembrokeshire			1964		

Place name	County	Layout	Flange	Closed	Auction	Survived
OAKENGATES	Shropshire		HF			✓
OAKLE STREET	Gloucestershire					
OLDBURY & LANGLEY GREEN	Worcestershire	1/2 line	FF		✓	✓
OLDFIELD PARK	Somerset		FF		✓	✓
OLD HILL	Staffordshire		FF			✓
OLD HILL (HIGH STREET) HALT	Staffordshire	LP	FF	1964		✓
OLTON	Warwickshire		FF		✓	✓
OSWESTRY	Shropshire		HF	1966	✓	✓
OXFORD	Oxfordshire		FF		✓	✓
PADDINGTON	London		FF		✓	✓
PAIGNTON	Devonshire		FF		✓	✓
PANGBOURNE	Berkshire		FF		✓	✓
PAR	Cornwall		HF/FF		✓	✓
PARSON STREET	Bristol		FF		✓	✓
PEMBURY & BURRY PORT	Carmarthenshire		HF			✓
PEMBROKE	Pembrokeshire		HF			✓
PEMBROKE DOCK	Pembrokeshire		FF		✓	✓
PENCOED * reopened 1992	Glamorgan			1964*		
PENGAM (GLAM)	Glamorgan	LP	FF		✓	✓
PENTREBACH	Glamorgan		FF		✓	✓
PENYCHAIN unique blue & yellow	Caernarvonshire		FF			✓
PENZANCE	Cornwall		HF			✓
PERRANPORTH	Cornwall		FF	1963	✓	✓
PERSHORE	Worcestershire		HF		✓	✓
PEWSEY	Wiltshire					
PILNING (HIGH LEVEL)	Gloucestershire	LP	FF		✓	✓
PONTHIR	Monmouthshire			1962		
PONTLOTTYN	Glamorgan		FF			
PONTRILAS	Herefordshire		FF	1958		✓
PONTYPOOL (CRANE STREET)	Monmouthshire	LP	FF	1962		✓
PONTYPOOL ROAD	Monmouthshire		FF		✓	✓

Place name	County	Layout	Flange	Closed	Auction	Survived
PONTYPRIDD	Glamorgan		HF		✓	✓
PORTH	Glamorgan		FF		✓	✓
PORTHCAWL	Glamorgan		FF	1963	✓	✓
PORTISHEAD	Somerset		HF	1964	✓	✓
PORTMADOC	Caernarvonshire		HF		✓	✓
PORT TALBOT	Glamorgan		FF			✓
POYLE ESTATE HALT	Middlesex		FF	1965		✓
PRIESTFIELD	Staffordshire		FF	1972		✓
PRINCES END AND COSELEY	Staffordshire		HF	1962		
PRINCES RISBOROUGH	Buckinghamshire		FF		✓	✓
PURTON	Wiltshire		FF	1964	✓	✓
PWLLHELI	Caernarvonshire		HF		✓	✓
PYLE	Glamorgan		FF	1964	✓	✓
QUAKERS YARD (LOW LEVEL)	Glamorgan	LP	FF			✓
RADSTOCK WEST *early design	Somerset		Flat*	1959		✓
RADYR	Glamorgan		FF		✓	✓
READING GENERAL	Berkshire		HF		✓	✓
READING WEST	Berkshire		FF		✓	✓
REDLAND	Bristol		FF			✓
REDRUTH	Cornwall		HF		✓	✓
RHAYADER	Radnorshire		FF	1962	✓	✓
RHOOSE	Glamorgan		FF	1964	✓	✓
RHYMNEY	Glamorgan		FF		✓	✓
RISCA	Monmouthshire		FF	1962	✓	✓
ROSS-ON-WYE	Herefordshire		FF	1964		✓
ROUND OAK	Staffordshire		FF			✓
ROWLEY REGIS & BLACKHEATH	Worcestershire		FF		✓	✓
ROYAL OAK Underground open	London		HF	1962		✓
RUABON	Denbighshire		FF		✓	✓

Place name	County	Layout	Flange	Closed	Auction	Survived
ST. ANNES PARK	Bristol		FF	1970	✓	✓
ST. AUSTELL	Cornwall		HF		✓	✓
ST. BUDEAUX FERRY ROAD	Devonshire	LP	FF		✓	✓
ST.CLEARS	Carmarthenshire		FF	1964		✓
ST.ERTH	Cornwall		FF		✓	✓
ST. FAGANS	Glamorgan		HF	1962		✓
ST. IVES	Cornwall		FF			✓
SALTASH	Cornwall					✓
SALTFORD	Somerset		HF	1970	✓	✓
SAUNDERSFOOT	Pembrokeshire					
SEA MILLS	Bristol		FF		✓	✓
SEER GREEN AND JORDANS also '&'	Buckinghamshire		FF		✓	✓
SEVERN TUNNEL JUNCTION	Monmouthshire	LP	FF		✓	✓
SHIFNAL brown flanges	Shropshire		HF		✓	✓
SHIPTON FOR BURFORD	Oxfordshire	LP	FF		✓	✓
SHIREHAMPTON	Bristol		FF		✓	✓
SHIRLEY	Warwickshire		FF		✓	✓
SHREWSBURY	Shropshire		HF/FF		✓	✓
SKEWEN	Glamorgan			1964		
SLOUGH	Berkshire		HF/FF		✓	✓
SMALL HEATH & SPARKBROOK	Warwickshire		FF		✓	✓
SMETHWICK WEST	Staffordshire		FF		✓	✓
SOHO & WINSON GREEN	Warwickshire		FF	1972	✓	✓
SOLIHULL	Warwickshire		HF/FF		✓	✓
SOUTHALL	Middlesex		HF/FF		✓	✓
SOUTH MOLTON	Devonshire		FF	1966		
SPRING ROAD	Warwickshire		FF		✓	✓
STAINES WEST	Middlesex		HF	1965	✓	✓
STARCROSS	Devonshire		FF			✓
STONEHOUSE (BURDETT ROAD)	Gloucestershire	LP	FF			✓
STOURBRIDGE JUNCTION	Worcestershire	1 line/LP	HF/FF		✓	✓
STOURBRIDGE TOWN	Worcestershire		FF		✓	✓
STRATFORD-UPON-AVON	Warwickshire		HF		✓	✓

Place name		County	Layout	Flange	Closed	Auction	Survived
STROUD	brown flanges	Gloucestershire		HF*		✓	✓
SWANSEA HIGH STREET		Glamorgan	LP	HF/FF		✓	✓
SWANSEA (VICTORIA)		Glamorgan	LP	FF	1964	✓	✓
SWAN VILLAGE		Staffordshire		FF	1972	✓	✓
SWINDON		Wiltshire		HF		✓	✓
TAFFS WELL		Glamorgan		FF		✓	✓
TAPLOW		Buckinghamshire		HF/FF		✓	✓
TAUNTON		Somerset		HF		✓	✓
TEIGNMOUTH		Devonshire		HF			
TENBY		Pembrokeshire		FF		✓	✓
THAME		Oxfordshire		HF	1963	✓	✓
THEALE		Berkshire		FF			✓
THE LAKES HALT		Warwickshire		FF			✓
TILEHURST		Berkshire		FF		✓	✓
TIPTON FIVE WAYS		Staffordshire		FF			✓
TIR PHIL		Glamorgan		FF			
TIVERTON JUNCTION		Devonshire		FF	1986	✓	✓
TONYPANDY & TREALAW		Glamorgan		FF		✓	✓
TORQUAY	plastic B&W only	Devonshire		**		✓	✓
TORRE		Devonshire		FF		✓	✓
TOTNES		Devonshire		FF		✓	✓
TOWYN		Merionethshire		FF			✓
TREFOREST		Glamorgan		FF		✓	✓
TREFOREST ESTATE		Glamorgan		FF			✓
TREHAFOD		Glamorgan		FF		✓	✓
TREHERBERT		Glamorgan		FF			✓
TREORCHY		Glamorgan		FF			
TROEDYRHIW		Glamorgan		FF		✓	✓
TROWBRIDGE		Wiltshire		HF		✓	✓
TRURO		Cornwall		HF/FF		✓	✓
TWYFORD		Berkshire		FF		✓	✓
TYLORSTOWN		Glamorgan		FF			

Place name	County	Layout	Flange	Closed	Auction	Survived
TYSELEY	Warwickshire		FF		✓	✓
UPPER PONTNEWYDD	Monmouthshire			1962		
UXBRIDGE VINE STREET	Middlesex	LP	HF	1962	✓	✓
WARGARVE	Berkshire		FF			✓
WARWICK	Warwickshire		FF		✓	✓
WEDNESBURY (CENTRAL)	Staffordshire	LP	FF	1972	✓	✓
WELLINGTON	Somerset		HF		✓	✓
WELLINGTON SALOP	Shropshire	LP	HF		✓	✓
WELLINGTON (SALOP)	Shropshire	LP	FF		✓	✓
WELSHPOOL	Montgomeryshire		HF		✓	✓
WESTBOURNE PARK	London		HF/FF		✓	✓
WEST BROMWICH	Staffordshire		FF	1972	✓	✓
WESTBURY WILTS	Wiltshire	LP	HF		✓	✓
WEST DRAYTON & YIEWSLEY	Middlesex		HF		✓	✓
WEST EALING	Middlesex		HF		✓	✓
WESTON MILTON	Somerset					
WESTON-SUPER-MARE GENERAL	Somerset	LP	HF		✓	✓
WESTON-SUPER-MARE LOCKING RD.	Somerset	LP	to confirm	1964		
WEST RUISLIP	Middlesex		HF		✓	✓
WHITLAND	Carmarthenshire		FF		✓	✓
WHITLOCKS END HALT	Warwickshire	LP	FF?			
WIDNEY MANOR	Warwickshire		FF		✓	✓
WILMCOTE	Warwickshire		FF		✓	✓
WINDMILL END HALT	Staffordshire	LP	FF	1964		✓
WINDSOR & ETON CENTRAL	Berkshire	LP	HF		✓	✓
WOLVERHAMPTON (LOW LEVEL)	Staffordshire	LP	FF	1972	✓	✓
WOOD END	Warwickshire		FF			✓
WOOTTON BASSETT	Wiltshire		FF	1965		✓
WOOTTON WAWEN PLATFORM	Warwickshire	2 line	FF		✓	✓
WORCESTER FOREGATE STREET	Worcestershire	LP	HF		✓	✓
WORCESTER SHRUB HILL	Worcestershire	LP	HF		✓	✓

Place name	County	Layout	Flange	Closed	Auction	Survived
WREXHAM (EXCHANGE)	Denbighshire	LP	FF		✓	✓
WREXHAM GENERAL	Denbighshire		FF		✓	✓
YARDLEY WOOD	Warwickshire		FF			✓
YATE	Gloucestershire			1965		
YATTON	Bristol		FF		✓	✓
YNYSHIR	Glamorgan		FF	1964		
YSTRAD MYNACH	Glamorgan		FF		✓	✓
YSTRAD (RHONDDA)	Glamorgan	LP	FF		✓	✓

(Tim Clarke)

YNYSHIR – a very elusive totem from Glamorgan. (Dawlish Museum)

(Tim Clarke)

EASTERN REGION TOTEMS

CHAPTER 8

The Eastern Region

Introduction

This area draws together the counties of Lincolnshire, Cambridgeshire, Huntingdonshire, Essex, Suffolk and Norfolk, along with smaller parts of South Yorkshire, Nottinghamshire, Northamptonshire, Bedfordshire, Hertfordshire, Middlesex and north-east London. While there were nearly a thousand stations in this area, only 360 or so were equipped with totems, and some of those were only in place for a couple of years. This means that some ER totems are in fact rarer than the highly prized NE totems, where records show that of the 128 stations equipped, only five or six are not known to have any surviving examples. The ER, however, has some 80+ stations where we do not currently know of any surviving totems! This region also developed prime links to the continent and has the greatest concentration of major ports in Britain.

(South Devon Railway – Tindale Collection)

The history of the region

The first passenger line in the region was the Sheffield & Rotherham Railway (S&RR). This was only 5 miles in length and opened in 1838. This line connected with the North Midland Railway from Derby in 1840, providing Sheffield with its first service to London.

That was closely followed in 1839 by the Eastern Counties Railway, who chose the slums of East London for their Devonshire Street terminus. The line crossed what was then mainly marshes and fields to a temporary terminus at Romford, before Brentwood was attained the following year. The steep incline beyond Brentwood and financial problems delayed opening to **Colchester** for another three years. The line was originally built to a gauge of 5ft, but as the system expanded the directors realised that the 4ft 8in standard should be adopted to connect with other railways. They completed this in 1844.

East London was also the home to another very early developer, the London & Blackwall Railway, who in 1840 used rope haulage, because of the close proximity of the ships in the docks. It was thought that sparks from steam engines would ignite the sails, then the ships. They countered this problem in 1849 by erecting a roof over the railway in corrugated iron! Fortunately, only a mile or so had to be treated in this fashion, then steam traction took over until the demise of passenger services in 1926. Most of the line is still in use today, as after many years of neglect the Docklands Light Railway started running services again over this historic railway in 1987. What a wonderful sight a West India Docks or Millwall Junction totem in ER blue would have made. Sadly the line was in limbo during the totem era, as was the North London Railway branch from Victoria Park to Poplar East India Dock Road, which would have made superb MR totems! Yes, we do mean MR. While we are in East London, we cannot overlook one of the smallest but most interesting of the London termini – Fenchurch Street – opened by the London & Blackwall Railway in 1841 to replace Minories station.

At first, with only two platforms, it soon became swamped by passengers – what a nuisance! Another two platforms were added in 1854 to cope with increased traffic which, amazingly, was accepted from both the Great Eastern and North London Railway's, on top of the London, Tilbury & Southend Railway's own trains! The situation eased slightly with the opening of Liverpool Street in 1874, and by this time NLR services were using **Broad Street**. There was not such collaboration, however, when it came to the development of Southend-on-Sea as a resort. The LT&SR first gained access to this lucrative business in 1856, but the GER waited until 1889 to open its rival service from Shenfield to **Southend-on-Sea Victoria**.

(Author's collection)

The development of railways in East Anglia was largely motivated by the need to move large quantities of farm produce to the markets in the cities. This task was made easier for the railway engineers by the huge areas of flat terrain that had to be crossed. The roads of that time were hopelessly inadequate, with mud-filled tracks a common sight.

The Yarmouth & Norwich Railway opened in 1844, giving the residents of Norwich a much quicker, more comfortable ride to the sea. The annual outing to the seaside that became such an event during the Victorian era was inextricably linked to the coming of the railways. Relatively cheap excursions were a considerable money-spinner for the early railway companies, and gave rise to a huge hotel building programme. Many families looked forward to their summer holiday with excitement and anticipation as the time approached. The railway companies laid on hundreds of extra services to cope with the huge holiday demand. East Anglia saw many of these trains, and what would we give today to recreate the true heyday of the holiday expresses? Unfortunately we have now seen a move away from the traditional British seaside holiday that generations of us grew up with, and many of the Victorian hotels are neglected today, as families are lured abroad by warmer climates. Totems from our favourite holiday haunts keep those memories alive, however, and they are probably the most popular collecting theme.

The latter half of the 1840s was known as the Railway Mania years, when massive expansion of the network took place. East Anglia saw new lines open from **Stratford** to **Bishops Stortford**, then on to **Cambridge** and Norwich via **Ely** in 1845. The more direct route from London to Norwich via **Ipswich** was not completed until 1849.

The **Ely** to **Peterborough** line was opened by the Eastern Counties Railway in 1847, and while East Anglia was dominated by the ECR, they were not so fortunate in gaining a foothold in Lincolnshire. This was a stronghold of the East Lincolnshire Railway and the Manchester, Sheffield & Lincolnshire Railway. The mid-19th century was a time of immense rivalry between the railway companies, and take-overs were commonplace.

One of the early giants was the Midland Railway owned by the 'Railway King', George Hudson, who also had the ECR under his control. He was a very influential man who made huge sums of money from railway operation. His empire at its height stretched from Rugby in the south to Newcastle in the north. A journey from London to York in 1848 would have been via Derby, and most of the fare would have been pocketed by the MR. The Great Northern Railway exploited this with their direct line in 1852 via **Grantham**, which saved over an hour on the London to Edinburgh times offered by its rivals. The great station at **Kings Cross** also opened in the same year. Doncaster, which has always held a place in the hearts of all ER followers, was ironically overlooked by the GNR in their original plans for a direct line from **Peterborough** to **York**. The original plan was to run via **Lincoln**, **Gainsborough**, then on to **Selby**, thus avoiding Doncaster. This was noticed by the local MP Edmund Becket Denison, who persuaded the GNR along with other prominent townsfolk that it would be a terrible folly to miss Doncaster. Fortunately his plea was heeded and the line was built through **Grantham** and Doncaster. Soon afterwards Doncaster became the major locomotive and rolling stock works.

Pure Lincolnshire nostalgia, 1974. (Alan Young)

What wonderful and magnificent machines have emerged from the 'Plant' over the years. Some of the greatest locomotive engineers who ever lived worked at Doncaster. The likes of Gresley, Ivatt and Thompson built legendary locomotives here. Despite its status, the station never received totems because of early fluorescent lighting.

Rapid expansion took place throughout the region in the 1850s, with branch lines opening for the residents of hitherto unheard-of hamlets and quaint villages, giving local people the chance to find employment other than farming for the first time. The branch lines fed into the national network and kept the railway coffers in a fairly healthy state. The major industrial town of the time was Sheffield, and this soon became a hub of the network. The coal mines of South Yorkshire and Nottinghamshire were the basis for much railway building, as the railways quickly saw the potential for huge traffic flows from the mines to commercial and domestic customers. The diversity of freight traffic and a wondrous array of lines heading off in all directions coupled with the cumbersome, but infinitely more nostalgic, semaphore signalling and its accompanying boxes were images that captured the imagination of many a young lad as he sat watching the trains go by. Nowadays we try to rekindle those memories by surrounding ourselves with totems.

The railways of Lincolnshire were formed by the need to move goods to the docks in the north and exploit the seaside resorts in the east. Lincolnshire suffered huge losses during the Beeching years, but surprisingly a good number of totems from the area survive, and only a handful have yet to appear on the open market.

Although the majority of lines were in place by the end of the 1850s, there were some lines where agreement was not reached for several decades – the most notable being the GNR & GER Joint line opening in stages between 1879 and 1882. The last and most certainly short-lived was the Midland & Great Northern Railway, which did not open until 1893. It stretched from **Peterborough** across north Norfolk to Norwich and Yarmouth. Not many stations on the line received totems, but one of the few that did was **Melton Constable**, where the headquarters and locomotive works were situated. Unfortunately the M&GN system closed in 1959, but again totems do survive. There were obviously some very early pioneers of our hobby active over 40 years ago!

The railways of East Anglia, with the exception of the M&GN, became part of the giant Great Eastern system in 1862. The London terminus then was Bishopsgate, which was woefully inadequate for the thousands pouring into the capital every day. Liverpool Street was opened in 1874 and even this proved inadequate after a few decades. The East Side was added in 1894, making Liverpool Street the largest station in London until Victoria was enlarged in 1908. The railways formed by the Victorians were enjoyed by people from all walks of life for over a century; although there were class distinctions, the services provided were affordable in an age where the motor car did not reign supreme. The arrival of cars gave people the freedom to explore hitherto unknown territories, but the loss of revenue to the railway companies could not be ignored indefinitely. Then along came one Dr Beeching with his document entitled 'The Reshaping of British Railways' in 1963. The decisions taken at that time have been well publicised, and the arguments will rage on forever, but was Beeching really the heartless axeman he was portrayed to be? Could it be argued that the weapon he used was more of a double-edged sword?

Cressing station lies unspoilt, 1975. (Alan Young)

Many of the branch lines axed by Dr Beeching left whole communities isolated from the railway network, but today they could be considered fortunate. Just consider how modernisation has led to massive housing development, giant superstores, acres of car parks and inevitable road 'improvements' anywhere considered to be within easy commuting distance of the cities. Would the rural delights of **Long Melford**, **Cavendish** and **Lavenham** in Suffolk have retained tofay's timeless charm if they were still rail-connected and electrified, with express services to Cambridge and Colchester?

The saddest aspect aside from the severe inconvenience to passengers, was the loss of some very picturesque lines along with classic station architecture throughout the country. East Anglia and Lincolnshire suffered during the Beeching years, but maybe this little tale may provide a light-hearted insight into the mind of Dr Beeching. A friend, who is now 80 years old, wrote to Dr Beeching's office in 1964 requesting the opportunity to purchase a totem from **Saffron Walden**, which was about to close. There were only three totems on the station, and to his great surprise all three were delivered to his local station for the meagre sum of a few shillings each! The story does not end there – as within a few days Dr Beeching's office asked for one of the totems back! My friend obliged, but kept the other two for over thirty years. Was Dr Beeching, therefore, a secret totem collector? Have we finally discovered the reason for all those station closures?

The geography of the region

From the Thames in the south to the Humber in the north, and the coastal resorts in the east to the coalfields of South Yorkshire, this region covers a large expanse of England. The area has distinctive architecture and mainly agricultural and maritime traditions, much of which has remained unspoilt by the Industrial Revolution. The area provided fewer obstacles for railway engineers than any other, as nowhere in East Anglia is much more than 2,000ft above sea level. The whole area has a gently undulating landscape, exposed to stiff easterly winds off the North Sea, which were exploited by the many windmills in the region. These have appeared on numerous railway posters advertising the delights of rural Suffolk and the Norfolk Broads as holiday destinations.

East Anglia produces a third of the nation's vegetables from the rich arable soils that abound in the region. Most of this produce was formerly moved by the railway, and the vast marshalling yards at **March** were built to cope with such traffic – sadly the railway has declined, and **March** is no longer a hub of the network.

The area in the triangle between **Peterborough**, **Cambridge** and **King's Lynn** – known as The Fens – is largely reclaimed swampland and was notoriously difficult to build and live on. The building of the city of **Ely** was only possible because of the location of a chalk hill to build upon. The Norfolk Broads lie to the east of Norwich, and provide a relaxing backdrop for the boating fraternity as they meander around miles of unspoilt waterway. The tranquillity is only punctuated by the sounds of wild birds and the wind whispering through the reeds. Norwich is one of our finest preserved cities, dominated by the second tallest cathedral spire in England, only surpassed by **Salisbury**. Fine old cobbled streets give an air of times gone by, and the area around Elm Hill and Tombland is medieval. Sadly none of Norwich's stations ever carried totems.

The north Norfolk coast is an Area of Outstanding Natural Beauty, and just occasionally we find small towns dotted along the sandy stretches, the most notable being **Hunstanto**n, where 60ft cliffs hold back the sea (famously visited by Sir John Betjeman in the early '60s on a DMU). To the east lie Wells and Cromer.

Further south are the once bustling fishing ports of Great Yarmouth and Lowestoft, which both formerly boasted two main line stations, but only one carried totems – namely **Lowestoft North**. The others had early electric lighting. Further down the coast we find the unspoilt delights of Southwold and **Aldeburgh** before reaching the busy ports of **Felixstowe** and **Harwich**. These both handle vast amounts of container traffic, which is mainly moved by rail – apparently! This will surprise anyone who commutes along the A12 in Essex. These two ports, along with Tilbury, have seen enormous expansion since the demise of the once mighty Royal Albert Docks in East London.

Further inland, near **Manningtree**, we come to Constable country, the Stour Valley, an area of peaceful scenery and pink washed cottages with thatched roofs. Much of the artist's work was inspired by such locations as Flatford Mill and Dedham Vale, which are now owned by the National Trust. We can find, if we are lucky, some wonderfully named totems in this area, such as **Sible** and **Castle Hedingham**, **Lavenham**, **White Colne**, **Bury St Edmunds**, **Thorpe-le-Soken** and the seaside town of **Clacton-on-Sea**.

Moving south we find an area of very elusive totems. The **Wickford** to Southminster branch line was, until 10 years ago, still semaphore signalled and operated by ageing DMUs. The only intermediate station with totems was **Burnham-on-Crouch**, probably because of its popularity with yachtsmen (and women of course). It is still very much a sailing centre today, but with electrification it has taken on many former city dwellers looking for 'the quiet life' on the Crouch estuary in expanding housing developments.

Almost as popular as ever are the resorts of **Southend-on-Sea**, **Thorpe Bay**, **Westcliff** and **Leigh-on-Sea**, as we head towards London along the Thames estuary. Sandy beaches quickly give way to the industrial grime that oil refineries inflict upon the eye, as we come to Canvey Island, **Purfleet** and the giant Ford car plant at Dagenham.

Leaving London, the ECML cuts mainly through gravel, then tunnels through the chalk hills of Hertfordshire, crossing the viaduct at Welwyn, then skirting Bedfordshire, with clay deposits and brickfields on either side.

To the east lies the university city of **Cambridge**, which according to history was founded by disgruntled Oxford scholars. Here we find some spectacular college architecture, which spans the tree-lined River Cam in several places. The cathedral city of **Peterborough** is the next major town northwards and was, in its heyday, a magnet for trainspotters, with the large New England shed (35A) just to the north and lines radiating to all points of the compass. Here we enter the flat Lincolnshire wolds, and to the west lies Cotswold limestone extended through Northamptonshire to form the Lincoln Edge range of hills, hence tunnels at Stoke and Peascliffe near **Grantham**.

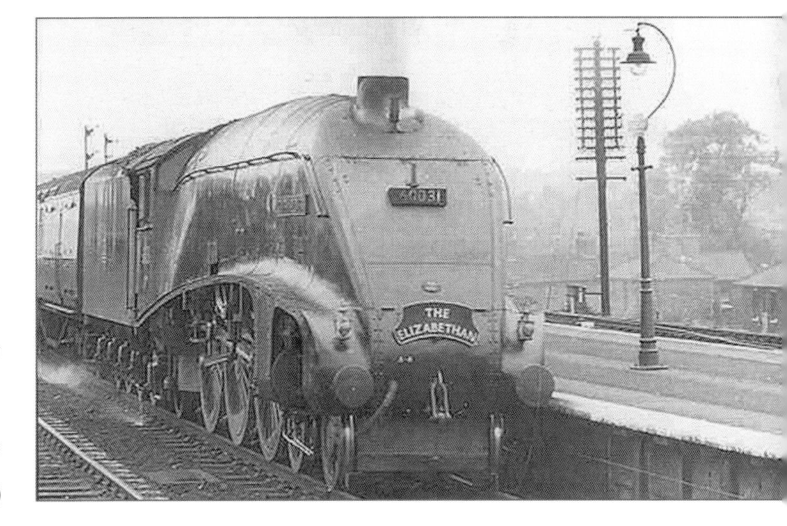

Golden Plover at full flight thundering through Grantham in the 1950s. (Alf Miles collection)

The Derbyshire peaks lie temptingly to the west in the Midland territory that borders the ECML. To the east, the coming of the Great Northern and Great Central railways created the coastal resorts of **Skegness** and Cleethorpes respectively. Other resorts now devoid of railway access are **Mablethorpe** and **Sutton-on-Sea**.

The city of **Lincoln** has one of England's most imposing cathedral frontages and like **Ely** rises above the local flatlands on a rocky escarpment. In medieval times Lincoln was England's fourth largest city after London, York and Winchester. The wool trade generated its wealth.

North Lincolnshire is much more industrialised, with a large steelworks at Scunthorpe, and dock complexes at Immingham and Grimsby on the Humber estuary. To the north-west of the region lie Sheffield, **Barnsley** and **Chesterfield** – home to a once mighty steel and coal industry – the evidence of which scars the landscape for miles around. A complex network of railways and an endless variety of freight traffic provided a spotters paradise to many young enthusiasts as we hunted down those elusive 'cops' hidden away in locosheds.

In the '50s and '60s you had the choice of **Darnall** (41A), **Millhouses** (41C), **Barrow Hill** (41E), **Staveley** (41H) and **Mexborough** (41F) all within a few miles radius, and all bedecked with totems. With the demise of steam, however, **Darnall**, **Millhouses**, **Staveley** and **Mexborough** closed, then new diesel depots appeared at Tinsley (41A), and **Shirebrook** (41J). At the eastern end of the Woodhead route, home to Class 76 electric locos, was **Wath** (41C) depot.

To possess a totem from any of these stations provides us with a tenuous link to our heritage. Our fondest memories are of adventurous days spent 'bunking' into the hallowed ground of the locoshed: armed with the cunning of a fox, a camera, some crisps and a bottle of pop we dodged the shed foreman as we crept quietly among awesome mechanical beasts. Happy days indeed!

Neither Sheffield Midland or Victoria was fitted with totems, but the surrounding suburbs were liberally doused with them – some of them very rare, which brings us nicely to the next section.

The Eastern Region database

This is a region of fascinating contrasts. On the one hand, some stations had their totems unceremoniously dumped at a very early date. **Grantham**, **Newark** and **Retford** had been stripped by the late 1950s, while in East Anglia totems survived at **Woodbridge** on the East Suffolk line until 1984. **Goxhill** in Lincolnshire holds the accolade of being the last station on the entire BR network to retain its totems – amazingly as recent as 1988! We shall now highlight some of the rarest ER totems.

A: The Tendring Hundred Railway opened **Alresford** on the Clacton branch in 1866. We are unaware of any survivors. **Appleby** in Lincolnshire was a very short-lived station, opened by the LNER in 1923 and closed in 1967. **Audley End** has a famous stately home nearby. (An LNER Sandringham class 4-6-0 also carried the name.) Opened in 1848 by the ECR, it was the junction for the branch line to **Saffron Walden**.

B: **Baldock** is one of the rarer stations on the ex-GNR **Hitchin** to **Cambridge** line. Opening in 1850, it only had totems briefly, but Ashwell & Morden and Royston did not. **Barking** is very elusive. Originally an LT&SR station, it opened in 1854 and was enlarged gradually until it became a major BR/LT interchange in 1961 with the addition of a flyover to alleviate conflicting movements. The majority of totems were removed by this time, but a few clung on for several years on the **Kentish Town** service platforms.

Heading north to Yorkshire, we find **Barnsley Exchange**, which reputedly had totems briefly until fluorescent lighting was installed. The first station north of Cambridge was **Barnwell Junction**, which opened in 1884. It was the first stop on the Mildenhall branch and closed in 1962, but survives as a private residence. The totems are rare, as is nearby **Bartlow**. The former locoshed station of **Barrow Hill** in Derbyshire closed very early in 1954 and a few totems survive. **Beccles** totems are known to survive, but few in good condition – many are faded and they have larger letters. **Bentley** in Suffolk was on the Norwich main line. It was opened in 1846 by the Eastern Union Railway and only had four or five totems. A creased example is shown below.

In East London the first station out of Liverpool Street is **Bethnal Green** where one of us spent many hours scribbling numbers as a 'spotty' youth (DB). It opened in 1872 and was known as Bethnal Green Junction until 1895. The totems were all removed during electrification work in 1960. Further along the line to Southend we come to **Billericay**, which along with **Wickford**, **Rayleigh**, **Rochford** and **Prittlewell** opened in 1889. All these stations were de-totemised in 1957 so it is very doubtful that any survive. The former Colne Valley line in Essex had some of the most delightful names imaginable. The line opened in sections between 1860 and 1863, and consisted of stations at **White Colne**, **Earls Colne**, **Halstead**, **Sible and Castle Hedingham**, **Yeldham** and **Birdbrook** which all had totems.

Amazingly, despite early closure in 1962, we know of a survivor from every station! **Bishops Stortford** is rare – a one-time junction for the line to Braintree. **Boston** and **Bowes Park** have both yet to appear at auction. The **Brightside** totem shown below is a rare Sheffield area totem, which may well have given inspiration to the Monty Python team. Michael Palin was raised in Sheffield and might have thought of his roots when 'Always look on the Bright Side of Life' was sung at the end of the film *The Life of Brian*, or perhaps it is just a coincidence!

North-east London is the home to many rarities. As discussed elsewhere in this book, the electrification of Liverpool Street to Enfield Town, **Hertford East** and Chingford lines in 1961 caused many early totem casualties, hence **Broxbourne**, **Bruce Grove**, **Burnt Mill** and **Bush Hill Park** are rare. The Lea Valley line was not dealt with until 1969, therefore totems from this section, like **Brimsdown**, do survive. Lastly, we have found no survivors from **Bury St Edmunds**, opened in 1846 by the Ipswich & Bury Railway.

C: The totems at **Cambridge** were removed by 1958, when fluorescent lighting was installed. Opening in 1845 it has seen a huge variety of motive power over the years, with even such locomotives as A4s, A3s and A1s passing through with expresses diverted from the GN main line during the steam era. On the Great Eastern section there are several rarities. We have yet to see **Cantley**, **Chadwell Heath**, **Chelmsford**, **Cheshunt**, **Clacton**, **Clapton**, **Colchester** or **Cressing** at auction. As at Cambridge, early electric lighting caused the premature demise of most of these, except **Cantley** and **Cressing**, which both lasted until the mid-'70s. The totems at **Clare** on the Stour Valley line in Essex lasted until closure in 1967. The station came into existence in 1845. The Edgware, Highgate & London Railway opened the station at **Crouch End** in 1867. The totems were fitted in the early '50s, but closure took place in 1954, so the survival of one of these is quite remarkable. Note the early narrow style, which measured half an inch less from top to bottom than later totems.

Waiting for the scrapman, north-east London, 1961. (Tony Wright)

D: **Dagenham Dock** was opened by the LT&SR in 1908 to serve the expanding docks area. It is a rare totem. The pair shown below are both rare South Yorkshire items. **Darfield** was on the **Wath** to Cudworth line, opened by the North Midland in 1840 and resited in 1901. **Dodworth** was located between **Penistone** and Barnsley – a MS&LR station which arrived on the scene in 1854 and made an early departure in 1959. The one shown below has since been restored. **Deepcar** is another early closure (1959), although the totems remained up for some years after, and **Dronfield**, opened in 1840, closed in 1967, and reopened in 1981, has yet to make a public appearance.

E: The LMS station at **East Tilbury** opened in 1936 as a halt, and was promoted to station status in 1949 by BR. We have evidence of totems, but are unaware when they were removed or if any survive. Other South Yorkshire rarities are **Ecclesfield West**, which the MR opened as Ecclesfield in 1897; it became West in 1950 and closed in 1967. Also opening in 1897 was **Elsecar & Hoyland** between Sheffield and Barnsley. Despite its size, the station at **Ely**, which was opened by the ECR in 1845, lost all its totems very early and we are unaware of any preserved.

In situ during 1973, and known to survive. (Alan Young)

The only intermediate station between Romford and Upminster is **Emerson Park Halt** – one of only two 'totemed' halts on the ER – opened by the LT&SR in 1909 as Emerson Park & Great Nelmes. The gas lamps and totems were removed in 1977. On the GNR we have two rarities. **Enfield Chase** on the Hertford Loop was opened as Enfield to replace an earlier station in 1910, and gained its current title in 1923. On the main line, **Essendine** opened in 1852 and closed in 1959. The totems seem to have vanished.

F: **Fakenham East** was an ECR station that opened in 1849 as Fakenham. BR added East in 1948, whereas **Fakenham West** (M&GN) was originally opened by the Lynn & Fakenham Railway in 1880 as Fakenham Town, and became West, also in 1948. Neither station had many totems, nor are we unaware of any survivors from the M&GN station that closed in 1959. The ECR station at **Forest Gate**, opened in 1840, strangely only had totems affixed to one of the four platforms, while the others retained LNER electric lamps with the name incorporated in the perspex cover.

G: Lincolnshire dominates this section with four rarities. **Gainsborough Central** opened in 1849 and forms part of an important crossroads. To date, only two totems have been auctioned. **Goxhill** (opened in 1848) was the last station to be de-totemised, whereas **Grantham** (opened in 1852) was one of the first. The latter is still an interchange for the Nottingham to Skegness service, but in its heyday boasted a locoshed (35B), and several mainline engines were allocated here. **Grimsby Docks** (opened by the MS&L in 1853) boasted totems, but the major station at Grimsby Town was not equipped. The coming of the railways in 1848 caused a huge expansion of the fishing port, and by 1939 there were 500 vessels catching over 190,000 tons per annum. **Great Bentley** on the Colchester to Clacton line, which opened in 1878, has yet to yield any of its totems.

H: **Hackney Downs** was opened by the GER in 1872 as Hackney Downs Junction, and the word Junction was dropped in 1896. There were many totems, but few survivors. **Harlow** (opened in 1841 by the Northern & Eastern Railway) was relatively rural until the expansion of Harlow New Town, when a new station called Harlow Town was built further south on the site of **Burnt Mill** in 1960. The original **Harlow** station became Harlow Mill and the totems were removed. **Harringay Park** was opened by the GER in 1878 as Green Lanes & Noel Park. It became Harringay Park & Green Lanes in 1883, **Harringay Park** in 1951, then Harringay Stadium in 1958 when the totems were removed. In 1990 it became Harringay East.

Another early GNR re-signing was **Hatfield**, which opened in 1850. It was a former junction for the St Albans branch which closed in 1951. It has been the location of several disasters, of which the years 1860, 1870 and very recently 2000 stand out. North of **Ipswich** is the junction for **Bury St Edmunds** at **Haughley**, which opened in 1849 courtesy of the Eastern Union Railway. It was also known as the southern terminus of the closed Mid-Suffolk Light Railway, which had aspired to reach **Halesworth** on the East Suffolk line. Unfortunately money ran out, so Laxfield became the terminus, and closure of the whole line took place in 1952. The station at **Haughley** (BR) finally succumbed to closure in 1967.

Hertford North totems are very rare because of early removal. The LNER opened the station in 1924 to replace an earlier station further south. **Highams Park** is the penultimate station on the Liverpool Street to Chingford line. It was opened by the GER as Hale End in 1873 and renamed Highams Park & Hale End in 1899. The LNER seat-names carried the full title until the mid-'70s, although the Hale End was officially dropped in 1969. The totems were removed in about 1961 during electrification, and are therefore very rare. This also applies to **Hoe Street** on the same line. This became Walthamstow Central upon the opening of an interchange with the Underground Victoria Line in 1968. At **Hitchin** the Cambridge line parts company with the ECML, and until 1962 another line connected from there to Bedford, via **Henlow Camp** and **Shefford**. Very few **Hitchin** totems are known to survive. **Holbeach** is a great Lincolnshire rarity. It opened in 1858 and closed along with the rest of the M&GN system in 1959. In South Yorkshire the station at **Holmes** was opened in 1858 by the Midland Railway and closed in 1955, so the survival of one is astounding. The last rarity is **Hythe**, just north of Colchester, which was opened by the EUR in 1849. We are unaware of any survivors.

I: Only two names and both are rarities. **Ingatestone** is a lovingly restored ECR station, which opened in 1846. The totems were made and stored on the station pending re-signing, which never took place. They are therefore usually in mint condition. Further down the line is **Ipswich** – opened by the EUR in 1846 as Ipswich Stoke Hill (re-sited in 1860). It once boasted a busy docks railway system that has now declined.

K: A curious station in Essex on the GER main line is **Kelvedon** (opened by the ECR in 1843), which had totems, and before that, LNER horseshoe-shaped enamel lamp signs. Several of the much older horseshoes survive, but the totems have disappeared – probably dislodged by Sandringhams and Britannias thundering through!

Rare **Killamarsh Central** was opened in 1892 by the MS&L and closed in 1963. Neither **Kings Cross** or **Kings Cross York Road** are easy to find, as there were very few totems installed; despite the size of Kings Cross only platform 16 had totems. Opened by the GNR in 1852 and designed by Lewis Cubitt, the station still retains a magnificent double arch roof and has always been a magnet for enthusiasts. What sights could once be savoured, as magnificent Gresley Pacifics and mighty Deltics stormed the gradient between Gasworks and Copenhagen Tunnels and engines busied themselves in the yard at Top Shed (34A). These images only live on because of the photos and films that our predecessors fortunately had the foresight to take – not to mention the odd totem. **Kirby Cross** lies between **Thorpe-le-Soken** and **Walton-on-Naze** in Essex. Opened by the Tendring Hundred Railway in 1866, it still retains some of its rural charm and provides a passing point on the single line branch. A totem has not been seen at auction thus far, and neither has **Kirton** in Lincolnshire, which was opened by the GNR in 1849. It was a small station just south of **Boston** near the Wash, closing to passengers in 1961.

L: We moved **Langwith** from our MR database. This was a Midland Railway station of 1875 and once had a large locoshed nearby (40E/41J). One of the best-preserved medieval villages in Suffolk is **Lavenham**, which has a superb street of timber-built houses and a 15th-century guildhall. It was provided with a station by the GER in 1865; this closed rather prematurely before Beeching in 1961. In Essex on the Thames estuary lies quaint **Leigh-on-Sea** (opened in 1855 by the LT&SR). The town still attracts a large number of visitors who stroll along the path between the railway and the sea, then rest a while at the pubs and seafood stalls. We believe that totems were very short lived here and none have resurfaced, yet!

In Cambridgeshire we find **Linton** has yet to give up any of its totems. Reference to the database will show that several names have yet to appear at auction in this section, although a few examples are known in collections. The Lincolnshire station of **Louth** lost its totems in the late 1950s, and **Lowdham** (Notts) is proving very elusive also.

An N7 enters Lower Edmonton with a Liverpool Street train, 1960. (Tony Wright)

M: **Maldon East** is a curious survivor, as none of the many photos showing the station in its heyday show any totems *in situ*, although the totem shown here has obvious signs of being used. The ECR Witham to Maldon line opened in 1848 and had a rural appeal with minor halts at Wickham Bishops and Langford & Ulting. Two old weak wooden bridges near the former station were one of the reasons cited during closure proposals in 1964. The Mayor of Maldon was quoted as saying 'this is a disastrous and retrograde step' when commenting on the closure. How true his words were: the town has now doubled in size!

Further north lies **Manningtree** – junction for Harwich. Opened in 1846 by the EUR, it is located on the picturesque Stour estuary. The totems were removed by 1958, which also applies to **March**, another junction station and famous locoshed (31B). Opened by the ECR in 1847, it grew as vast amounts of agricultural traffic passed through the yards at Whitemoor – now the site of a prison! In East London we find **Maryland** – opened by the GER in 1873 as Maryland Point. The LNER renamed it **Maryland** in 1940, and totems are scarce.

The former junction for the Eye branch was **Mellis**, which opened in 1849 (EUR). The branch closed to passengers in 1931 and freight in 1964. **Mellis** closed two years later. The erstwhile hub of the M&GN at **Melton Constable** closed in 1959. Several totems are known, but one has not yet appeared at auction; neither have **Mexborough** or **Millhouses & Ecclesall**.

N: The elusive pair of **Newark Castle** and **Newark Northgate** dominate the rarity stakes as neither is known to survive for sure at present. The first station opened in 1846 as part of the Nottingham to Lincoln line, and gained the Castle title in 1950. The GNR station came into being in 1852, and became Northgate in 1950. The Newmarket Railway opened **Newmarket** in 1848. The station was replaced in 1902 by a new station further south, to cope with the demand. One of the leading horse racing centres, it was also the last place to use horses for shunting (retired racehorses perhaps!). Early re-signing has led to the totems being scarce.

Noel Park was on the former GER **Seven Sisters** to **Palace Gates** line, opening in 1878 as Green Lanes. It became Green Lanes & Noel Park in 1884, then Noel Park & Wood Green in 1902. Nearby **Northumberland Park** is curious as Park is abbreviated to just **'PK.'** on the totem. Opened by the Northern & Eastern Railway in 1842 as Marsh Lane, it became Park in 1852, and retained this unusual title until receiving its current name from the LNER in 1923.

O: **Ockendon** station was opened by the LT&SR in 1892, and was until very recently the only intermediate station on the Grays to Upminster line. The totems are rare. A new station at Chafford Hundred has opened nearby to serve the retail park at Lakeside. **Orwell** shared its name with the nearby river. Located on the **Westerfield** to **Felixstowe** branch line, it opened in 1877 and closed in 1959, hence no totems are known to survive. Another 1959 closure was the Sheffield area station of **Oughty Bridge**, which was believed to have had totems.

P: **Palace Gates** was opened by the GER in 1878 to take some traffic from its rival the GNR, who had a monopoly up to that point, with **Wood Green** being used by all passengers for Alexandra Palace. The GER line never lived up to expectations, because of the long uphill walk facing passengers arriving at Palace Gates, and it closed in 1963. Nearby **Palmers Green** was opened by the GNR in 1871. It lost its totems in the late 1950s, and we are unaware of any survivors. The same story applies to **Potters Bar**, opened by the GNR in 1852 as Potters Bar & South Mimms. The station was reconstructed in 1955, and the totems, which had only been up about five years, were reputedly scrapped. Those at **Purfleet** may also have gone the same way. Opened by the LT&SR in 1854, this station serves a mainly industrial area on the River Thames.

R: **Rainham** in Essex seems to have lost its totems at about the same time, when Purfleet and Dagenham Dock were 'blitzed'. It was an LT&SR station, opening in 1854 and remained largely intact until rebuilding in 1962, when the totems came down. **Rayleigh** and **Rectory Road** were re-signed in 1957 and 1961 respectively. **Renishaw Central** was opened as Eckington & Renishaw by the North Midland Railway in 1840, and was renamed and re-sited three times before finally closing in 1963. As totems survive from the adjacent two stations (**Killamarsh Central** and **Staveley Central**), it would be logical to assume that examples from Renishaw Central may still be around, but the evidence does not support this argument so far. The **Retford** totem shown here is very rare, and only surfaced for the first time in 2000, after reputedly being bought at a boot sale and entered into a Yorkshire auction. While it made a considerable sum of money, many more common totems have achieved higher prices, so upon reflection it could be considered to be a bargain!

Rochford (ex-GER) opened in 1889. It lost its totems in about 1957. **Rolleston Junction** has appeared once at auction, albeit creased, but it is the only ER totem with 'Junction' in the lower panel. The station was opened by the MR in 1847 as Southwell Junction, and received the later name in 1860. It is believed that **Rotherham Central** may have briefly had totems, but we await photos taken between 1950 and 1956 to prove this. In Essex the staggered platforms of **Roydon** have not changed much over the years. Opened by the Northern & Eastern in 1841, it is a charming station with a canal alongside. We are only aware of one restored totem. Very close by is **Rye House** on the Broxbourne Junction to **Hertford East** line (opened in 1846 by the ECR) of which none are known, but the next station, **St Margarets**, certainly does exist (above).

S: Colchester has two stations serving the town centre. The lesser known, but more convenient, is **St Botolph's**, which was opened by the Tendring Hundred in 1866, and renamed Colchester Town in 1991. Along with many of its neighbours it was re-signed in the late 1950s. We are unaware of any survivors, but would welcome some news to the contrary. The rather sad looking **St James Street** shown below is rare enough to warrant inclusion again. The Liverpool Street to Chingford line is one of the author's favourites (DB), so we thought you might like to see it before restoration. The station was opened in 1870 by the GER and is often referred to locally as 'Jimmy St'. This may be the only survivor.

Just down the road is **Seven Sisters**, which was the junction for **Palace Gates**, opened in 1872 (GER). If you have one of these, then DB would adopt you as a friend for life. This also applies to **Silver Street** on the same line. The **Sible and Castle Hedingham** (shown on the previous page) is a true classic. Opened by the Colne Valley & Halstead Railway in 1867, the line disappeared from the railway map in 1962, but fortunately the Colne Valley Railway preserves a small section. The wonderfully named **Six Mile Bottom** has not yet been auctioned, but a few are known. It was opened by the Newmarket Railway as Westley in 1848, but was renamed after only six months. We know which name we prefer. We have mentioned how all the three **Southend-on-Sea** stations had totems, and how strange it is that none are known at this time, so the picture below is something to drool over.

A truly remarkable *in situ* shot from 1956. (British Rail)

This totem was on the ex-GER line at **Victoria** station. The town has two other stations, both ex-LT&SR (**Central** and **East**) which were part of the LMS system. In 1948 the Fenchurch Street to **Shoeburyness** lines were added to the London Midland Region. As it was formerly LMS this made sense, but geographically it was out on a limb. After only 12 months this arrangement ceased, and the line came under ER control. Managers therefore went ahead in 1948 and ordered some maroon enamels for their stations. One of these, an MR maroon **Southend-on-Sea Central** fascia board is known to survive!

We can only speculate whether MR totems were ever made for this line, or more interestingly, do they survive? Some stations lost their ER totems by 1956, mainly towards the eastern end of the line, while west of **Upminster** they remained up until the mid-'70s. Of special note was the use of totems on the Underground platforms between **Upminster** and **Bromley (by Bow)**, where the totems had stickers over Bromley to avoid confusion with Bromley in Kent!

The branch line from **Rolleston Junction** to **Southwell** closed to passengers in 1959, but the totems at Rolleston retained the junction title until they were removed. This was unusual, as we have often found the appendage painted out

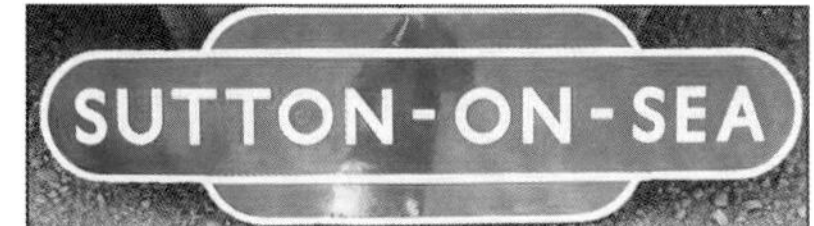

elsewhere. **Southwell** had a struggle to obtain patronage originally, as it opened and closed twice between 1847 and 1860 and was finally laid to rest in 1959. Are there any survivors?

One of the rarest Lincolnshire totems is **Stallingborough**, with 15 letters and no example known by us. The MS&L opened it in 1848. **Stamford Hill** and **Stoke Newington** (on the Liverpool Street to Enfield Town line) opened in 1872 and lost their totems by 1961. The architectural delight that is **Stamford Town** station was opened by the MR as Stamford in 1848, and became 'Town' in 1950 to distinguish it from Stamford East (closed in 1957) when all trains were routed to the Town station. It is believed that there were only four to six totems here. **Stratford** totems, although not very rare, were only fitted to platforms 11, 12 and 13. This was formerly the largest shed (30A) in the country, with an allocation of nearly 400 locos in 1950. The depot finally closed in 2001, as the site is required for the Channel Tunnel Rail Link. A new depot has now opened in Temple Mills yard nearby. Opened by the GNR in 1881 was **Stroud Green** on the Highgate branch, which along with **Crouch End** had totems very briefly until closure in 1954. However, unlike **Crouch End**, we are unaware of any survivors.

Sturmer, on the former Stour Valley line from **Sudbury** to **Haverhill**, stands out, with no survivors seen by us as yet. All the other stations on the line have produced several examples. The station was opened by the GER in 1865 and met its demise in 1967. The MS&L opened the station at **Summer Lane** in 1855 but closed it in 1859, only to open it again in 1867. After this rather shaky start it continued in use until official closure in 1959. The station remained in use for occasional specials, and the totems were still up in 1966! Despite the closure of much of the M&GN in 1959 another totem to survive is **Sutton Bridge**, which was opened in 1862 but re-sited in 1866.

The market town of **Swaffham** was once a focal point of rural Norfolk's railways. The Lynn & Dereham Railway first connected it to the outside world in 1847. While we can speculate that some old swede farmer may have a barn full of **Swaffham** totems, they are at present somewhat elusive. The final rarity is **Swinton Central**, which the MS&L opened in 1872 as Swinton, was known as 'Central' from 1950, and closed in 1958.

T: The LT&SR originally opened **Thorpe Bay** on 1 July 1910 as Southchurch-on-Sea. This lasted precisely 17 days before being renamed **Thorpe Bay**. We are only aware of one surviving totem. **Thurgarton** is a rare beast, with no example at auction but a couple in private hands. The delightful Suffolk station at **Thurston** still retains a rather stately looking Tudor building by Frederick Barnes. It opened in 1846 courtesy of the Ipswich, Bury & Newmarket Railway. One of the first Lea Valley line stations to lose its totems was **Tottenham**, which has been known as Tottenham Hale at various times. The Northern & Eastern Railway opened it in 1840.

U: The LT&SR station at **Upminster** opened in 1885 and became much larger with the arrival of Underground services in 1932 and the building of car sheds in 1959. The totems all seem to have been scrapped, whereas the next station towards London, at **Upminster Bridge**, retained totems until the early 1970s.

Steam has returned to Upminster! The totems have not. (Author's collection)

On the same line is **Upton Park**, which opened in 1877 – most famous for being the home of West Ham United FC. Some stations on this line have given up their totems more often than others. **Upton Park**, **East Ham** and **West Ham (Manor Road)** are seen very infrequently, so the picture that follows will give fellow LT&SR collectors a rare treat.

W: **Wadsley Bridge** was opened in 1845 by the Sheffield, Ashton-under-Lyme & Manchester Railway and closed officially in 1959, but lingered on for many years because of its close proximity to Sheffield Wednesday's football ground. Special trains used the station during home games, and we have evidence showing the totems still *in situ* in 1975, although by this time they were very faded. The Essex resort of **Walton-on-Naze** lies next to Clacton. The railway arrived here in 1867 because of the efforts of the Tendring Hundred Railway, who gave Victorian passengers the treat of cliff top views on setting foot outside the station. The totems are very elusive, with none seen by us. The Northern & Eastern Railway opened **Ware** in 1843, and to date the totems have not resurfaced, though at the time of going to press one is rumoured to exist.

The totems at **Wath Central** remained *in situ* in 1970, despite official closure in 1959. It opened in 1841 as Wath, then Wath & Bolton in 1850, becoming Wath-on-Dearne in 1914, and finally Wath Central in 1950. Several steam locos were cut up by W. George Ltd adjacent to the station – most famously the A1 Pacific No. 60130 *Kestrel*. There are photos showing the totems extant long after they should have been removed. The totems from nearby **Wath North**, however, were not so fortunate. This station closed in 1968 and we are unaware of any survivors. **Weeley** on the Clacton line was re-signed in the late 1950s and the totems have not resurfaced – yet. It was a Tendring Hundred station, which opened in 1866.

Welwyn North is slightly rarer than **Welwyn Garden City**, having made fewer appearances in public. The 'North' station opened as Welwyn in 1850 and became Welwyn North to distinguish it from Welwyn Garden City when the LNER opened the latter in 1926, replacing an earlier halt.

On the LT&SR line, the 1895 station of **Westcliff on Sea** lost its totems to fluorescent lighting in the mid-1950s and none are known. The intermediate station of **West Green** on the erstwhile **Palace Gates** branch opened in 1878 and while the totems lasted until closure in 1963, we have been unable to locate any survivors. **White Hart Lane** is best known for Tottenham Hotspur's football ground and a totem may be hanging on a supporter's lounge wall somewhere, but as it was the victim of early removal (1961) we doubt it. The totems at **Wickford** were taken down even earlier (1957), so one of these in a collection is even less likely. Just south of Cambridge lies **Whittlesford** (opened in 1845 by the ECR), and fortunately we have just been shown one of these elusive beasts.

In Derbyshire, **Whitwell** is now believed to have been ER. A colour photo would help. The Midland Railway opened it in 1875 and no totems have been located yet. The M&GN station of **Wisbech North** opened in 1877 and along with the majority of this much lamented cross-country route it disappeared in 1959, but unlike many of the other stations closed at the same time, Wisbech North totems are conspicuously unknown. Another of the Tendring Hundred stations, **Wivenhoe** (formerly Wyvenhoe), lies on the River Colne. Early re-signing once again has deprived collectors of another treasure. To the east of Sheffield lies **Woodhouse** (opened by the Sheffield & Lincolnshire Junction Railway in 1850). Like so many South Yorkshire dark blue totems, this is very elusive. **Wood Street** was a former GER locoshed on the Liverpool Street to Chingford line (opened in 1873). It was re-signed in 1961 and we are unaware of any survivors.

Y: Only one name here, but what a treasure to finish on. **Yeldham** was opened by the Colne Valley & Halstead Railway in 1862 and had a life-span of exactly 100 years during which time it hardly altered. A totem is known to survive from this 1962 closure.

Large lettered totems *in situ* at Wickford, *c.* 1957. (LCGB Ken Nunn Collection)

Yeldham, damp and deserted. (Malcolm Root GRA)

Above: March 1973. (Alan Young)

Left: July 1975. (Alan Young)

Chapter 8 Totem Listing

Place name	County	Eastern Region			Totem in	Totem
		Layout	Flange	Closed	Auction	Survived
ACLE	Norfolk		HF		✓	✓
ALDEBURGH	Suffolk		HF	1966	✓	✓
ALFORD TOWN	Lincolnshire		HF/FF	1970	✓	✓
ALRESFORD	Essex		HF			
ALTHORPE	Lincolnshire		HF		✓	✓
ANGEL ROAD	Middlesex		FF		✓	✓
APPLEBY	Lincolnshire		FF	1967		✓
ATTERCLIFFE ROAD	Yorkshire		FF		✓	✓
ATTLEBOROUGH	Norfolk		HF		✓	✓
AUDLEY END	Essex		HF			✓
BALDOCK	Hertfordshire		HF			
BARKING	Essex		HF			
BARNETBY	Lincolnshire		HF		✓	✓
BARNSLEY EXCHANGE to confirm	Yorkshire	2 line				
BARNWELL JUNCTION	Cambridgeshire	2 line	HF	1962		✓
BARROW HILL	Derbyshire		HF	1954	✓	✓
BARTLOW	Essex		FF	1967		✓
BEAUCHIEF	Yorkshire		HF	1961	✓	✓
BECCLES large letters	Suffolk		HF			✓
BECONTREE	Essex		HF		✓	✓
BENFLEET	Essex		HF			
BENTLEY	Suffolk		FF	1966		✓
BETHNAL GREEN	London		HF			
BIGGLESWADE	Bedfordshire		HF		✓	✓
BILLERICAY	Essex		HF			
BIRDBROOK	Essex		HF	1962	✓	✓
BISHOPS STORTFORD	Hertfordshire		HF			✓
BLACKHORSE ROAD	Essex		HF		✓	✓
BLEASBY	Nottinghamshire		HF		✓	✓
BOSTON	Lincolnshire		HF			✓
BOWES PARK	Middlesex		HF			✓
BRAMPTON	Suffolk		FF		✓	✓

Place name	County	Layout	Flange	Closed	Auction	Survived
BRANDON	Norfolk		HF		✓	✓
BRAUGHING	Hertfordshire		HF/FF	1964	✓	✓
BRIGG	Lincolnshire		FF		✓	✓
BRIGHTSIDE	Yorkshire		FF			✓
BRIMSDOWN	Middlesex		FF			✓
BROMLEY	London		HF		✓	✓
BROOKMANS PARK	Hertfordshire		HF		✓	✓
BROXBOURNE	Hertfordshire		HF			✓
BRUCE GROVE	Middlesex		FF			
BRUNDALL	Norfolk		HF		✓	✓
BRUNDALL GARDENS HALT	Norfolk	LP	FF			✓
BUNTINGFORD	Hertfordshire		HF	1964	✓	✓
BURES	Essex		HF		✓	✓
BURNHAM-ON-CROUCH	Essex		HF			✓
BURNT MILL	Essex		FF			✓
BURSTON	Norfolk		HF	1966	✓	✓
BURTON JOYCE	Nottinghamshire		HF			✓
BURY ST. EDMUNDS	Suffolk		HF			
BUSH HILL PARK	Middlesex		FF			
CAMBRIDGE	Cambridgeshire		HF			
CANTLEY	Norfolk		HF			✓
CARLTON & NETHERFIELD	Nottinghamshire	LP	HF		✓	✓
CAVENDISH	Suffolk		HF	1967	✓	✓
CHADWELL HEATH	Essex		HF			✓
CHALKWELL	Essex		HF			
CHAPELTOWN SOUTH	Yorkshire	2 line	HF		✓	✓
CHATTERIS	Cambridgeshire		HF	1967	✓	✓
CHELMSFORD	Essex		HF			✓
CHESHUNT	Hertfordshire		FF			✓
CHESTERFIELD CENTRAL	Derbyshire	2 line	HF	1963	✓	✓
CHESTERFIELD MIDLAND	Derbyshire	LP	HF			✓
CLACTON-ON-SEA	Essex	LP	HF			✓
CLAPTON	London		FF			

Place name	County	Layout	Flange	Closed	Auction	Survived
CLARE	Suffolk		HF	1967		✓
COLCHESTER	Essex		HF			
COLLINGHAM	Nottinghamshire		HF		✓	✓
CONISBOROUGH	Yorkshire		HF			✓
CORTON	Suffolk		HF	1970	✓	✓
COTTAM	Nottinghamshire		FF	1959	✓	✓
CRESSING	Essex		HF			✓
CREWS HILL	Middlesex		HF			✓
CROUCH END	Middlesex		HF	1954	✓	✓
CROWLE CENTRAL	Lincolnshire	LP	HF		✓	✓
CUFFLEY	Hertfordshire		HF		✓	✓
DAGENHAM DOCK	Essex		HF			
DAGENHAM EAST	Essex		HF		✓	✓
DAGENHAM HEATHWAY	Essex		HF		✓	✓
DARFIELD	Yorkshire		HF	1963		✓
DARNALL	Yorkshire		HF/FF		✓	✓
DAYBROOK	Nottinghamshire		HF	1960	✓	✓
DEEPCAR	Yorkshire		HF	1959	✓	✓
DERBY ROAD	Suffolk		HF		✓	✓
DERSINGHAM	Norfolk		FF	1969	✓	✓
DISS large letters	Norfolk		HF		✓	✓
DODWORTH	Yorkshire		HF	1959		✓
DORE & TOTLEY also 'and'	Derbyshire		HF		✓	✓
DOVERCOURT BAY	Essex		HF		✓	✓
DOWNHAM	Norfolk		HF/FF		✓	✓
DRONFIELD	Derbyshire			1967		✓
DULLINGHAM	Cambridgeshire		HF		✓	✓
EARLS COLNE	Essex		HF	1962		✓
EAST HAM	London		FF		✓	✓
EAST TILBURY	Essex		HF			
ECCLESFIELD WEST	Yorkshire	2 line	HF	1967		

Place name	County	Layout	Flange	Closed	Auction	Survived
ECCLES ROAD	Norfolk		HF		✓	✓
ELM PARK large letters	Essex		HF		✓	✓
ELMSWELL	Suffolk		HF		✓	✓
ELSECAR AND HOYLAND	Yorkshire	2 line	HF			
ELSENHAM	Essex		FF		✓	✓
ELY	Cambridgeshire		HF			
EMERSON PARK HALT	Essex		HF			✓
ENFIELD CHASE	Middlesex		HF			
ENFIELD LOCK	Middlesex		FF		✓	✓
ESSENDINE	Rutland		HF	1959		
FAKENHAM EAST	Norfolk	LP	HF	1964		✓
FAKENHAM WEST	Norfolk	LP	HF	1959		
FELIXSTOWE BEACH	Suffolk	LP	HF	1967		✓
FELIXSTOWE TOWN	Suffolk		HF		✓	✓
FINNINGHAM	Suffolk		HF	1966	✓	✓
FIRSBY	Lincolnshire		HF	1970	✓	✓
FISKERTON	Nottinghamshire		HF			✓
FLORDON	Norfolk		FF	1966		✓
FORDHAM	Cambridgeshire		HF	1965		✓
FOREST GATE	London		HF		✓	✓
FORNCETT	Norfolk		FF	1966	✓	✓
FOXTON	Cambridgeshire		HF			✓
FRINTON-ON-SEA	Essex		HF			✓
FULBOURNE	Cambridgeshire		HF	1967	✓	✓
GAINSBOROUGH CENTRAL	Lincolnshire	2 line	HF		✓	✓
GEDLING	Nottinghamshire		HF	1960	✓	✓
GLEMSFORD	Suffolk		HF	1967	✓	✓
GORLESTON-ON-SEA	Norfolk		HF	1970	✓	✓
GOXHILL	Lincolnshire		HF		✓	✓
GRANTHAM	Lincolnshire		HF			
GRAYS	Essex		HF		✓	✓

Place name	County	Layout	Flange	Closed	Auction	Survived
GREAT BENTLEY	Essex		HF			
GREAT CHESTERFORD	Cambridgeshire		FF			✓
GRIMSBY DOCKS	Lincolnshire		HF			✓
HABROUGH	Lincolnshire		FF		✓	✓
HACKNEY DOWNS	London		FF			✓
HADDISCOE	Norfolk		FF		✓	✓
HADHAM	Hertfordshire		HF	1964	✓	✓
HALESWORTH	Suffolk		HF		✓	✓
HALSTEAD	Essex		HF	1962		✓
HARLING ROAD	Norfolk		FF		✓	✓
HARLOW	Essex		HF			✓
HARRINGAY (was Harringay West)	London		HF		✓	✓
HARRINGAY PARK	London		HF			
HARRINGAY WEST (renamed)	London	LP	HF		✓	✓
HARSTON	Cambridgeshire		FF	1963		✓
HARWICH TOWN	Essex		HF		✓	✓
HATFIELD	Hertfordshire		HF			
HATFIELD PEVEREL	Essex		HF			✓
HAUGHLEY	Suffolk		HF	1967		✓
HAVERHILL	Suffolk		HF	1967	✓	✓
HEACHAM	Norfolk		FF	1969	✓	✓
HEATH	Derbyshire		HF	1963		✓
HECKINGTON	Lincolnshire		HF			✓
HEELEY	Yorkshire		HF	1968	✓	✓
HERTFORD EAST	Hertfordshire		HF		✓	✓
HERTFORD NORTH	Hertfordshire		HF			
HIGHAM	Suffolk		HF	1967		✓
HIGHAMS PARK	Essex		FF			✓
HISTON	Cambridgeshire		HF	1970		✓
HITCHIN	Hertfordshire		HF			✓
HOE STREET	Essex		FF			

Place name		County	Layout	Flange	Closed	Auction	Survived
HOLBEACH		Lincolnshire		HF	1959		
HOLMES	large letters	Yorkshire		HF	1955		✓
HOLT		Norfolk		HF	1964	✓	✓
HOPTON ON SEA	small 'on'	Suffolk		HF	1970	✓	✓
HORNCHURCH		Essex		HF		✓	✓
HORNSEY		Middlesex		HF		✓	✓
HUNSTANTON		Norfolk		HF	1969	✓	✓
HYKEHAM		Lincolnshire		HF		✓	✓
HYTHE		Essex		HF			
INGATESTONE		Essex		FF			✓
IPSWICH		Suffolk		HF		✓	✓
KELVEDON		Essex		FF			
KENNETT		Cambridgeshire		HF		✓	✓
KILLAMARSH CENTRAL		Derbyshire	2 line	HF	1963		✓
KILNHURST CENTRAL		Yorkshire	LP	HF	1968	✓	✓
KILNHURST WEST		Yorkshire	LP	HF	1968	✓	✓
KINGS CROSS		London		HF		✓	✓
KINGS CROSS YORK ROAD		London	LP	FF	1977	✓	✓
KING'S LYNN		Norfolk		FF		✓	✓
KIRBY CROSS		Essex		HF			✓
KIRTON		Lincolnshire		HF	1961		✓
KIVETON BRIDGE		Yorkshire		FF		✓	✓
KNEBWORTH		Hertfordshire		FF		✓	✓
LAINDON		Essex		HF			
LANGWITH		Derbyshire			1964		
LAVENHAM		Suffolk		HF	1961		✓
LEA BRIDGE		London		HF/FF	1985	✓	✓
LEIGH-ON-SEA		Essex		HF			
LEISTON		Suffolk		HF	1966	✓	✓
LETCHWORTH		Hertfordshire		HF			✓
LEVERTON		Nottinghamshire		FF	1959		✓

Place name	County	Layout	Flange	Closed	Auction	Survived
LEYTON MIDLAND ROAD	Essex	LP	HF		✓	✓
LEYTONSTONE HIGH ROAD	Essex	LP	FF			✓
LINCOLN CENTRAL	Lincolnshire	LP	HF			✓
LINCOLN ST. MARKS	Lincolnshire		HF	1986		✓
LINGWOOD	Norfolk		HF		✓	✓
LINTON	Cambridgeshire		HF	1967		
LITTLEPORT	Cambridgeshire		FF		✓	✓
LITTLEWORTH	Lincolnshire		FF	1961		✓
LONG MELFORD	Suffolk		HF	1967		✓
LONG STANTON	Cambridgeshire		HF	1970	✓	✓
LOUTH poss large letters	Lincolnshire		HF	1970		
LOWDHAM	Nottinghamshire					
LOWER EDMONTON	Middlesex		FF			✓
LOWESTOFT NORTH	Norfolk	2 line	HF	1970	✓	✓
MABLETHORPE	Lincolnshire		HF/FF	1970	✓	✓
MAGDALEN ROAD	Norfolk		FF	1968	✓	✓
MALDON EAST	Essex	LP	HF	1964		✓
MANNINGTREE	Essex		HF			
MANOR PARK	Essex		HF		✓	✓
MARCH	Cambridgeshire		HF			
MARKET RASEN	Lincolnshire		HF		✓	✓
MARKS TEY	Essex		HF		✓	✓
MARYLAND	London		HF			✓
MELDRETH	Cambridgeshire		HF		✓	✓
MELLIS	Suffolk		HF	1966		✓
MELTON CONSTABLE	Norfolk		FF	1964		✓
MEXBOROUGH	Yorkshire		HF			✓
MILLHOUSES & ECCLESALL	Yorkshire	LP	HF	1968		✓
MISTLEY	Essex		HF		✓	✓
MOULTON	Lincolnshire		HF	1959	✓	✓
NARBOROUGH AND PENTNEY	Norfolk	LP	FF	1968	✓	✓

Place name	County	Layout	Flange	Closed	Auction	Survived
NEEDHAM	Suffolk		FF		✓	✓
NEWARK CASTLE	Nottinghamshire		HF			
NEWARK NORTHGATE	Nottinghamshire	2 line	HF			
NEW HOLLAND TOWN	Lincolnshire		HF		✓	✓
NEWMARKET	Cambridgeshire		HF			
NEWPORT	Essex		FF		✓	✓
NEW SOUTHGATE	Middlesex		HF		✓	✓
NOEL PARK	Middlesex		HF	1963		✓
NORTHUMBERLAND PK.	Middlesex		FF			✓
NORTH WALSHAM MAIN	Norfolk	LP	HF			✓
OAKINGTON	Cambridgeshire		HF	1970	✓	✓
OAKLEIGH PARK	Hertfordshire		HF		✓	✓
OCKENDON	Essex		HF			✓
ORWELL	Suffolk		HF	1959		
OUGHTY BRIDGE	Yorkshire			1959		
OULTON BROAD NORTH	Norfolk	2 line	HF		✓	✓
OULTON BROAD SOUTH	Norfolk	2 line	FF		✓	✓
PALACE GATES	Middlesex		HF	1963		✓
PALMERS GREEN	Middlesex		HF			
PARKGATE & RAWMARSH	Yorkshire	LP	HF	1968	✓	✓
PENISTONE	Yorkshire		HF			✓
PETERBOROUGH EAST	Cambridgeshire	LP	HF	1966	✓	✓
PETERBOROUGH EAST	Cambridgeshire	2 line	FF	1966	✓	✓
PETERBOROUGH NORTH	Cambridgeshire	2 line	HF		✓	✓
PITSEA	Essex		HF			✓
PLAISTOW	Essex		HF		✓	✓
PONDERS END	Middlesex		FF		✓	✓
POTTERS BAR	Hertfordshire		HF			
PRITTLEWELL	Essex		HF			
PURFLEET	Essex		HF			

Place name	County	Layout	Flange	Closed	Auction	Survived
RADCLIFFE ON TRENT	Nottinghamshire		HF		✓	✓
RAINHAM	Essex		HF			
RAYLEIGH large letters	Essex		HF			
RECTORY ROAD	London		FF			
REEDHAM	Norfolk		HF		✓	✓
RENISHAW CENTRAL	Derbyshire	LP	HF	1963		
RETFORD	Nottinghamshire		HF		✓	✓
ROCHFORD large letters	Essex		HF			
ROLLESTON JUNCTION	Nottinghamshire	LP	HF		✓	✓
ROTHERHAM CENTRAL	Yorkshire	?		1966		
ROTHERHAM MASBOROUGH	Yorkshire	LP	FF	1988	✓	✓
ROYDON	Essex		HF			✓
RYE HOUSE	Hertfordshire		HF			
SAFFRON WALDEN	Essex		FF	1964		✓
ST. BOTOLPHS	Essex		HF			
ST. IVES	Cambridgeshire		HF	1970	✓	✓
ST. JAMES STREET	Essex		FF			✓
ST. MARGARETS	Hertfordshire		HF			✓
ST. NEOTS	Cambridgeshire		HF		✓	✓
SALHOUSE	Norfolk		FF		✓	✓
SANDY	Bedfordshire		HF		✓	✓
SAWBRIDGEWORTH	Hertfordshire		FF			✓
SAXHAM AND RISBY small 'and'	Suffolk		HF	1967	✓	✓
SAXMUNDHAM	Suffolk		HF			✓
SEVEN SISTERS	Middlesex		FF			
SHEEPBRIDGE	Derbyshire		HF	1967	✓	✓
SHELFORD	Cambridgeshire		FF		✓	✓
SHEPRETH	Cambridgeshire		HF		✓	✓
SHIREBROOK WEST	Derbyshire	LP	HF	1964		✓
SHOEBURYNESS	Essex		HF			✓
SIBLE AND CASTLE HEDINGHAM	Essex	2 line	HF	1962		✓
SILVER STREET	Middlesex		FF			

Place name	County	Layout	Flange	Closed	Auction	Survived
SILVERTOWN	Essex		FF		✓	✓
SIX MILE BOTTOM	Cambridgeshire		HF	1967		✓
SKEGNESS large letters	Lincolnshire		HF		✓	✓
SLEAFORD	Lincolnshire		HF		✓	✓
SNETTISHAM	Norfolk		FF	1969	✓	✓
SOHAM	Cambridgeshire		HF	1965	✓	✓
SOMERLEYTON	Suffolk		HF		✓	✓
SOMERSHAM	Huntingdon		HF	1967		✓
SOUTHEND-ON-SEA CENTRAL	Essex	LP	HF			
SOUTHEND-ON-SEA EAST	Essex	LP	HF			
SOUTHEND-ON-SEA VICTORIA	Essex	LP	HF			
SOUTH TOTTENHAM	Middlesex		HF			✓
SOUTHWELL	Nottinghamshire		HF	1959		
SPALDING TOWN	Lincolnshire		HF			✓
STAINFORTH	Yorkshire		HF			✓
STALLINGBOROUGH	Lincolnshire					
STAMFORD HILL	Middlesex		FF			
STAMFORD TOWN	Lincolnshire	2 line	HF			
STANDON	Hertfordshire		HF	1964	✓	✓
STANFORD-LE-HOPE	Essex		HF			✓
STANSTED	Essex		FF		✓	✓
STAVELEY CENTRAL	Derbyshire	LP	HF	1963	✓	✓
STEVENAGE	Hertfordshire		HF		✓	✓
STOKE	Suffolk		HF	1967	✓	✓
STOKE NEWINGTON	London		FF			
STOWMARKET	Suffolk		HF		✓	✓
STRATFORD	London		FF		✓	✓
STROUD GREEN	Middlesex		HF	1954		
STURMER	Essex		HF	1967		
SUDBURY	Suffolk		HF			✓
SUMMER LANE *still up in 1966	Yorkshire		HF	1959*		
SUTTON BRIDGE	Lincolnshire		HF	1959	✓	✓
SUTTON-ON-SEA	Lincolnshire		HF/FF	1970	✓	✓

Place name	County	Layout	Flange	Closed	Auction	Survived
SWAFFHAM	Norfolk		HF	1968		
SWINDERBY	Lincolnshire		HF/FF		✓	✓
SWINTON CENTRAL	Yorkshire	LP?	HF	1957		
THETFORD large letters	Norfolk		HF		✓	✓
THORNE NORTH	Lincolnshire		HF		✓	✓
THORNE SOUTH To confirm	Lincolnshire					
THORPE BAY	Essex		HF			✓
THORPE-LE-SOKEN	Essex		HF		✓	✓
THURGARTON	Nottinghamshire		HF			✓
THURSTON	Suffolk		HF			✓
TILBURY TOWN	Essex		HF		✓	✓
TIVETSHALL	Norfolk		FF	1966	✓	✓
TORKSEY 'Torkesey' on totem	Lincolnshire		HF	1959	✓	✓
TOTTENHAM	Middlesex		HF			✓
TRIMLEY	Suffolk		HF		✓	✓
UPMINSTER	Essex		HF			
UPMINSTER BRIDGE	Essex		HF		✓	✓
UPNEY	Essex		HF		✓	✓
UPTON PARK	Essex		HF		✓	✓
WADSLEY BRIDGE	Yorkshire		HF	1959	✓	✓
WAINFLEET	Lincolnshire		HF		✓	✓
WALTHAM CROSS	Hertfordshire		HF		✓	✓
WALTHAMSTOW	Essex		HF		✓	✓
WALTON-ON-NAZE	Essex		HF			
WANSTEAD PARK	Essex		HF			✓
WARE	Hertfordshire		HF			
WATH CENTRAL *still up in 1970	Yorkshire	LP	HF	1959*	✓	✓
WATH NORTH	Yorkshire	2 line?	HF	1968		
WEELEY	Essex		HF			
WELWYN GARDEN CITY	Hertfordshire		HF		✓	✓

Place name		County	Layout	Flange	Closed	Auction	Survived
WELWYN NORTH		Hertfordshire		HF		✓	✓
WESTCLIFF ON SEA		Essex	LP	HF			
WESTERFIELD		Suffolk		HF			✓
WEST GREEN		Middlesex		HF	1963		
WEST HAM (MANOR ROAD)		Essex	LP	HF			✓
WEST HORNDON		Essex		HF			
WEST RUNTON		Norfolk		HF		✓	✓
WEYBOURNE		Norfolk		HF	1964	✓	✓
WHITE COLNE		Essex		HF	1962		✓
WHITE HART LANE		Middlesex		FF			
WHITE NOTLEY		Essex		HF			✓
WHITTLESEA		Cambridgeshire		HF		✓	✓
WHITTLESFORD		Cambridgeshire		FF			✓
WHITWELL		Derbyshire			1964		
WICKFORD	large letters	Essex		HF			
WICKHAM MARKET		Suffolk		HF		✓	✓
WINCHMORE HILL		Middlesex		HF			✓
WISBECH NORTH		Cambridgeshire	LP	HF	1959		
WITHAM	large letters	Essex		HF		✓	✓
WIVENHOE		Essex		HF			
WOMBWELL CENTRAL		Yorkshire	LP	HF	1959		✓
WOMBWELL WEST		Yorkshire	2 line	HF			✓
WOODBRIDGE		Suffolk		HF		✓	✓
WOODGRANGE PARK		Essex		HF		✓	✓
WOOD GREEN		Middlesex		HF		✓	✓
WOODHALL JUNCTION		Lincolnshire		FF	1970	✓	✓
WOODHOUSE		Yorkshire					
WOOD STREET		Essex		FF			
WORSTEAD		Norfolk		HF			✓
WRABNESS		Essex		HF		✓	✓
WROXHAM		Norfolk		HF/FF		✓	✓
WYMONDHAM		Norfolk		HF		✓	✓
YELDHAM		Essex		HF	1962		✓

HAWARDEN BRIDGE
CHESTER GENERAL
NOTTINGHAM MIDLAND
WEMBLEY CENTRAL
WHITCHURCH
CHEDDINGTON
COALVILLE TOWN
ASHTON CHARLESTOWN
CHERRY TREE
LICHFIELD
KENSAL RISE
WATFORD WEST
NORTHAMPTON CASTLE
DERBY MIDLAND
PRESTON ROAD
NEWTON-LE-WILLOWS
LONDON MIDLAND REGION TOTEMS

CHAPTER 9

The London Midland Region

Introduction

The formation of the London, Midland and Scottish Railway in the 1923 Grouping created the largest of the 'Big Four' Companies. The network stretched from London to the Central Highlands of Scotland, including the whole of England west of the Pennines and the whole of North Wales. At 7,790 route miles it was more than 1,200 miles larger than the LNER and virtually twice the size of the GWR. However, the LMS covered such a diverse and large area that it was decided to create this region for administration and identity purposes. The London Midland Region (hereafter called the LMR), at just under 5,000 route miles, was still a mighty large company, covering the area from the Scottish Border down to London (north to south) and Bedfordshire to Anglesey (east to west). The four totems below help to illustrate the extent of the Region.

This chapter concentrates on the London Midland Region portion of the old LMS and the reader is referred to Chapter 11 for the ex-LMS Scottish section.

The history of the London Midland Region

The southern portion of the former LMS was the result of amalgamating some 16 companies over a period of about 100 years. Some of these names may appear surprising, the London, Tilbury and Southend Railway (LT&SR) for example. The companies that formed the LMR were, in alphabetical order:

Birkenhead Joint	(BJR)
Cheshire Lines Committee	(CLC)
Cockermouth, Keswick and Penrith Railway	(CK&PR)
Cromford and High Peak	(C&HPR)
Furness Railway	(FR)
Lancashire and Yorkshire Railway	(L&YR)
London and North Western Railway	(LNWR)
London, Tilbury and Southend	(LT&SR)
Maryport and Carlisle Railway	(M&CR)
Mersey Railway	(MeR)
Midland Railway	(MR)
North London Railway	(NLR)
North Staffordshire Railway	(NSR)
Stratford-on-Avon and Midland Junction Railway	(S&MJR)
Whitehaven, Cleator and Egremont Railway	(WC&ER)
Wirral Railway	(WR)

With such an amalgamation, the history is clearly complicated and will only be briefly reviewed in this book, merely to help set the historical perspective for the work. In this list there were some giants (LNWR) and some minnows (BJR), but together they formed the north-western arm of the British Railways network in 1948.

The BJR is an old railway company dating back to the 1830s. It had a chequered history, being joined to and then broken from several companies in that area. It was eventually drawn into the LNWR in 1860, but was jointly administered by the GWR, who wanted access to the lucrative traffic into Liverpool. Thus **Birkenhead** became a joint GWR/LNWR station and remained so until Nationalisation.

The CLC was formed in 1865 when railway companies around the Manchester, Sheffield and even Lincolnshire areas decided to pool some of their assets and expertise for economic reasons. Two ex-CLC totems are shown below.

They were joined a year later by elements of the MR. This pooling of interest led to the development of commuter lines in Cheshire, the Wirral and South Lancashire. It eventually became a compact and powerful railway, serving the Liverpool, Manchester and Chester triangle. In the 1870s the CLC expanded north of the Mersey and the last significant expansion occurred in 1884 when they reached Southport. Surprisingly, in the 1923 grouping the CLC retained independence and it was finally merged into the LMR in the 1948 Act of Nationalisation. Pruning occurred after this date, as duplicated routings in the area were thinned. The major losses were essentially the **Liverpool Central** and **Manchester Central** stations along with the lovely station of **Chester Northgate**.

The CK&P ran through some superb scenery. Their line between **Penrith** and **Cockermouth** was opened to mineral traffic in 1864. The North Eastern Railway initially operated this freight traffic. Once the LNWR had acquired other routes into **Workington** and **Whitehaven**, it began to operate passenger traffic over the CK&P from 1866. This gave the LNWR good access to the most northerly area of its 'empire'. In 1923 the LMS took over the route and steam ran until the mid-'50s when, to plagiarise that great traveller/personality Michael Palin, 'the lesser spotted DMU' arrived. Economics forced the closure of freight working in 1964, and two years later passenger trains also stopped. This meant that the train journey along the banks of Bassenthwaite Lake ceased and the former trackbed is now the dual carriageway A66. The super station at **Bassenthwaite Lake** is still in place, although now totally overgrown and barely visible. Two ex-CK&P totems are seen below.

The C&HPR was one of the very first railways in existence. An Act of Parliament created the company in 1825, and by 1831 some 33 miles of track were operational between **Cromford** and **Whaley Bridge**. It was not until 20 years later a connection was eventually made to the main line at **Whaley Bridge**. The company was leased to the LNWR in 1862 and taken over completely in 1887.

The Furness Railway was a small regional company that the new LMS inherited in 1923. It constructed its first lines in 1844, and passenger services started two years later. It operated the now famous Cumbrian Coast line between **Barrow** and **Whitehaven**. Further south it developed lines to **Carnforth** and **Lancaster**. Two tourist routes into **Windermere** (from **Ulverston**) and Coniston Lake (from **Foxfield**) were also added. **Barrow** became a freight traffic centre as iron ore was extracted in the region. As a result of the increased income Barrow Central station became the centrepiece of the FR. Before nationalisation portions of the FR were axed. The branch to **Lake Side** closed to passengers in 1965 (reopened by the Lakeside & Haverthwaite Railway in 1973). The FR contained some wonderfully named stations such as **Cark** and **Cartmel**, Furness Abbey, **Windermere** and **Ravenglass**. Below are two ex-Furness totems.

The narrow gauge Ravenglass Railway still uses 'totem type' signs for its museum, and the nearby railway pub (the Ratty Arms) has a similar sign. We could not pass up the chance of including a pair of most unusual 'totems' still *in situ*!

One of the larger companies in the LMS was the L&YR. This, as the name implies, covered the area across the Pennines, and the railway was responsible for linking the two industrial areas of Manchester and Leeds. The construction of the line took place from both Leeds and Manchester ends simultaneously. The last section to be finished was the most problematic, the mile long Summit Tunnel section, north of **Littleborough**. On the Lancashire side a complex network of lines was built around **Bury**, **Blackburn**, **Preston**, **Burnley** and across towards Liverpool. The area south-west of Preston towards Southport and **Ormskirk** was heavily developed and the L&Y joined with the LNWR to develop the system to Blackpool and the Fylde Coast. All this was achieved in the ten-year period 1840–50.

On the Yorkshire side lines opened into **Halifax**, **Bradford**, and west from **Todmorden** towards **Burnley**. In the early years, the L&Y had a poor reputation for service and punctuality, but as the network grew and passenger loading increased it began to establish the reverse reputation – a strong reliable railway company. It finally merged with the LNWR in 1922. At the 1923 Grouping the newly enlarged LNWR was the major constituent of the LMS, and some of the traditions of the L&Y helped establish the LMS reputation in the north-west.

When nationalisation arrived many of the eastern stations of the old L&Y passed into the hands of the North Eastern Region of BR, so that lines running east from **Sowerby Bridge** and **Halifax** through **Brighouse** and into **Bradford Exchange** were fitted with tangerine totems. (The westerly section from **Hebden Bridge** and **Todmorden** across to **Burnley** remained LMR). We have many examples of totems from this company, so our apologies if we have not selected your favourites!

The LNWR was the real heavyweight in the 1923 formation of the LMS. It also has its origins right at the start of the railway era. The LNWR Company formed in 1846, but the constituents were the Liverpool and Manchester (1830 Rainhill trials and all that), the Grand Junction Railway, the Manchester & Birmingham and the London & Birmingham. These four early companies were all pioneers for the lines from London north to the industrial heartland of England and to the northern cities of Manchester and Liverpool.

Once all these four had amalgamated expansion really began in earnest, first north towards **Lancaster** and **Carlisle** (1846), west to **Chester** and **Holyhead** (1848), east through **Bedford** and **Cambridge** (1865) and into South and Central Wales (1865–8). They even had lines into **Leeds** (1847), **Workington** and **Whitehaven** (1866), then into Ruthin and **Corwen** in North Wales (1879). This was expansion on a scale not witnessed before or since, and they became, for a time, the world's largest stock company. Before the 1923 grouping there were joint developments with the GWR (around **Shrewsbury** and **Hereford**), the FR in northern Lancashire and into Cumberland, across the border in Scotland with the Caledonian Railway, the Glasgow & South Western and the Portpatrick & Wigtownshire Joint. Consequently the LNWR influence was very considerable in most of the western parts of England and Wales, (with the footholds in the east and in Scotland) by the start of the 20th century.

The really telling acquisition, however, was the L&Y in 1922, giving the Company all the routes in the north-west of England, with the exception of some interloping lines of its great and long term rival, the Midland Railway. Imagine the reaction, therefore, a year after acquiring the L&Y, at the news that it was to be grouped with its rival the MR. However, out of this union came arguably the strongest of the 'Big Four' railway companies.

In 1948 the old LNWR was the cornerstone of the new LMR. The tradition and good management practices continued to exert influence through the 1950s and 1960s. With few exceptions most of the lines remained intact and were considerably upgraded. This includes the WCML, the North Wales Coast line to **Holyhead**, the main spurs through the Midlands, the Potteries, lines into Liverpool and Manchester and sections of the trans-Pennine lines. Two of the many wonderful BR(M) posters, characteristic of the region, follow.

(South Devon Railway – Tindale Collection)

(South Devon Railway – Tindale Collection)

As with the L&Y, we have a plethora of totems to choose from showing the heritage of the LNWR in the LMR. Pictures of many of the rarer totems are already shown in the database that follows, so we have chosen stations that are interesting and desirable to the LNWR collector in our opinion.

The LT&SR came into being in 1854 when the **Forest Gate** to **Tilbury** line opened. By 1856 **Southend-on-Sea** had been reached and the London terminus at Fenchurch Street was also operational. The Great Eastern Railway declined to operate the line in 1875, so the LT&SR ran its own operations until taken over by the MR in 1912.

It seems slightly curious that the Southend line was under LMR control even after the 1948 Nationalisation, and control did not pass to the ER until 1949. Thus in the era of the totem this company really fell under the ER umbrella, and the reader will find the history and developments in Chapter 8.

The M&CR was one of this country's smallest railway bodies, with only 43 route miles, and fewer than 30 engines passing into the control of the LMS in 1923. It formed early (1837) mainly to feed goods and services from **Carlisle**, through **Dalston** and **Aspatria**, to the port of **Maryport**. Extensions looped through Mealsgate and a spur was built down to Papcastle to link with the CK&PR. However, part of this loop closed before 1923 and the LMS closed the rest in 1930.

The Mersey Railway linking Liverpool and the Wirral opened in 1886. Its northern extension into **Birkenhead Park** joined with the Wirral Railway, so this short historical review will look at both the MeR and WR. The WR dates back to the 1860s, and was built to serve the growing communities at the northern end of the Wirral Peninsula. Lines ran to New Brighton (1888) and **Hoylake** (1881). However, the two had quite distinctly different fates at the 1923 grouping. The MeR was excluded from the grouping and retained independence until Nationalisation. The WR was grouped and as a result was upgraded and electrified. The complexity of the companies and lines around the Birkenhead/Liverpool conurbation is shown below.

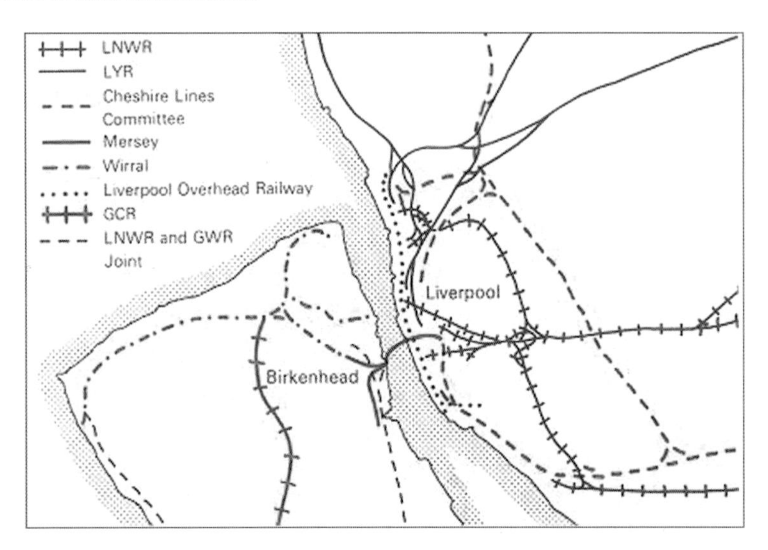

Parts of the WR closed in 1963. The ex-MeR line into **Liverpool Central (Low Level)** became Merseyrail, who then upgraded the whole area to give an electrified network that spreads further out into the Wirral Peninsula and down towards **Chester**. Four of the Mersey area stations are illustrated below.

The Midland Railway (MR) was for years the bitter rival of the LNWR. They both had the same ideals and aspirations, and it was an interesting early marriage when they were grouped together in 1923. The formation of the MR in 1844, which amalgamated smaller regional companies, represented the first of the major Victorian Age railway 'giants' to emerge. In 1844 they took over the Bristol & Gloucester to move west, then the Leeds & Bradford (1847) to move north. In a shrewd move they took over the line from **Hitchin** to **Leicester**, and after agreements with the GNR finally made it to London St Pancras. In their bitter rivalry with the LNWR and the desire to reach Scotland they built probably the most famous line in Britain, the **Settle** to **Carlisle**.

Expansion occurred throughout the 19th century, and by the end of the Victorian Age the MR was a force to be reckoned with. Routes stretched through the West Midlands, the East Midlands, Somerset, Dorset, Cheshire and Cambridgeshire. This was in addition to the main route up the spine of England to Carlisle. Their headquarters were in **Derby** and at the 1923 grouping Midland Railway executives filled many of the senior positions in the new LMS. The best routes and working practices came from the LNWR and it was these routes that were developed. Four ex-MR totems are included below.

After Nationalisation wholesale closure of MR metals ensued: for example, Manchester through the Peak District to **Matlock**, **Great Malvern** down to Tewkesbury and **Northampton** to **Bedford**. It is very gratifying, however, that Railtrack investment in the **Settle** to **Carlisle** route has ensured that this famous and scenic journey can be taken by steam or modern traction. One of the best sights of the steam age today is the mighty Pacifics still pounding up through the moors to the north. In the 1923 grouping the MR contributed over 2,100 route miles to the LMR total of nearly 7,800. However, in the years since over a third of those miles have been lost. Nevertheless, it was the perpetual struggle between the MR and the LNWR that gave rise to much of the network from which Dr Beeching was able to make the economic (but not social) judgements.

The North London Railway (NLR) was developed to provide transport links between Camden Yards and the East India Dock area of East London in about 1850. After successive developments it linked Bow, Poplar, Islington and Hampstead. After signing agreements with the LNWR it ran services to **Primrose Hill** with access to the main route to the north (1852). Access to the city was gained in 1865 with the opening of the line to **Broad Street**. It was absorbed into the LNWR in 1922, prior to the formation of the LMS. Two of its stations are shown below.

The North Staffordshire Railway was one of the small companies incorporated into the LMS basket in 1923. It was formed in the mid-1840s to provide a network of lines around the **Newcastle** and **Stoke-on-Trent** area. But within a few years it had spread construction to include **Uttoxeter**, Cheadle, **Congleton**, Crewe and **Macclesfield**. The pottery industry and the local coal mining industry provided steady freight revenue. It built standard gauge and narrow gauge tracks (narrow gauge to Leek). Once it had been taken over by the LMS, the cuts started, including the narrow gauge line to Leek, with links to Cheadle and **Sandbach** in Cheshire. The bulk of the old NSR was axed during the Beeching era, with routes throughout the network being chopped. Today the routes are but a shadow of the 220 miles inherited by the LMS.

The Stratford-on-Avon and Midland Junction (S&MJR) was formed late in comparison with many companies, amalgamating three small firms south of Birmingham in 1908. They ran east as far as **Towcester** with small spurs both north and south. The final minor company that was merged to form the LMS was the Whitehaven, Cleator and Egremont Railway in Cumberland. It was built solely to support mineral traffic in the area during the 1850s, but eventually started carrying passengers in 1857. Extensions were built east towards Rowrah and south to Lowca. They also linked with the M&C at Linefoot to provide a compact network for the then-thriving west Cumberland. The final extension was driven south through Egremont and **Sellafield** to the coast in 1869. They worked closely with the Furness Railway, which was the major financial backer. Much of the network has gone, first attacked by the LMS and then more savagely in the Beeching years by BR.

This review of a complex series of mergers and take-overs is intended to give the reader a flavour of the heritage of all these wonderful maroon totems. The layouts of the hundreds of totems are many and varied, like the terrain over which LMR tracks were laid. How many of us have stood on the old LMR stations and seen sights such as the one below?

(Alan Young)

We now look at the geography of the region as this played a major part in station developments across the entire LMR network.

The geography of the region

With a vast 5,000-mile network and terrain as varied as the accents of their customers, the LMR certainly inherited a mixture of coaching stock, motive power and railway heritage. Its lines passed through a mixture of industrial and rural landscapes, and can be found in more than half the English counties, including probably the most beautiful scenery in England, the Lake District. The backbone of the LMR is the WCML. By taking a footplate ride on the 'Royal Scot' from Euston to **Carlisle**, we can cover much of the geography of the region. Our locomotive today is No. 46253 *City of St Albans*, built at Crewe in 1946.

CITY OF ST ALBANS

The guard blows the whistle at Euston station and we are off, away up Camden bank, past the shed (1B), through **Primrose Hill** tunnel, the north London suburbs and past **Willesden** sheds (1A). It is not long before we are moving apace into Hertfordshire and through the chalk cuttings of the Chiltern Hills. This is southern rural England at its best and, although a commuter area these days, many of the villages retain the charm of bygone times. The Grand Union Canal is alongside, another reminder of times past. We cross into Bedfordshire, through **Wolverton**, with its great carriage works, and into the heart of England. This is great engine driving country and the rolling English countryside slips by as we reach 80 miles an hour. We don't even stop for water so the scoop goes down at **Castlethorpe**. We head through Kilsby tunnel and into Warwickshire, where industry starts to appear. The whole of the East Midlands on our right has three distinct regions: in the north we have the craggy hills and moors of the Peak District, further south the farmlands of Leicestershire and north Staffordshire, then down to historic **Coventry** and industrial middle England.

Further north we pass through **Nuneaton** and into coal mining country. This part of Staffordshire is a maze of underground tunnels and mine shafts – industry is everywhere. To the south of us is **Birmingham** and the West Midlands, a great industrial base in Victorian times. Just over 120 miles from London, we pass through **Lichfield** with the unique three-spired cathedral, then on up the valley of the Trent through **Rugeley** and into **Stafford**. To our right are the Potteries, a union of six towns, the setting for many famous novels and the home of world-class ceramic designers, Wedgwood, Spode, Minton and others. Parts of Staffordshire are very appealing, and many a country estate and mansion can be found here. We make a final rush into Cheshire and the huge railway complex at Crewe, which has always been a magnet for trainspotters. For many years hundreds of enthusiasts – young and old alike – have descended on the station like ants to watch, photograph and record anything that moves. To the south lay Basford Hall freight yards. Steam sheds, both North (5A) and South (5B), were near the station and the expanse of Crewe Locomotive Works but a short walk away. The shot that follows shows the extent of the railway and station in 1953.

(Courtesy of Aerofilms)

Towards the top of this picture can be seen the lines to **Chester** (left) and **Manchester** (right). Anyone visiting Crewe today, will not see the fields to the right of the station. Further north from Crewe to the left are the salt mines of **Winsford** and the beautiful walled city of **Chester**. Cheshire is very typical of English countryside, full of Roman ruins, medieval churches and elegant Tudor, Georgian and Victorian homes. The Cheshire plains fall away both left and right as we head north across the Mersey and into Lancashire. All we can see now is industry on both sides, the great port of Liverpool to the left, from where many thousands left to start new lives abroad. On our right is the mighty industrial centre of **Manchester**, where much of the nation's wealth was created. The industrial landscape is a stark contrast with the charms of the picturesque villages only a few miles to the south, where many of the wealth creators lived, well away from the areas of their good fortune. The cotton towns around Manchester are not as bustling as in former times, but this is still the industrial and trade capital of the north.

Warrington and **Wigan** were centres of coal, but not today. At **Farington**, 207 miles from London, we pass the Up 'Royal Scot'. She left Glasgow at 10 o'clock, the time we steamed out of Euston. We cross the South Lancashire plain on our left, home to some fertile soils and wonderful produce, while on the right we can see the hills of the Pennine Chain, the backbone of England. Lancashire is a very diverse county, full of seaside haunts, wild landscapes, heavy industry and lovely rural villages. A tall spire marks our arrival at **Preston** and we check speed to pass through the station complex.

The hills to our right soon become mountains, full of heather-covered moorland and fir tree-laden slopes. So far we have burned 4 tons of coal and steamed away almost 8,000 gallons of water, but *St Albans* is still not tired. Away on our left is **Blackpool** and to the right the Forest of Bowland. These were once the playgrounds of the industrial north, with amusements and solitude in equal measures.

Soon after **Lancaster** a steel bridge carries us over the Lune and we see the first signs of the mountains of Cumbria (sorry, it was Westmorland and Cumberland in totem times!). We can see the Irish Sea, the Furness Fells and Morecambe Bay to the left and an eighth set of water troughs for our thirsty engine ahead. **Carnforth** is the start of the real work, as we climb into the hills, a 20-mile hard drive for our crew. This is the southern Lake District, a cluster of jewel-like lakes, of spring daffodils, wonderful walks and a land of real beauty that inspired some of England's finest literature. Wordsworth and Beatrix Potter chose to live here, and it is not difficult to see why. It is a breathtaking place to explore and admire. Its turbulent past, with Vikings, Scots and other marauders, is a real contrast with the landscape. Desirable totems here include **Kendal**, **Windermere** and **Oxenholme**.

In front is **Tebay**, and the infamous climb up **Shap**, so *St Albans* has no time to rest as the next 4 miles are going to be hard. This is no country for the railway builder, and wintertime here is not for the faint hearted. Once we pass the signal box at **Shap**, some 920ft above sea level, it is downhill for the last 31 miles into the border city of **Carlisle** and the end of the journey. The last 50 miles have taken their toll on both engine and crew, so they go away to their respective sheds for a well-earned rest! To the north is the Solway Firth, Hadrian's Wall and Scotland, a region of perpetual conflict until James I arrived (not No. 6011, we mean James VI of Scotland), where even the churches had fortifications! Our route north has taken us over bridges, viaducts and through tunnels, all built on wealth to generate more wealth.

Since leaving London we have been through 13 English counties, seen a real variety of landscapes and passed through many historical places. The diversity of architecture, and the hustle and bustle of English life, makes this journey one of life's great pleasures and one of the great railway journeys of the world.

Other areas that the LMR served include the North Wales route to **Holyhead**. Again, wonderful scenery is found on this line travelling west from **Chester**. In the '50s and '60s many a tourist used the LMR stations as a starting point for the long trek to the peaks of Snowdonia. Another picturesque route is that from **Llandudno Junction** down through the Conway Valley to **Betws-y-Coed** and Blaenau Festiniog. In later years the LMR spread south into mid-Wales, as the WR lost its foothold in North Wales, but the WR gained lines in Devon and Cornwall to compensate. The geography of the region is almost the geography of England. Just like the scenery, we totem collectors have a wonderful diversity to enjoy.

The London Midland Region database

Being the largest of the regions in terms of totem count, the Midland database took most effort in the compilation stage. Well over 800 totems are individually listed on the 26 pages that follow, with over 150 photographs in the data section alone. In each of the alphabetical listings there are some wonderful names, but places such as **Carlisle**, **Coventry**, **Derby Friargate**, **Manchester Central** and **Shap** are really quite special. There are so many stations under every letter that each set of notes below is restricted to quite a select group.

A: **Abergele and Pensarn** is one of those romantic names from North Wales. It has appeared in auction, but is still very collectable. The station opened in 1848.

Two Midland stations that were very early closures are **Albio**n and **Alcester**. **Albion** is on the existing main line across the region and is due west of **West Bromwich**. With one of us being a 'Baggies' fan, it is a real must, but sadly one is not known to have survived. It was opened by the LNWR in 1852, but was closed to passenger traffic in 1960. **Alcester** was opened by the Midland Railway in 1866 but closed in 1962. **Althorp Park** in Northamptonshire has now become a real collector's piece because of the association with the late Diana, Princess of Wales. This station was an early closure (in 1960) and is located on the now electrified line between Northampton and Rugby. **Amlwch** was the terminus of the Anglesey branch line, which closed in 1964, leaving only one line (that to Holyhead) across the entire island. Another branch to Red Wharf Bay existed until 1930. Both **Appleby East** and **Appleby West** are very collectable. The former (opened by the North Eastern Railway in 1862) closed almost a hundred years later in 1962, when the entire line between Bowes and Clifton Moor was axed. The Midland Railway opened Appleby West in 1876 (as Appleby). The station was given its totem name in 1952. It is now just Appleby again (BR in 1968). Totems from **Armitage** (opened by the LNWR in 1847) are not known, but as this station was closed in 1960, it seems probable they were all put in the skip! **Ashby-de-la-Zouch** is one of those unusual names with a triple hyphen. Some of the fully flanged totems are face drilled. Totems from **Aylesbury High Street** are not known, but this station did close in 1953. Any totems from here were not more than three years old at disposal!

B: **Balshaw Lane & Euxton** (ex-LNWR) and **Banks** (ex-L&Y), located within 15 miles of each other in Lancashire, have a great number of similarities. Both have yet to appear in auction, and both closed in the '60s. Totems from these stations are not thought to have survived. **Barnoldswick** is one of the few Yorkshire stations in the LMR database. It has yet to appear in auction and we have yet to confirm its flange type. It was an ex-Midland station that closed in 1965.

Totems from both the stations in Bedford are always keenly sought. **Bedford Midland Road** has not appeared in auction and is the present main station for the town. The station opened in 1859 as Bedford but the 'Midland Road' was added between 1924 and 1978. In 1978 it was renamed Bedford Midland. **Bedford St Johns** opened three years after the Midland station and closed in 1984. Bedford St Johns Halt replaced it in 1984. This section of the database contains some rare items not yet seen in auction. They include **Belle Vue**, **Belmont**, **Belper**, **Berkswell & Balsall Common** and **Bescot**. At least we have been able to confirm the existence of totems from these locations.

Besses o' th' Barn is most desirable, and one of the top five classic names. It was discussed in more detail in Chapter 5. This was one of the last stations to be built by the LMS, opening in 1933. It closed in 1991 only to be reopened by the Greater Manchester Passenger Transport Executive a year later. Another collector's piece is **Betws-y-Coed** in North Wales. We have yet to confirm the existence of totems and the flange type from **Birch Vale** and **Birkenhead Central**. **Birmingham New Street** was heavily rebuilt when the centre of the city was redeveloped in the '60s, at which time most of the totems were lost. It opened in 1854 and replaced the old Birmingham Curzon Street station of 1838. We know of the existence of only a few totems from **Blackpool Central**. This was a wonderful station beneath the Tower, and for years saw millions of tourists arrive and depart. It was demolished to make way for a car park in 1964. Sacrilege!

Brooklands opened in 1859 and closed in 1991. The first totem from here reappeared in 2001 when it was advertised in a railway magazine. The station was re-opened by the GMPTE in 1992. **Burton-on-Trent** is a rare survivor that we mentioned in Chapter 5. **Burnley** had three stations in the town but the totems from **Burnley Manchester Road** (closed 1961 and reopened 1986) are the most sought after.

C: We have not been able to confirm the flange type for **Caergwrle** in Flintshire. This is a shortened form of the full station name of Caergwrle Castle and Wells. **Caledonian Road & Barnsbury** is a totem that has not appeared in auction, nor have the totems from **Calvert** (on the main line north of Aylesbury). **Canley Halt** (near **Coventry**) appeared for the first time in auction in 2001. **Carlisle** is a rare item, even though one appeared in auction at Stoneleigh a few years ago. This wonderful station opened in 1847 and has been depicted in many great railway photographs. **Carpenders Park** had a few flangeless totems, most unusual for the LMR. Totems from **Chapel-en-le-Frith Central** and **South** have yet to appear in auction and other rarities include **Chassen Road**, **Chatburn** and **Cheadle Heath** in particular.

Neither **Chester General** nor **Chester Northgate** are common, though both appeared in the same auction (Kidlington, January 2001). The LNWR station that became **Chester General** opened in 1849 and became simply Chester in 1969. **Chester Northgate** is an ex-CLC station that closed in 1969 after 90 years. We have been able to find out very little about totems from either **Clifton Junction** or **Clitheroe** in Lancashire. Both are ex-L&Y stations and the former is still open as Clifton. BR reopened Clitheroe in 1990. We know little about totems from the ex-CLC station **Clubmoor** near Liverpool. The station was only open between 1927 and 1960. **Corkickle**, just south of **Whitehaven** is a most unusual name and one of the rarest totems in Cumberland.

Coventry station was extensively rebuilt in the early 1960s and we suspect most of the totems ended their days in dump trucks. At least one totem is known to have survived and is pictured below. The station was first opened by the L&B in 1838 and is an ex-L&NW structure. We also know little about totems from **Crouch Hill** in North London. Other interesting names include **Coseley (Deepfields)**, **Cressington & Grassendale**, **Cromford and Culcheth**, none of which have been seen in public auction.

D: **Daimler Halt** is situated just north of **Coventry** and was the station for the old Daimler Company. Curiously, it opened during the First World War (in 1917) and was closed by BR in 1965. Totems from another West Midlands station, **Darlaston**, have not thought to have survived. Below is a photograph of a totem *in situ* at **Denbigh** (closed early in 1962) but none are known to have survived. If any were taken off the station, they would be prizes indeed!

(Tom Sherratt)

We have mentioned in Chapter 5 about the overpainted **Dent** totems, but the ordinary totems from this location are classics in their own right. **Derby** had three stations, two MR and one GNR. **Derby Friargate** is highly prized by collectors and for a time held the record price for a totem. This was the GNR station that opened as Derby in 1878, being renamed ten years later and closed in 1964. **Derby Midland** first opened in 1840 also as Derby and was renamed in 1950. It was renamed Derby again in 1968. **Derby Nottingham Road** was open for 111 years before closing in 1967. It is the only Derby totem not to have appeared yet in auction. Other real rarities are **Droylesden** and **Dukinfield Central**, only a couple of miles from each other in the suburbs of east Manchester. **Dukinfield Central** was an early BR closure (1959) and one of the most westerly LNER stations. Others not appearing publicly include **Dolgarrog**, **Draycott & Breaston** and **Dunstable North**.

E: **Earby** totems have not been confirmed as survivors. This ex-Midland station is very near Barnoldswick. It is only very recently that a totem from the station at **Ettingshall Road & Bilston**, just south-east of Wolverhampton on the mainline across the region appeared in an auction (June 2001, SRA). This small station closed in June 1964. Stations worthy of mention in this section include **Eccleston Park**, **Edale** and the two-lined **Elstree & Borehamwood**.

F: Several totems in the Greater Manchester area are rarities. These are **Fallowfield**, **Farington** and **Farnworth & Halshaw Moor**. The first two stations were closed early in 1958 and 1960 respectively. It is therefore probable that all signs from here were destroyed. The last named has not appeared in auction. **Finmere** is not common, appearing for the first time in auction during 2000. This former GCR station took this name in 1922. All other totems here are relatively common, though **Furness Vale** in north Derbyshire has not appeared in auction.

G: **Glendon & Rushton** first opened as Rushton in 1857, but was an early closure in 1960. It seems unlikely anything survived from this small station. **Golbourne** in south Lancashire had two stations, both of which closed. No totems from either have been confirmed. **Golbourne North** was on the GCR line to St Helens and only held this name for three years (1949–52). **Golbourne South** is on the WCML. It too was renamed in 1949, but closed in 1961. **Green Lane** is a Wirral station that opened in 1886. We are not sure if any totems survived the re-signing. Desirable totems here include **Gospel Oak**, an NLR station and **Great Longstone** on the northern section of the Peak Line.

H: Totems from two Derbyshire stations, **Hadfield** and **Hayfield**, are not confirmed survivors. The first station near **Dinting** is still open, but **Hayfield** (closed in 1970) was the terminus on the branch from **New Mills Central**. The other station that is missing from many collections is **Heaton Mersey**, just south of Manchester. This ex-MR station opened in 1880 and closed in 1961. **Hampstead Heath** in North London is a comparative rarity, as is **Hartford & Greenbank** on the WCML between Crewe and **Warrington**. **Hest Bank** is a famous location, north of Carnforth on the WCML. We have not confirmed that totems survived from this ex-LNWR station that opened in 1846. BR closed it in 1969. Only the flat variety of totem was hung at **Highbury & Islington** and the London collectors among us (and Arsenal supporters) eagerly seek this totem. The harbour town and station at **Holyhead** is a familiar location for the boat train to Ireland. No totems have been confirmed to survive from the second station that the LNWR opened in 1866 to replace the first 1851 station. (That station had also replaced another station that the C&HR opened in 1848).

We mention in detail the wooden totems that hung at **Horton-in-Ribblesdale** and the strange history of the 'transient' **Hough Green** totem in the Appendix. Both **Hucknall Byron** and **Hucknall Central** were casualties of the Beeching era, but the naming history in this town is long and complicated. **Hyde Junction** opened in 1863 and was renamed in 1951 as **Hyde North**. Totems from **Hyde Junction** are not known, but any would have only been up three years, so we feel they are unlikely to have survived. **Hyde North** totems are also not that common.

I: An **Ilkeston North** totem would fit into several Derbyshire collections that exist, but none have appeared in auction. Totems bearing this name were only up for 14 years (1950–64) as the station was renamed from the GNR station that opened in 1878. **Irchester** has appeared in auction but is not common. It opened in 1857 and closed in 1960. Between 1881 and 1888 it was named Irchester for Rushden & Higham Ferrers. This name would have produced a most interesting layout for a totem!

K: Most of the totems here have appeared in auction. The only exceptions are **Kentish Town West**, **Kimberley**, **Kirkby Muxloe** and **Knotty Ash**. This last named totem is sought by quite a few of the serious 'aficionados'. Other collectors' totems here might include the two-lined **Kidsgrove Liverpool Road** (a rare totem with the word 'Liverpool' on the sign), **Kilsby & Crick**, an ex-LNWR station that closed early in 1960, or **Knott Mill and Deansgate**, a two-line totem from suburban Manchester.

L: Lancaster had two superbly named stations in **Lancaster Castle** and **Lancaster Green Ayre**. The first named was opened by the LNWR in 1846, and is the present-day station (becoming just Lancaster in 1969). The second station was first named Lancaster in 1848 by the L&CR before becoming Lancaster Green Area in 1850. It kept this name until 1870 when the Green Area became Green Ayre (closed in 1966).

We doubt the existence of totems at **Leek**, so any information would be gratefully received. This ex-NSR station closed in 1965. Totems from **Leire Halt**, a small Leicestershire station, have not appeared in auction. While we are in this county, totems from either **Leicester Central** or **Leicester London Road** would grace any Midland collection. **Central** was a former GCR station that was open for exactly 70 years (1899–1969), while **London Road** is still open as Leicester (named in 1969). It had also been named Leicester Campbell Street between 1867 and 1892. **Liverpool Central Low Level** is the only totem beginning with the word 'Liverpool'. These totems were 4ft long and none have appeared in auction. **Llanfairfechan** is on the North Wales coast route, and even though totems have been in auction these signs are scarce. While we are in North Wales, the two totems from **Llandudno** and **Llandudno Junction** always create a stir at auction, and what about the superbly named **Llanwrst & Trefriw**, not far from **Conway**? We complement a superb Welsh quartet below with some wonderful scenery on a 1960s LMR poster!

(South Devon Railway Trust – Tindale Collection)

London Road High Level (closed in 1967) is not in the capital, as the name implies, but in **Nottingham**, just east of the city centre. The totem has not appeared in auction, nor have those from **Longport** in the Potteries. We have confirmed the existence of totems from these locations and from **Lower Darwen** in Lancashire.

M: We have been unable to find any evidence of surviving totems from **Macclesfield Central**, an 1873 GC/NS station that is open today as the main station for the town. Totems from the 1960 closure at **Macclesfield Hibel Road** have appeared in auction. Totems known to have survived but not appearing yet publicly include **Mansfield Woodhouse**, **Marple**, **Maryport** and **Mobberley**. We have no information on **Mersey Road and Aigburth**, **Middlewood**, **Mill Hill Broadway**, **Milnthorpe**, **Mold** or **Mollington**. We know these stations had totems from old photographs, but the fact that some are still open makes us curious to learn why no totems are currently known to have survived. Here we have the only LMR three-line totem that was produced – **Marsh Lane & Strand Road** (an ex-L&Y station) in Liverpool first opened in 1850. It was actually closed between 1941 and 1943, and is currently named Bootle New Strand. One of the more evocative Welsh names is **Menai Bridge**. The LNWR opened this beautiful station (shown below) in 1858. BR sadly closed it in 1966.

(Tom Sherratt)

Totems from both **Morecambe Euston Road** and **Morecambe Promenade** are rare. **Euston Road** was an early closure (1963), and is the only totem including the word 'Euston'. Promenade (ex-MR) remains open as plain Morecambe. We have no data on **Mossley Hill**, or, to give it its full title, Mossley Hill for Aigburth. The ex-LNWR station totem just read **Mossley Hill**. We also have no data on **Mouldsworth**, the ex-CLC station on the line from Chester to Manchester.

N: There are some real collectors' items under this letter. Neston on the Wirral had two stations – **Neston North**, the ex-GC station on the line north from Chester, and **Neston South**, the Birkenhead Railway station that only had this name between 1952 and 1956. This may account for the fact that we have not seen totems from this location. **Neston North** is rare and has not appeared in auction, nor has **New Basford**, just north of Nottingham (ex-GCR, opened in 1899, closed in 1964 by Dr Beeching).

Both **New Mills Newtown** and **Northampton Bridge Street** have yet to appear in auction, while we have no data on **Newsholme**, an ex-L&Y station south of Hellifield that closed in 1957. The early closure may account for this.

Finally, we have not been able to confirm the survival of totems from **Northenden** or **Northwich**. The former is in south Manchester and the latter on the cross-country route to Chester. Both are ex-CLC stations closed by Beeching in 1964.

O: **Oakham** was the county town of Rutland and one of only five stations in that former county. These totems and those from **Oakley** and **Oldham Werneth** have yet to be seen in auction. **Oakley** was on the line from **Bedford** to **Wellingborough**, where intermediate stations progressively closed. **Oldham Werneth** (ex-L&YR) is one of three stations in that town, and we have included a picture of this rare totem in our database.

P: Our research for LMR totems beginning with 'P' proved difficult. We have not confirmed the existence of totems from five locations (**Partington**, **Penyffordd**, **Pleasington**, **Prees** or **Prestbury**). In fact we have no photo evidence on **Penyffordd** and have yet to confirm that totems were ever made for this station. The Derbyshire station of **Pilsley** has been the subject of debate, but for now it is not in the database. Several other 'P' totems have not appeared in auction, as listed in the database pages. Below we have included photos of some of the more elusive items!

Q: Only three names here, with **Quorn & Woodhouse** the pick of the trio. The 4ft **Queens Park** totems hung on the shared BR/Underground platforms as shown below in Alan Young's atmospheric shot. (The last 'Q' is **Queensferry** near Chester.)

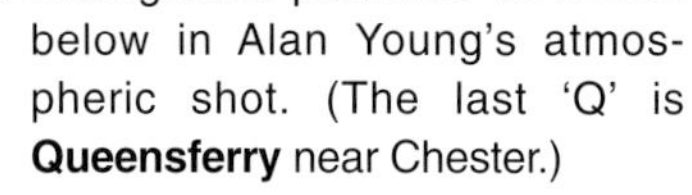

May 1973. (Alan Young)

R: **Radcliffe Black Lane** is an elusive totem from south-east Lancashire. It opened as Black Lane in 1848 and was given its totem name by the LMS in 1933 before being closed in 1970. There were two stations in Reddish, east of Manchester. Both opened as Reddish, the LNWR station (later **Reddish South**) in 1849 and the S&M station (later **Reddish North**) in 1875. We have no data on **Reddish North**, but **Reddish South** has appeared in auction.

We have yet to find evidence of surviving totems for **Rickmansworth Church Street**, a very early closure in 1952. It only held this name for two years, being simply Rickmansworth between 1862 and 1950. We have no data on **Rose Hill**, renamed from Marple (Rose Hill). It was a very early Macclesfield Committee station, opening in 1869. A totem from **Rugby Midland** would be a prize in anybody's collection. We do not know of a surviving example and suspect 'corporate cleansing' accounted for all of them. The station opened in 1885 and held the name Rugby Midland for twenty years (1950–70). Before and after these dates it was simply Rugby. Rugeley had two stations in the town, **Rugeley Town** and **Trent Valley**, the latter being on the WCML to the north. **Trent Valley** opened in 1847 and **Rugeley Town** (closed in 1965) in 1870. Totems from **Runcorn** are scarce because of early station redevelopment, and we have been unable to uncover a survivor – yet!

S: There are 82 different MR totems beginning with the letter 'S', so we are going to restrict comment to the rare, elusive or desirable items. Of these, 11 have not been confirmed as survivors, and a further 20 known totems have not appeared in public. The unknown survivors are **St Helens Central**, **St Helens Shaw Street**, **Saltney Ferry (Mold Junction)**, **Sandycroft**, **Sharnbrook**, **Smithy Bridge**, **Stacksteads**, **Stanmore Village**, **Stockport Edgeley** and **Strines**. Note that these are located throughout the LMR region and show how haphazard removal and survival was. Below we show a selection of the elusive non-appearers in auction.

Other sought-after items include **St Albans Abbey** (opened in 1858 and fully named in 1924 from St Albans), **Shap** (opened in 1846 and closed in 1968), **Stockport Tiviot Dale** (ex-CLC, opened in 1865 and closed in 1967) and **Stoke-on-Trent** (opened by the NSR in 1848).

T: Totems from **Thatto Heath** are known, but have not appeared in auction. This is also the situation for **Tile Hill** (near Coventry) and **Todd Lane Junction**.

We use **Todd Lane Junction** in the photo below to show that the LMR had four different layouts when the word 'Junction' was used on the totem. **Town Green & Aughton** (ex-L&Y, opened in 1849) was unique in this region with its small letters, and **Trafford Park** was a late opening station (ex-CLC in 1904).

Upholland, Lancashire, April 1974. (Alan Young)

U: All six totems in this part of the database have appeared in auction but we have a wonderful shot of **Upholland** still *in situ* in 1974. Between 1900 and 1902 this station was given the unusual name Pimbo Lane.

V: In 1999 a totem from **Vauxhall & Duddeston** suddenly appeared in auction. Up to that time we thought this station did not have totems! This is an ex-LNWR station just north of **Birmingham New Street** on the line to **Lichfield**.

W: This is another large group of totems to review (73 in all) but there are some real rarities in this section. We have been able to confirm the survival of all but 12, and again they are all over the LMR area. **Warwick Road** is a Manchester suburban station that is now part of the new light rail Metro system for the city. **Watford North** (opened in 1910 as Callowland) is on the branch line to St Albans. **Wellingborough London Road** took its name (from Wellingborough) in 1924. The station closed in 1964 when many stations in that area were axed. **Wennington** (opened in 1849) is located east of **Carnforth**, and **West Derby** is just north of **Knotty Ash** in suburban Liverpool. Both would grace Lancashire collections. **West Kirby** was the terminus of Wirral Railway's line from Birkenhead. **Whalley and Whetstone** (both closed in the early '60s) are two more survivors to confirm. A totem from **Widnes South** would enhance several Lancashire collections. The station only had this name for three years (1959–62) so it seems unlikely we will see this item. **Willesden Junction High Level** stands above the site of the former **Willesden Junction** on the WCML. The final survivor to confirm is **Worsley**, in the western suburbs of Greater Manchester. This was a casualty along with seven other stations in the area in 1969. There are many totems here sought by an army of collectors. The desirable names include **Watford Junction**, **Wednesbury Town**, **Wembley Stadium**, **West End Lane**, **Whitehaven Bransty**, **Wigston Glen Parva**, **Willenhall**, **Windermere**, **Wolverhampton High Level** and **Wyrley & Cheslyn Hay**.

We close this chapter with two images that epitomise the LMR at the time totems came down. The shot of **Warrington Central** shows the full beauty of the spandrels and brickwork. **Walton Junction** is a Merseyside station and we rather liked the shot!

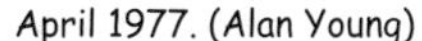

April 1977. (Alan Young)

August 1973. (Alan Young)

Chapter 9 Totem Listing

** = some face drilled (throughout this database)

Place name		County	London Midland Region			Totem in	Totem
			Layout	Flange	Closed	Auction	Survived
ABERGELE AND PENSARN		Denbighshire	2 line	FF		✓	✓
ACCRINGTON		Lancashire		FF		✓	✓
ACTON BRIDGE		Cheshire		FF		✓	✓
ACTON CENTRAL		Middlesex		HF		✓	✓
ADDERLEY PARK	some face drilled	Cheshire		FF		✓	✓
ADLINGTON		Cheshire		FF		✓	✓
AINSDALE		Lancashire		HF			✓
AINTREE SEFTON ARMS		Lancashire	2 line	HF		✓	✓
ALBION		Staffordshire			1960		
ALCESTER		Warwickshire			1962		
ALDERLEY EDGE		Cheshire		FF		✓	✓
ALDRIDGE		Staffordshire		FF	1965	✓	✓
ALFRETON & SOUTH NORMANTON		Derbyshire	2 line	FF	1967	✓	✓
ALLERTON		Lancashire		FF		✓	✓
ALREWAS	some face drilled	Staffordshire		FF	1965	✓	✓
ALSAGER		Staffordshire		FF		✓	✓
ALTHORP PARK		Northamptonshire		FF	1960	✓	✓
ALTON TOWERS		Staffordshire		FF		✓	✓
ALTRICHAM AND BOWDON		Cheshire	2 line	FF		✓	✓
AMBERGATE		Derbyshire		FF		✓	✓
AMLWCH		Anglesey		FF	1964	✓	✓
AMPTHILL		Bedfordshire		FF	1959		✓
ANSDALE & FAIRHAVEN		Lancashire		HF		✓	✓
APPLEBY EAST		Westmoreland			1962		
APPLEBY WEST		Westmoreland		HF			✓
APSLEY		Hertfordshire		HF		✓	✓
ARDWICK		Lancashire				✓	✓
ARLEY & FILLONGLEY		Leicestershire	2 line	FF	1960		✓
ARMITAGE		Staffordshire			1960		
ARNSIDE		Lancashire					✓
ASHBURYS		Lancashire		FF		✓	✓
ASHBURYS FOR BELLE VUE		Lancashire	2 line	HF		✓	✓

Place name		County	Layout	Flange	Closed	Auction	Survived
ASHBY-DE-LA-ZOUCH	some face drilled	Leicestershire		FF	1964	✓	✓
ASHBY MAGNA		Leicestershire		FF	1969		✓
ASHLEY		Cheshire		FF			✓
ASHTON CHARLESTOWN		Lancashire	2 line	FF		✓	✓
ASHWELL		Rutland		FF	1966	✓	✓
ASKAM		Lancashire		FF		✓	✓
ASPATRIA		Cumberland		FF		✓	✓
ASTON		Warwickshire		FF		✓	✓
ATHERSTONE		Warwickshire		FF		✓	✓
ATHERTON CENTRAL		Lancashire	2 line	FF		✓	✓
ATTENBOROUGH		Nottinghamshire		FF		✓	✓
AUGHTON PARK		Lancashire		HF		✓	✓
AWSWORTH		Nottinghamshire		FF	1964	✓	✓
AYLESBURY TOWN		Buckinghamshire		FF		✓	✓
AYLESBURY HIGH STREET		Buckinghamshire		HF	1953		

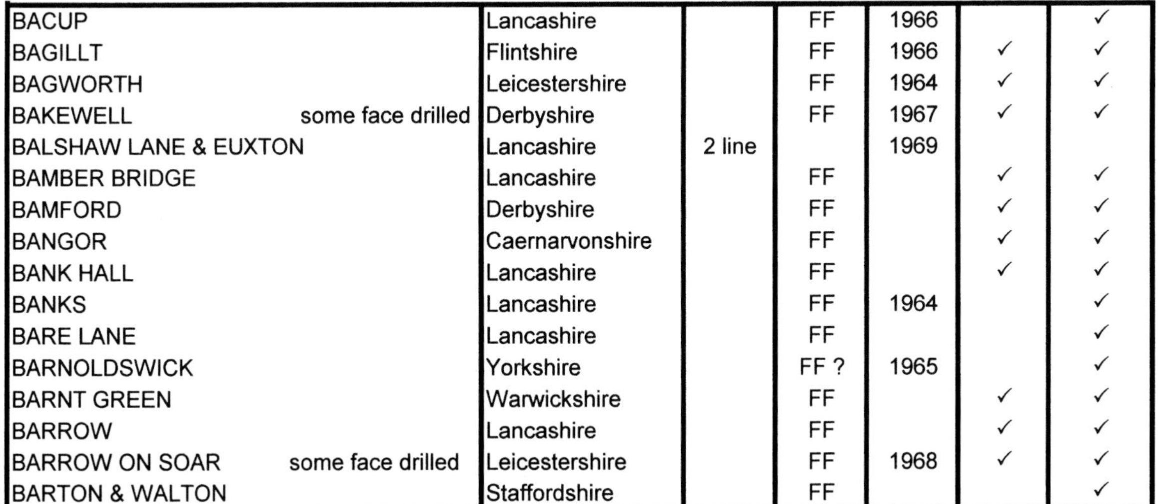

Place name		County	Layout	Flange	Closed	Auction	Survived
BACUP		Lancashire		FF	1966		✓
BAGILLT		Flintshire		FF	1966	✓	✓
BAGWORTH		Leicestershire		FF	1964	✓	✓
BAKEWELL	some face drilled	Derbyshire		FF	1967	✓	✓
BALSHAW LANE & EUXTON		Lancashire	2 line		1969		
BAMBER BRIDGE		Lancashire		FF		✓	✓
BAMFORD		Derbyshire		FF		✓	✓
BANGOR		Caernarvonshire		FF		✓	✓
BANK HALL		Lancashire		FF		✓	✓
BANKS		Lancashire		FF	1964		✓
BARE LANE		Lancashire		FF			✓
BARNOLDSWICK		Yorkshire		FF ?	1965		✓
BARNT GREEN		Warwickshire		FF		✓	✓
BARROW		Lancashire		FF		✓	✓
BARROW ON SOAR	some face drilled	Leicestershire		FF	1968	✓	✓
BARTON & WALTON		Staffordshire		FF			✓

Place name		County	Layout	Flange	Closed	Auction	Survived
BASFORD NORTH		Nottinghamshire		HF	1964	✓	✓
BASFORD VERNON		Nottinghamshire		HF	1967	✓	✓
BASSENTHWAITE LAKE	some face drilled	Cumberland	2 line	FF	1966	✓	✓
BEBINGTON & NEW FERRY		Cheshire	2 line	HF		✓	✓
BEDFORD MIDLAND ROAD		Bedfordshire	2 line	HF			✓
BEDFORD ST. JOHNS		Bedfordshire	2 line	FF		✓	✓
BEDWORTH		Warwickshire		FF	1965	✓	✓
BEESTON		Nottinghamshire		FF		✓	✓
BEESTON CASTLE AND TARPORLEY		Cheshire	2 line	FF	1966	✓	✓
BELGRAVE & BIRSTALL		Leicestershire	2 line	FF	1963	✓	✓
BELLE VUE		Cheshire		FF			✓
BELMONT		Middlesex		FF	1964		✓
BELPER		Derbyshire		FF			✓
BENTHAM		Lancashire		HF		✓	✓
BERKHAMPSTEAD		Hertfordshire		HF		✓	✓
BERKSWELL & BALSALL COMMON		Warwickshire	2 line	FF		✓	✓
BESCAR LANE		Lancashire		FF		✓	✓
BESCOT		Staffordshire		FF			✓
Besses o' th' Barn	some face drilled	Lancashire		FF		✓	✓
BETWS-Y-COED		Caernarvonshire		HF		✓	✓
BIDSTON		Cheshire		FF		✓	✓
BIRCH VALE		Derbyshire			1970		
BIRKDALE	some face drilled	Lancashire		FF		✓	✓
BIRKENHEAD CENTRAL		Cheshire	2 line				
BIRKENHEAD NORTH		Cheshire	2 line	FF		✓	✓
BIRKENHEAD PARK		Cheshire		FF		✓	✓
BIRMINGHAM NEW STREET		Warwickshire	2 line	HF		✓	✓
BLABY		Leicestershire		FF	1968	✓	✓
BLACKBURN		Lancashire		FF		✓	✓
BLACKPOOL CENTRAL		Lancashire		HF	1964	✓	✓
BLACKPOOL NORTH		Lancashire		HF		✓	✓
BLACKPOOL SOUTH		Lancashire		HF		✓	✓
BLACKROD		Lancashire		FF		✓	✓

Place name		County	Layout	Flange	Closed	Auction	Survived
BLACON		Cheshire		FF	1968		✓
BLAKE STREET		Staffordshire		FF		✓	✓
BLENCOW		Cumberland		FF	1972	✓	✓
BLETCHLEY	some o/p on Berkhampstead	Buckinghamshire		HF		✓	✓
BLISWORTH		Northampton		HF	1960	✓	✓
BLOXWICH		Staffordshire		FF	1965	✓	✓
BLUNDELLSANDS AND CROSBY		Lancashire	2 line	FF		✓	✓
BLYTHE BRIDGE		Staffordshire		FF			✓
BOLLINGTON		Cheshire		FF	1970		✓
BOLTON-LE-SANDS		Lancashire		FF	1969	✓	✓
BOLTON TRINITY STREET		Lancashire	2 line	FF		✓	✓
BOOTLE		Cumberland		FF		✓	✓
BOOTLE ORIEL ROAD		Lancashire	2 line	FF		✓	✓
BORROWASH		Derbyshire		FF	1966		✓
BOURNVILLE		Warwickshire		FF		✓	✓
BOWKER VALE		Lancashire		FF		✓	✓
BRACKLEY CENTRAL		Northampton	2 line	FF	1966	✓	✓
BRADLEY FOLD		Lancashire		FF	1970	✓	✓
BRAMHALL		Cheshire		HF/FF		✓	✓
BRANDON & WOLSTON		Warwickshire		FF	1960	✓	✓
BREDBURY		Cheshire		FF		✓	✓
BRICKET WOOD		Hertfordshire		HF			✓
BRIERFIELD		Lancashire		FF		✓	✓
BRINDLEY HEATH		Staffordshire					
BROADBOTTOM		Derbyshire		HF		✓	✓
BROADFIELD		Lancashire		FF	1970	✓	✓
BROAD GREEN		Lancashire		FF		✓	✓
BROAD STREET	(also 4' totems FF)	London		HF*	1986	✓	✓
BROMBOROUGH		Cheshire		FF		✓	✓
BROMFORD BRIDGE		Staffordshire		FF	1965	✓	✓
BROMLEY CROSS		Lancashire		FF			✓
BRONDESBURY	(also 4' totems FF)	Middlesex		HF/FF		✓	✓
BRONDESBURY PARK		Middlesex		HF		✓	✓

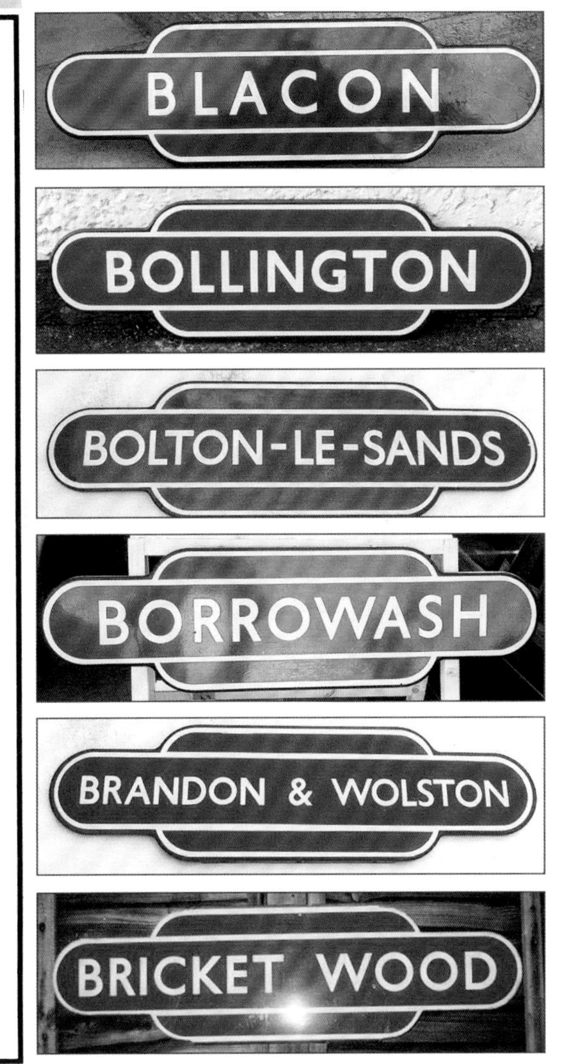

Place name		County	Layout	Flange	Closed	Auction	Survived
BROOKLANDS	* reopened 1992	Cheshire		FF	1991*		✓
BROUGHTON ASTLEY		Leicestershire		FF	1962		✓
BROWNHILLS		Staffordshire		FF		✓	✓
BRYN		Lancashire		FF			✓
BUCKINGHAM		Buckinghamshire		FF		✓	✓
BUCKLEY JUNCTION		Flintshire		FF		✓	✓
BULWELL COMMON		Nottinghamshire		FF	1963	✓	✓
BULWELL MARKET		Nottinghamshire		HF	1960	✓	✓
BURNAGE		Cheshire		FF		✓	✓
BURNESIDE		Westmoreland		FF		✓	✓
BURNLEY BARRACKS		Lancashire		FF		✓	✓
BURNLEY CENTRAL		Lancashire		FF		✓	✓
BURNLEY MANCHESTER RD.	reopen 86	Lancashire	2 line	FF	1961*		✓
BURN NAZE		Lancashire		FF		✓	✓
BURSCOUGH BRIDGE		Lancashire		FF		✓	✓
BURSCOUGH JUNCTION		Lancashire	2 line	FF		✓	✓
BURTON-ON-TRENT		Staffordshire		HF		✓	✓
BURY BOLTON STREET		Lancashire		HF	1980	✓	✓
BURY KNOWSLEY STREET		Lancashire	2 line	FF	1970	✓	✓
BUSHEY & OXHEY		Hertfordshire	2 line	FF		✓	✓
BUTLERS LANE		Staffordshire		FF		✓	✓
BUXTON		Derbyshire		HF		✓	✓
CAERGWRLE		Flintshire		To confirm			✓
CAERNARVON		Caernarvonshire		HF	1970	✓	✓
CALEDONIAN ROAD & BARNSBURY		Middlesex	2 line	FF			✓
CALVERT		Buckinghamshire			1963		✓
CAMDEN ROAD		London		HF		✓	✓
CANLEY HALT	some face drilled	Warwickshire		FF			✓
CANNOCK		Staffordshire		FF	1965	✓	✓
CANONBURY		London		FF		✓	✓
CAPENHURST		Cheshire		FF		✓	✓
CARDINGTON		Bedfordshire		FF	1962	✓	✓

Place name		County	Layout	Flange	Closed	Auction	Survived
CARK & CARTMEL		Lancashire		FF		✓	✓
CARLISLE		Cumberland		HF		✓	✓
CARNFORTH		Lancashire		FF		✓	✓
CARPENDERS PARK		Hertfordshire		HF/Flat		✓	✓
CASTLE BROMWICH		Warwickshire		HF	1968	✓	✓
CASTLETHORPE		Buckinghamshire		FF	1964	✓	✓
CASTLETON		Derbyshire		FF		✓	✓
CEFN-Y-BEDD	small letters	Flintshire		FF		✓	✓
CHAPEL-EN-LE-FRITH CENTRAL		Derbyshire	LP	FF	1967		✓
CHAPEL-EN-LE-FRITH SOUTH		Derbyshire	2 line	FF			✓
CHARWELTON		Northamptonshire		FF	1963		✓
CHASSEN ROAD		Lancashire					✓
CHATBURN		Lancashire		FF	1962		✓
CHEADLE HEATH		Cheshire		HF	1967		✓
CHEADLE HULME		Cheshire		FF		✓	✓
CHEDDINGTON		Buckinghamshire		FF			✓
CHELFORD		Cheshire		FF		✓	✓
CHERRY TREE		Lancashire		FF		✓	✓
CHESTER GENERAL		Cheshire		HF		✓	✓
CHESTER NORTHGATE		Cheshire	2 line	HF	1969	✓	✓
CHESTER ROAD		Warwickshire		FF		✓	✓
CHILVERS COTON		Warwickshire		FF	1965	✓	✓
CHINLEY		Derbyshire		HF/FF		✓	✓
CHORLEY		Lancashire		FF		✓	✓
CHORLTON-CUM-HARDY **		Lancashire		FF*	1967	✓	✓
CHURCH AND OSWALDTWISTLE **		Lancashire	2 line	FF*		✓	✓
CHURCHTOWN		Lancashire		FF	1964	✓	✓
CLAY CROSS		Derbyshire		FF	1967	✓	✓
CLAYTON BRIDGE		Lancashire		FF	1968	✓	✓
CLIFTON JUNCTION		Lancashire					
CLITHEROE	* reopened 1990	Lancashire			1962*		✓
CLOUGH FOLD		Lancashire		HF	1966	✓	✓
CLUBMOOR		Lancashire			1960		

Place name	County	Layout	Flange	Closed	Auction	Survived
COALVILLE TOWN	Leicestershire		HF	1964		✓
COCKERMOUTH	Cumberland		FF	1966	✓	✓
CODNOR PARK & IRONVILLE	Derbyshire	2 line	FF	1967	✓	✓
COLESHILL	Warwickshire		FF	1968	✓	✓
COLNE	Lancashire		FF		✓	✓
COLWYN BAY	Denbighshire		FF		✓	✓
CONGLETON	Cheshire		HF		✓	✓
CONNAHS QUAY **	Flintshire		FF	1966	✓	✓
CONWAY **	Caernarvonshire		FF	1966		✓
COPPULL	Lancashire		FF	1969		✓
CORBY small letters	Northamptonshire		FF	1966	✓	✓
CORKICKLE	Cumberland					
COSELEY (DEEPFIELDS)	Staffordshire	2 line	FF ?			✓
COUNDON ROAD	Warwickshire		FF	1965		✓
COUNTESTHORPE	Leicestershire		FF	1962	✓	✓
COVENTRY	Warwickshire		HF			✓
CRESSINGTON & GRASSENDALE **	Lancashire	2 line	FF**	1972		✓
CRICKLEWOOD	Middlesex		FF		✓	✓
CROFT	Leicestershire		FF	1968	✓	✓
CROMFORD	Derbyshire		FF			✓
CROSSENS	Lancashire		FF	1964	✓	✓
CROSTON	Lancashire		FF		✓	✓
CROUCH HILL	London		FF			
CROXLEY GREEN	Hertfordshire		FF		✓	✓
CRUMPSALL	Lancashire		FF		✓	✓
CULCHETH	Lancashire		FF	1964		✓
DAIMLER HALT	Warwickshire		FF	1965		✓
DAISY HILL	Lancashire		FF		✓	✓
DALSTON	Cumberland		FF		✓	✓
DALSTON JUNCTION	London		FF	1986		✓
DALTON	Lancashire		FF		✓	✓
DANE ROAD	Cheshire		FF		✓	✓

Place name	County	Layout	Flange	Closed	Auction	Survived
DARLASTON	Staffordshire			1965		
DARLEY DALE	Derbyshire		FF	1967	✓	✓
DARWEN	Lancashire		FF		✓	✓
DAVENPORT	Cheshire		FF		✓	✓
DEAN LANE	Lancashire		FF		✓	✓
DEGANWY	Caernarvonshire		FF		✓	✓
DENBIGH	Denbighshire		FF	1962		
DENT + overpainted on Burnley Central	Yorkshire		FF		✓	✓
DENTON	Lancashire		FF		✓	✓
DERBY FRIARGATE	Derbyshire		HF	1964	✓	✓
DERBY MIDLAND	Derbyshire		HF/FF		✓	✓
DERBY NOTTINGHAM ROAD	Derbyshire	2 line	FF	1967		✓
DESBOROUGH & ROTHWELL	Northamptonshire	2 line	FF	1968	✓	✓
DESFORD	Leicestershire		FF	1964	✓	✓
DIDSBURY	Lancashire		FF	1967	✓	✓
DIGGLE	Yorkshire		FF	1968	✓	✓
DINTING	Derbyshire		HF		✓	✓
DISLEY	Cheshire		HF		✓	✓
DITTON JUNCTION	Lancashire		FF			✓
DOLGARROG	Caernarvonshire		FF			✓
DONNINGTON	Shropshire		FF	1964	✓	✓
DRAYCOTT & BREASTON	Derbyshire	2 line	FF	1966		✓
DRIGG	Cumberland		FF		✓	✓
DROYLSDEN	Lancashire			1968		
DUDLEY PORT	Staffordshire		HF/FF		✓	✓
DUFFIELD some face drilled	Derbyshire		FF		✓	✓
DUKINFIELD CENTRAL	Cheshire	LP		1959		
DUNSTABLE NORTH	Bedfordshire		HF	1965		✓

Place name	County	Layout	Flange	Closed	Auction	Survived
EARBY	Yorkshire			1970		
EARLESTOWN	Lancashire		FF		✓	✓
EAST DIDSBURY	Lancashire		FF		✓	✓
EAST LANGTON	Leicestershire		FF	1968		✓

Place name	County	Layout	Flange	Closed	Auction	Survived
EAST LEAKE	Nottinghamshire		FF	1969	✓	✓
ECCLES	Lancashire		HF			✓
ECCLESTON PARK	Lancashire		HF			✓
EDALE	Derbyshire		FF			✓
EDGE HILL	Lancashire		FF		✓	✓
EGGINTON JUNCTION	Derbyshire		FF	1962	✓	✓
ELLESMERE PORT	Cheshire		FF		✓	✓
ELMESTHORPE	Leicestershire		FF	1968	✓	✓
ELSTREE & BOREHAMWOOD	Hertfordshire	2 line	HF		✓	✓
ENTWHISTLE	Lancashire		FF		✓	✓
ERDINGTON	Warwickshire		FF		✓	✓
ETRURIA	Staffordshire		FF		✓	✓
ETTINGSHALL ROAD & BILSTON	Staffordshire	2 line	FF	1964	✓	✓
EWOOD BRIDGE	Lancashire		FF	1972	✓	✓

Place name	County	Layout	Flange	Closed	Auction	Survived
FAILSWORTH	Lancashire		FF		✓	✓
FAIRFIELD FOR DROYLESDEN	Lancashire	2 line	HF			✓
FALLOWFIELD	Lancashire			1958		
FARINGTON	Lancashire			1960		
FARNWORTH & HALSHAW MOOR	Lancashire	2 line	FF			✓
FAZAKERLEY	Lancashire		FF		✓	✓
FENNY STRATFORD	Buckinghamshire		HF		✓	✓
FENTON	Staffordshire		FF	1961	✓	✓
FINCHLEY ROAD & FROGNAL	London		HF		✓	✓
FINMERE	Buckinghamshire		FF	1963	✓	✓
FLEETWOOD	Lancashire		FF	1966	✓	✓
FLINT	Flintshire		FF		✓	✓
FLITWICK	Bedfordshire		FF		✓	✓
FLIXTON	Lancashire		FF		✓	✓
FOLESHILL	Warwickshire		FF	1965	✓	✓
FORMBY	Lancashire		FF		✓	✓
FOUR ASHES	Staffordshire		FF	1959	✓	✓
FOUR OAKS	Warwickshire		FF		✓	✓

Place name	County	Layout	Flange	Closed	Auction	Survived
FOXFIELD	Lancashire		FF		✓	✓
FRESHFIELD	Lancashire		FF		✓	✓
FRODSHAM	Cheshire		FF		✓	✓
FURNESS VALE	Derbyshire		FF			✓
GARSTON	Lancashire		FF		✓	✓
GARSWOOD	Lancashire		FF		✓	✓
GATEACRE	Lancashire		FF	1972	✓	✓
GATLEY	Cheshire		FF			✓
GLAZEBROOK	Lancashire		FF			✓
GLENDON & RUSHTON	Northamptonshire	2 line		1960		
GLOSSOP CENTRAL	Derbyshire					✓
GODLEY JUNCTION	Cheshire		FF		✓	✓
GOLBORNE NORTH	Lancashire			1952		
GOLBORNE SOUTH	Lancashire			1961		
GOOSTREY	Cheshire		FF		✓	✓
GORTON	Lancashire					
GOSPEL OAK	London		FF			✓
GRANGE-OVER-SANDS	Lancashire		FF		✓	✓
GRAVELLY HILL	Warwickshire		FF		✓	✓
GREAT BARR	Warwickshire		FF		✓	✓
GREAT BRIDGE NORTH	Staffordshire		FF	1964	✓	✓
GREAT HARWOOD	Lancashire		FF	1957	✓	✓
GREAT LONGSTONE some face drilled	Derbyshire		FF	1962		✓
GREAT MISSENDEN	Buckinghamshire		FF		✓	✓
GREENFIELD	Yorkshire		FF		✓	✓
GREEN LANE	Cheshire					
GRESLEY	Derbyshire		FF	1964	✓	✓
GRETTON	Northamptonshire		FF	1966	✓	✓
GRINDLEFORD	Derbyshire		FF		✓	✓
GUIDE BRIDGE	Lancashire		HF		✓	✓

Place name		County	Layout	Flange	Closed	Auction	Survived
HALE		Lancashire		FF		✓	✓
HALL ROAD		Lancashire		FF		✓	✓
HAMMERWICH		Staffordshire		FF	1965	✓	✓
HAMPSTEAD HEATH		London		FF			✓
HAMPTON IN ARDEN		Warwickshire		FF		✓	✓
HANDFORTH		Cheshire		FF			✓
HANLEY		Staffordshire		FF	1964	✓	✓
HAPTON		Lancashire		FF			✓
HARLESDEN		Middlesex		HF			✓
HARLINGTON		Middlesex		FF		✓	✓
HARPENDEN CENTRAL		Hertfordshire		HF		✓	✓
HARPENDEN EAST		Hertfordshire		HF	1965	✓	✓
HARRINGTON		Cumberland		FF		✓	✓
HARROW & WEALDSTONE		Middlesex	2 line	HF		✓	✓
HARROW & WEALDSTONE	4' totem	Middlesex		FF			✓
HARTFORD		Cheshire		FF		✓	✓
HARTFORD & GREENBANK		Cheshire	2 line	FF			✓
HASLINGDEN		Lancashire		FF	1960	✓	✓
HATCH END		Middlesex		FF		✓	✓
HATHERN		Nottinghamshire		FF	1960	✓	✓
HATHERSAGE		Derbyshire		FF		✓	✓
HAWARDEN		Flintshire		HF		✓	✓
HAWARDEN BRIDGE		Flintshire		FF		✓	✓
HAWKESBURY LANE		Warwickshire		FF	1965	✓	✓
HAYFIELD		Derbyshire		FF	1970		
HAZEL GROVE		Cheshire		FF			✓
HEADSTONE LANE		Middlesex		FF			✓
HEALD GREEN		Cheshire		FF		✓	✓
HEATON CHAPEL & HEATON MOOR		Lancashire	2 line	HF/FF		✓	✓
HEATON MERSEY		Lancashire			1961		
HEATON PARK	some face drilled	Lancashire		FF			✓
HEDNESFORD		Staffordshire		FF	1965	✓	✓
HELLIFIELD		Yorkshire		FF		✓	✓

Place name	County	Layout	Flange	Closed	Auction	Survived
HELMDON	Northamptonshire		FF	1963		✓
HELMSHORE	Lancashire		FF	1966	✓	✓
HELSBY	Cheshire		FF		✓	✓
HEMEL HEMPSTEAD & BOXMOOR	Hertfordshire	2 line	FF		✓	✓
HENDON	Middlesex		FF		✓	✓
HENLOW CAMP	Bedfordshire		FF	1962	✓	✓
HESKETH PARK	Lancashire		HF	1962		✓
HEST BANK	Lancashire		FF	1969		
HESWALL HILLS	Cheshire		FF			✓
HEYSHAM	Lancashire		HF	1970		✓
HEYWOOD	Lancashire		FF	1970		✓
HIGHBURY & ISLINGTON	London		Flat		✓	✓
HIGHTOWN	Lancashire		FF		✓	✓
HILLSIDE	Lancashire		HF		✓	✓
HINCKLEY	Leicestershire		FF		✓	✓
HINDLEY NORTH	Lancashire		FF		✓	✓
HINDLEY SOUTH	Lancashire			1964		✓
HOLLINWOOD	Lancashire		FF		✓	✓
HOLMES CHAPEL	Cheshire		FF		✓	✓
HOLYHEAD	Anglesey					
HOLYWELL JUNCTION	Flintshire		FF	1966	✓	✓
HOOTON	Cheshire		HF		✓	✓
HOPE	Derbyshire		FF		✓	✓
HOPE VILLAGE	Flintshire		FF		✓	✓
HORTON-IN-RIBBLESDALE (Wooden)	Yorkshire					✓
HOUGH GREEN	Lancashire		HF/FF			✓
HOYLAKE	Cheshire		FF			✓
HUCKNALL BYRON	Nottinghamshire		HF	1964	✓	✓
HUCKNALL CENTRAL	Nottinghamshire		FF	1963	✓	✓
HUMBERSTONE ROAD	Leicestershire		FF	1968	✓	✓
HUNCOAT	Lancashire		FF			✓
HUNTS CROSS	Lancashire		FF		✓	✓
HUYTON	Lancashire		FF		✓	✓

Place name		County	Layout	Flange	Closed	Auction	Survived
HYDE CENTRAL		Cheshire		FF		✓	✓
HYDE JUNCTION*	renamed Hyde North	Cheshire					
HYDE NORTH		Cheshire		FF			✓
ILKESTON JUNCTION		Derbyshire	2 line	FF	1967	✓	✓
ILKESTON NORTH		Derbyshire	2 line	FF	1964		✓
INCE		Lancashire		HF		✓	✓
IRCHESTER		Northamptonshire		FF	1960	✓	✓
IRLAM		Lancashire		FF		✓	✓
JACKSDALE		Nottinghamshire		HF	1963	✓	✓
KEARSLEY		Lancashire		HF		✓	✓
KEGWORTH		Nottinghamshire		FF	1968	✓	✓
KENDAL		Westmoreland		FF		✓	✓
KENILWORTH		Warwickshire		FF	1965	✓	✓
KENSAL GREEN		Middlesex		HF		✓	✓
KENSAL RISE		Middlesex		HF		✓	✓
KENTISH TOWN		London		HF		✓	✓
KENTISH TOWN WEST		London	2 line	HF			✓
KENTON		Middlesex		HF		✓	✓
KENTS BANK		Lancashire		FF		✓	✓
KESWICK		Cumberland		FF	1972	✓	✓
KETTERING		Northamptonshire		FF		✓	✓
KIBWORTH		Leicestershire		FF	1968	✓	✓
KIDSGROVE CENTRAL		Staffordshire		FF		✓	✓
KIDSGROVE LIVERPOOL ROAD		Staffordshire	2 line	FF	1964	✓	✓
KILBURN HIGH ROAD		Middlesex		HF		✓	✓
KILSBY & CRICK		Northamptonshire		FF	1960	✓	✓
KIMBERLEY		Nottinghamshire		FF	1964		✓
KINGSBURY		Warwickshire		FF	1968	✓	✓
KINGS LANGLEY & ABBOTTS LANGLEY		Hertfordshire	2 line	HF		✓	✓
KINGS NORTON		Warwickshire		FF		✓	✓

Place name	County	Layout	Flange	Closed	Auction	Survived
KIRBY MUXLOE	Leicestershire		FF	1964		✓
KIRKBY	Lancashire		FF		✓	✓
KIRKBY BENTINCK	Nottinghamshire		FF	1963	✓	✓
KIRKBY-IN-ASHFIELD	Nottinghamshire		FF	1965	✓	✓
KIRKBY IN FURNESS	Lancashire		FF		✓	✓
KIRKBY STEPHEN EAST	Westmoreland		HF	1962	✓	✓
KIRKDALE	Lancashire		FF		✓	✓
KIRKHAM AND WESHAM	Lancashire	2 line	FF		✓	✓
KNOTT MILL AND DEANSGATE	Lancashire	2 line	FF		✓	✓
KNOTTY ASH	Lancashire		FF	1960		✓
KNUTSFORD	Cheshire		FF		✓	✓

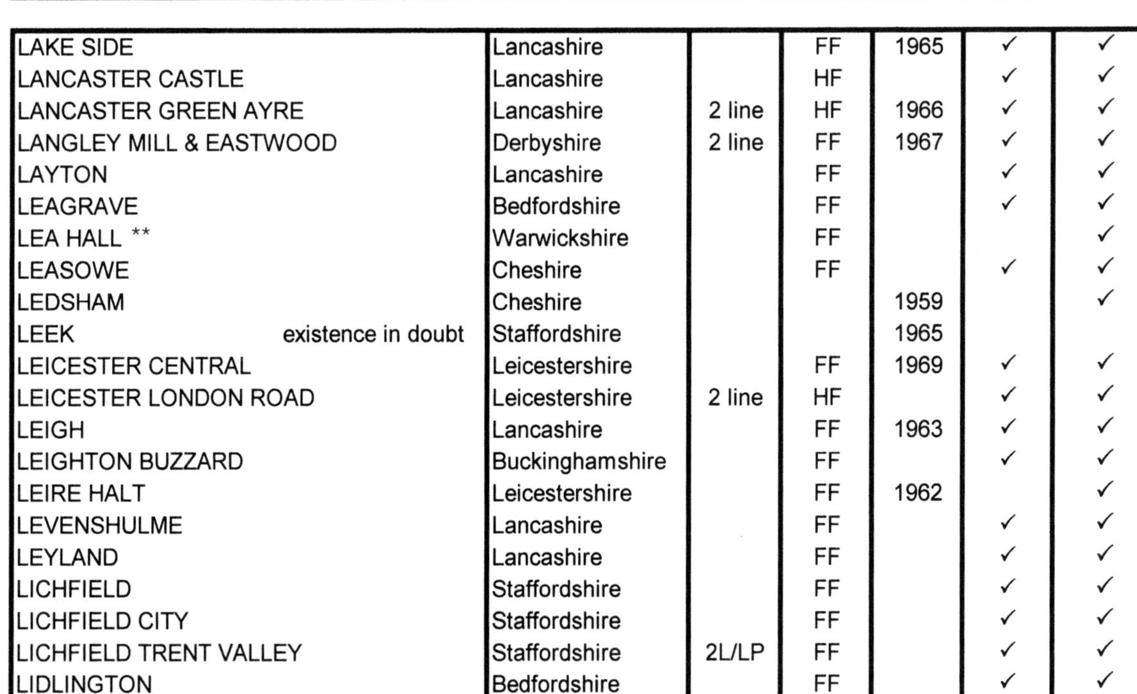

Place name	County	Layout	Flange	Closed	Auction	Survived
LAKE SIDE	Lancashire		FF	1965	✓	✓
LANCASTER CASTLE	Lancashire		HF		✓	✓
LANCASTER GREEN AYRE	Lancashire	2 line	HF	1966	✓	✓
LANGLEY MILL & EASTWOOD	Derbyshire	2 line	FF	1967	✓	✓
LAYTON	Lancashire		FF		✓	✓
LEAGRAVE	Bedfordshire		FF		✓	✓
LEA HALL **	Warwickshire		FF			✓
LEASOWE	Cheshire		FF		✓	✓
LEDSHAM	Cheshire			1959		✓
LEEK existence in doubt	Staffordshire			1965		
LEICESTER CENTRAL	Leicestershire		FF	1969	✓	✓
LEICESTER LONDON ROAD	Leicestershire	2 line	HF		✓	✓
LEIGH	Lancashire		FF	1963	✓	✓
LEIGHTON BUZZARD	Buckinghamshire		FF		✓	✓
LEIRE HALT	Leicestershire		FF	1962		✓
LEVENSHULME	Lancashire		FF		✓	✓
LEYLAND	Lancashire		FF		✓	✓
LICHFIELD	Staffordshire		FF		✓	✓
LICHFIELD CITY	Staffordshire		FF		✓	✓
LICHFIELD TRENT VALLEY	Staffordshire	2L/LP	FF		✓	✓
LIDLINGTON	Bedfordshire		FF		✓	✓

Place name	County	Layout	Flange	Closed	Auction	Survived
LINBY	Nottinghamshire		FF	1964	✓	✓
LITTLEBOROUGH **	Lancashire		FF		✓	✓
LITTLE SUTTON	Cheshire		FF		✓	✓
LIVERPOOL CENTRAL LOW LEVEL	Lancashire	2 line	4' only			✓
LLANDUDNO	Caernarvonshire		HF		✓	✓
LLANDUDNO JUNCTION	Caernarvonshire		FF		✓	✓
LLANFAIRFECHAN **	Caernarvonshire		FF		✓	✓
LLANGEFNI	Anglesey		FF	1964	✓	✓
LLANWRST AND TREFRIW	Denbighshire		FF		✓	✓
LONDON ROAD HIGH LEVEL	Nottinghamshire	2 line	FF	1967		✓
LONG BUCKBY	Northamptonshire		FF		✓	✓
LONG EATON	Derbyshire		FF		✓	✓
LONGPORT	Staffordshire		FF			✓
LONGSIGHT FOR BELLE VUE	Lancashire	2 line	HF	1958		✓
LONGTON	Staffordshire		FF		✓	✓
LONGTOWN	Cumberland		FF	1969	✓	✓
LOSTOCK GRALAM	Cheshire		FF		✓	✓
LOSTOCK HALL	Lancashire		FF	1969	✓	✓
LOSTOCK JUNCTION	Lancashire		FF	1966	✓	✓
LOUGHBOROUGH	Leicestershire		FF	1969	✓	✓
LOUGHBOROUGH MIDLAND	Leicestershire	2 line	HF		✓	✓
LOWER DARWEN	Lancashire			1958		✓
LUFFENHAM	Rutland		FF	1966	✓	✓
LUTON BUTE STREET	Bedfordshire		HF	1965	✓	✓
LUTON MIDLAND ROAD	Bedfordshire		HF		✓	✓
LUTTERWORTH	Leicestershire		FF	1969	✓	✓
LYTHAM	Lancashire		HF		✓	✓
MACCLESFIELD	Cheshire		FF		✓	✓
MACCLESFIELD CENTRAL	Cheshire	2 line				
MACCLESFIELD HIBEL ROAD	Cheshire	2 line	HF	1960	✓	✓
MAGHULL	Lancashire		FF		✓	✓
MANCHESTER CENTRAL + 4' totems 2L	Lancashire		FF*	1969	✓	✓

Place name	County	Layout	Flange	Closed	Auction	Survived
MANCHESTER EXCHANGE	Lancashire	2 line	FF	1969	✓	✓
MANCHESTER VICTORIA	Lancashire	2 line	FF		✓	✓
MANOR ROAD	Cheshire		FF		✓	✓
MANSFIELD TOWN	Nottinghamshire		HF	1964	✓	✓
MANSFIELD WOODHOUSE	Nottinghamshire		FF	1964		✓
MANTON **	Rutland		FF	1966	✓	✓
MARKET HARBOROUGH	Leicestershire		FF		✓	✓
MARPLE	Cheshire		FF			✓
MARSH LANE & STRAND ROAD	Lancashire	3 line	HF		✓	✓
MARSTON GREEN	Warwickshire		FF		✓	✓
MARYPORT	Cumberland		FF			✓
MATLOCK	Derbyshire		FF		✓	✓
MATLOCK BATH	Derbyshire		FF		✓	✓
MAULDETH ROAD	Lancashire		FF		✓	✓
MEIR	Staffordshire		FF	1966	✓	✓
MELTON MOWBRAY	Leicestershire		FF		✓	✓
MENAI BRIDGE	Caernarvonshire		FF	1966	✓	✓
MEOLS	Cheshire		FF		✓	✓
MEOLS COP	Lancashire		FF		✓	✓
MERSEY ROAD & AIGBURTH	Lancashire	2 line		1972		
MIDDLETON JUNCTION	Lancashire	2 line	FF	1966	✓	✓
MILES PLATTING	Lancashire		FF		✓	✓
MILLBROOK	Bedfordshire		FF		✓	✓
MILLERS DALE	Derbyshire		FF	1967	✓	✓
MILL HILL	Lancashire		FF		✓	✓
MILL HILL BROADWAY	Middlesex					
MILNROW	Lancashire		FF		✓	✓
MILNTHORPE	Westmoreland			1968		✓
MOBBERLEY	Cheshire		FF			✓
MOIRA	Leicestershire		FF	1964	✓	✓
MOLD	Flintshire		FF	1962		
MOLLINGTON	Cheshire			1960		
MONTON GREEN	Lancashire		HF	1969	✓	✓

Place name	County	Layout	Flange	Closed	Auction	Survived
MOORSIDE AND WARDLEY	Lancashire	2 line	FF		✓	✓
MORECAMBE EUSTON ROAD	Lancashire	2 line	HF	1963	✓	✓
MORECAMBE PROMENADE	Lancashire	2 line	HF			✓
MORETON	Cheshire		HF		✓	✓
MOSES GATE **	Lancashire		FF			✓
MOSSLEY	Lancashire		FF		✓	✓
MOSSLEY HILL	Lancashire					
MOSTON	Lancashire		FF		✓	✓
MOSTYN	Flintshire		FF	1966	✓	✓
MOULDSWORTH	Cheshire					
NANTWICH	Cheshire		FF		✓	✓
NARBOROUGH	Leicestershire		FF			✓
NAVIGATION ROAD	Cheshire		FF		✓	✓
NELSON **	Lancashire		FF		✓	✓
NESTON NORTH	Cheshire		HF		✓	✓
NESTON SOUTH	Cheshire					
NEW BASFORD	Nottinghamshire		FF	1964		✓
NEWCASTLE	Staffordshire		FF	1964	✓	✓
NEWCHAPEL & GOLDENHILL	Staffordshire	2 line	FF	1964	✓	✓
NEWCHURCH	Lancashire			1964		✓
NEW HEY	Lancashire		FF		✓	✓
NEW MILLS CENTRAL	Derbyshire		FF		✓	✓
NEW MILLS NEWTOWN	Derbyshire	2 line	HF			✓
NEWPORT	Shropshire		FF	1964	✓	✓
NEWSHOLME	Yorkshire			1957		
NEWSTEAD	Nottinghamshire		FF		✓	✓
NEWTON HEATH	Lancashire		FF	1966	✓	✓
NEWTON-LE-WILLOWS	Lancashire		HF		✓	✓
NORMACOT	Staffordshire		FF	1964	✓	✓
NORTHAMPTON BRIDGE ST.	Northamptonshire	2 line	FF	1964		✓
NORTHAMPTON CASTLE	Northamptonshire	2 line	FF		✓	✓
NORTHENDEN	Lancashire			1964		

Place name	County	Layout	Flange	Closed	Auction	Survived
NORTHFIELD	Warwickshire		FF		✓	✓
NORTHOLT PARK	Middlesex		FF		✓	✓
NORTH WEMBLEY	Middlesex		HF		✓	✓
NORTHWICH	Cheshire					
NOTTINGHAM MIDLAND	Nottinghamshire		HF		✓	✓
NUNEATON	Warwickshire		FF		✓	✓
OAKAMOOR to confirm	Staffordshire		?	1965	✓	✓
OAKHAM	Rutland		FF		✓	✓
OAKLEY	Bedfordshire		FF	1958		✓
OLDBURY & BROMFORD LANE	Worcestershire	2 line	FF		✓	✓
OLD DALBY	Leicestershire		FF	1966	✓	✓
OLDHAM CENTRAL	Lancashire	2 line	FF	1966	✓	✓
OLDHAM MUMPS	Lancashire		FF		✓	✓
OLDHAM WERNETH	Lancashire		FF			✓
OLD ROAN	Lancashire		FF		✓	✓
OLD TRAFFORD	Lancashire		FF		✓	✓
OLNEY	Buckinghamshire		FF	1962	✓	✓
ORMSKIRK	Lancashire		FF		✓	✓
ORRELL	Lancashire		FF		✓	✓
ORRELL PARK	Lancashire		FF		✓	✓
OXENHOLME	Westmoreland		FF		✓	✓
OXFORD ROAD	Lancashire		FF		✓	✓
PADGATE	Lancashire		FF		✓	✓
PARK STREET & FROGMORE	Hertfordshire	2 line	FF		✓	✓
PARTINGTON	Cheshire			1964		
PATRICROFT	Lancashire		FF		✓	✓
PEAK FOREST FOR PEAK DALE	Derbyshire	LP	FF	1967	✓	✓
PEAR TREE & NORMANTON	Derbyshire	2 line	FF		✓	✓
PELSALL	Staffordshire		FF	1965	✓	✓
PEMBERTON	Lancashire		FF			✓
PENDLEBURY	Lancashire		FF	1960		✓

Place name	County	Layout	Flange	Closed	Auction	Survived
PENDLETON	Lancashire		FF		✓	✓
PENDLETON BROAD STREET	Lancashire	2 line	FF	1966	✓	✓
PENKRIDGE	Staffordshire		FF		✓	✓
PENMAENMAWR	Caernarvonshire		FF		✓	✓
PENNS	Warwickshire		FF	1965		✓
PENRITH	Cumberland		FF		✓	✓
PENRUDDOCK	Cumberland		FF	1972	✓	✓
PENYFFORDD to Confirm	Flintshire					
PERRY BARR	Warwickshire		FF		✓	✓
PIDDINGTON	Northamptonshire		FF	1962		✓
PINXTON SOUTH	Nottinghamshire		HF	1963	✓	✓
PITTS HILL	Staffordshire		FF	1964	✓	✓
PLEASINGTON	Lancashire		FF			
PLECK	Staffordshire			1958		✓
POLESWORTH	Warwickshire		FF			✓
PORT SUNLIGHT	Cheshire		FF		✓	✓
POULTON	Lancashire		FF		✓	✓
POYNTON	Cheshire		FF			✓
PREES	Shropshire					
PRESCOT	Lancashire		FF		✓	✓
PRESTATYN	Flintshire		HF		✓	✓
PRESTBURY	Cheshire					
PRESTON	Lancashire		HF		✓	✓
PRESTON ROAD	Lancashire		FF		✓	✓
PRESTWICH	Lancashire		FF		✓	✓
PRIMROSE HILL	London		HF	1991		✓
PYE BRIDGE	Nottinghamshire		FF	1967	✓	✓

Place name	County	Layout	Flange	Closed	Auction	Survived
QUEENSFERRY	Flintshire		FF	1966	✓	✓
QUEENS PARK 4' totems only	Middlesex		FF		✓	✓
QUORN & WOODHOUSE	Leicestershire		FF	1963		✓

Place name	County	Layout	Flange	Closed	Auction	Survived
RADCLIFFE BLACK LANE	Lancashire	2 line	FF	1970		✓
RADCLIFFE CENTRAL	Lancashire		FF		✓	✓
RADFORD	Nottinghamshire		FF	1964	✓	✓
RADLETT	Hertfordshire		HF		✓	✓
RADWAY GREEN	Cheshire		FF	1966	✓	✓
RAINFORD JUNCTION	Lancashire		FF		✓	✓
RAINHILL	Lancashire		FF		✓	✓
RAMSBOTTAM	Lancashire		FF	1972	✓	✓
RAVENGLASS	Cumberland		FF		✓	✓
RAWTENSTALL	Lancashire		FF	1972	✓	✓
REDDISH NORTH	Lancashire					
REDDISH SOUTH	Lancashire		HF		✓	✓
REPTON & WILLINGTON	Derbyshire	2 line	FF	1968	✓	✓
RHYL	Flintshire		HF		✓	✓
RICKMANSWORTH CHURCH STREET	Hertfordshire	2 line	HF	1952		
RIDGMONT	Bedfordshire		FF		✓	✓
RISHTON	Lancashire		FF		✓	✓
ROADE	Northamptonshire		HF	1964		✓
ROBY	Lancashire		FF		✓	✓
ROCHDALE	Lancashire		HF		✓	✓
ROCK FERRY	Cheshire		HF		✓	✓
ROMILEY	Cheshire		FF		✓	✓
ROOSE	Lancashire		FF		✓	✓
ROSE GROVE	Lancashire		FF		✓	✓
ROSE HILL	Cheshire		FF			
ROWSLEY	Derbyshire		FF	1967	✓	✓
ROYTON	Lancashire		FF	1966	✓	✓
ROYTON JUNCTION	Lancashire		FF		✓	✓
RUDDINGTON	Nottinghamshire		FF	1963	✓	✓
RUGBY CENTRAL	Warwickshire		HF	1969	✓	✓
RUGBY MIDLAND	Warwickshire		HF			
RUGELEY TOWN	Staffordshire		FF	1965	✓	✓
RUGELEY TRENT VALLEY	Staffordshire	2 line	FF		✓	✓

Place name	County	Layout	Flange	Closed	Auction	Survived
RUNCORN	Cheshire					
RUSHCLIFFE HALT	Nottinghamshire		FF	1963		✓
SADDLEWORTH	Yorkshire		FF	1968		✓
ST. ALBANS ABBEY	Hertfordshire		HF			✓
ST. ALBANS CITY some o/p on Cheddington	Hertfordshire		HF/FF		✓	✓
ST. ANNES	Lancashire		FF		✓	✓
ST. HELENS CENTRAL	Lancashire			1952		
ST. HELENS JUNCTION	Lancashire	2 line	FF			✓
ST. HELENS SHAW STREET	Lancashire	2 line ?				
ST. LUKES	Lancashire		FF	1968	✓	✓
ST. MICHAELS	Lancashire		FF			✓
SALE	Cheshire					✓
SALFORD	Lancashire		HF/FF		✓	✓
SALTLEY	Warwickshire		FF	1968		✓
SALTNEY FERRY (MOLD JUNCTION)	Flintshire	2 line		1962		
SALWICK	Lancashire		FF		✓	✓
SANDBACH	Cheshire		FF		✓	✓
SANDHILLS also 4' totems FF	Lancashire		HF/FF		✓	✓
SANDYCROFT to confirm	Flintshire			1961		
SANKEY	Lancashire		FF		✓	✓
SAWLEY JUNCTION (renamed Long Eaton)	Derbyshire		FF		✓	✓
SAXBY	Leicestershire		FF	1961		✓
SCALE HALL	Lancashire		FF	1966		✓
SEAFORTH & LITHERLAND	Lancashire	2 line	FF		✓	✓
SEALAND	Flintshire		FF	1968	✓	✓
SEASCALE	Cumberland		FF		✓	✓
SEATON	Rutland		FF	1966	✓	✓
SEFTON PARK	Lancashire		FF	1960		✓
SELLAFIELD	Cumberland		FF		✓	✓
SELLY OAK	Warwickshire		FF		✓	✓
SETTLE	Yorkshire		FF		✓	✓
SHAP	Westmoreland		FF	1968	✓	✓

Place name	County	Layout	Flange	Closed	Auction	Survived
SHARNBROOK	Bedfordshire			1960		
SHAW & CROMPTON	Lancashire		FF		✓	✓
SHEFFORD	Bedfordshire		FF	1962	✓	✓
SHENSTONE	Staffordshire		FF		✓	✓
SHOTTON HIGH LEVEL	Flintshire	2 line	FF		✓	✓
SHOTTON LOW LEVEL	Flintshire		HF	1966		✓
SHUSTOKE	Warwickshire			1968		✓
SILEBY	Leicestershire		FF	1968	✓	✓
SILECROFT	Cumberland		FF		✓	✓
SILLOTH	Cumberland		FF	1964	✓	✓
SILVERDALE	Staffordshire		FF		✓	✓
SKIPTON	Yorkshire		FF			✓
SMETHWICK ROLFE STREET	Staffordshire	2 line	FF		✓	✓
SMITHY BRIDGE	Lancashire			1960		
SOUTH ACTON	Middlesex		FF			✓
SOUTH HAMPSTEAD	London		HF		✓	✓
SOUTH KENTON * (+4' totems)	Middlesex		FF*		✓	✓
SPITAL	Cheshire		HF		✓	✓
SPONDON	Derbyshire		FF			✓
SPON LANE	Staffordshire		FF	1964		✓
SQUIRES GATE	Lancashire		FF		✓	✓
STACKSTEADS	Lancashire			1966		
STAFFORD	Staffordshire		FF			✓
STALYBRIDGE	Lancashire		FF		✓	✓
STANLOW & THORNTON	Cheshire		FF		✓	✓
STANMORE VILLAGE	Middlesex		HF	1952		
STANTON GATE	Derbyshire		FF	1967	✓	✓
STAPLEFORD	Nottinghamshire		FF	1967	✓	✓
STAVELEY	Westmoreland		HF		✓	✓
STECHFORD	Warwickshire		HF		✓	✓
STOCKINGFORD	Warwickshire		FF	1968	✓	✓
STOCKPORT EDGELEY	Cheshire	2 line				
STOCKPORT TIVIOT DALE	Cheshire	2 line	FF	1967	✓	✓

Place name	County	Layout	Flange	Closed	Auction	Survived
STOKE MANDEVILLE	Buckinghamshire		FF			✓
STOKE-ON-TRENT	Staffordshire		HF		✓	✓
STONE	Staffordshire		FF		✓	✓
STONEBRIDGE PARK	Middlesex		HF			✓
STREETLY	Staffordshire		FF	1965	✓	✓
STRETFORD	Lancashire		FF			✓
STRETTON	Derbyshire		FF	1961	✓	✓
STRINES	Derbyshire					
STUBBINS	Lancashire		FF	1972	✓	✓
STYAL	Cheshire		FF		✓	✓
SUDBURY	Staffordshire		FF	1966	✓	✓
SUDBURY & HARROW ROAD	Middlesex	2 line	FF		✓	✓
SUDBURY HILL (HARROW)	Middlesex	LP	FF		✓	✓
SUMMERSEAT	Lancashire		FF	1972	✓	✓
SUTTON COLDFIELD	Warwickshire		FF		✓	✓
SUTTON JUNCTION	Nottinghamshire		FF	1964	✓	✓
SUTTON PARK	Warwickshire		FF	1965	✓	✓
SWINTON	Lancashire		HF		✓	✓
SYSTON	Leicestershire		FF	1968	✓	✓
TAMWORTH	Staffordshire		FF		✓	✓
TANHOUSE LANE	Lancashire		FF	1964	✓	✓
TEBAY	Westmoreland		FF	1968	✓	✓
THATTO HEATH	Lancashire		FF			✓
THORNTON - CLEVELEYS	Lancashire		HF	1970	✓	✓
THRELKELD **	Cumberland		FF	1972	✓	✓
TIBSHELF TOWN	Derbyshire		FF	1963		✓
TILE HILL	Warwickshire					✓
TIMPERLEY	Cheshire		FF		✓	✓
TIPTON OWEN STREET	Staffordshire	2 line				
TODD LANE JUNCTION	Lancashire	LP	HF	1968		✓
TODMORDEN	Yorkshire		HF/FF		✓	✓
TOWCESTER	Northamptonshire		HF	1952		

Place name	County	Layout	Flange	Closed	Auction	Survived
TOWN GREEN & AUGHTON small letters	Lancashire	2 line	HF			✓
TRAFFORD PARK	Lancashire		FF			✓
TRENCH CROSSING	Shropshire		FF	1964	✓	✓
TRENTHAM	Staffordshire		FF	1964	✓	✓
TRING	Hertfordshire		FF		✓	✓
TROUTBECK	Cumberland		FF	1972	✓	✓
TROWELL	Nottinghamshire		FF	1967	✓	✓
TUNSTALL	Staffordshire		FF	1964	✓	✓
TURVEY	Bedfordshire		FF	1962	✓	✓
TUTBURY	Derbyshire		FF	1966	✓	✓
TYLDESLEY	Lancashire		FF	1969	✓	✓
ULLESTHORPE	Leicestershire		FF	1962	✓	✓
ULVERSTON	Lancashire		FF		✓	✓
UPHOLLAND	Lancashire		FF		✓	✓
UPTON-BY-CHESTER	Cheshire		FF		✓	✓
URMSTON	Lancashire		FF		✓	✓
UTTOXETER	Staffordshire		FF		✓	✓
VAUXHALL & DUDDESTON	Warwickshire	2 line	FF		✓	✓
WALKDEN HIGH LEVEL	Lancashire	2 line	FF		✓	✓
WALLESEY GROVE ROAD	Cheshire	2 line	FF		✓	✓
WALLESEY VILLAGE	Cheshire		FF		✓	✓
WALSALL	Staffordshire		FF		✓	✓
WALTON JUNCTION **	Lancashire		FF		✓	✓
WARCOP	Westmoreland		FF	1962		✓
WARRINGTON	Lancashire		FF		✓	✓
WARRINGTON CENTRAL	Lancashire	2 line	FF		✓	✓
WARWICK ROAD	Lancashire		FF			
WATERFOOT	Lancashire		FF	1966	✓	✓
WATERLOO	Lancashire		FF		✓	✓

= Painted over Watford Junction

Place name	County	Layout	Flange	Closed	Auction	Survived
WATER ORTON	Warwickshire		FF		✓	✓
WATFORD HIGH STREET *(+4' totems FF)	Hertfordshire	2 line*	HF/FF			✓
WATFORD JUNCTION	Hertfordshire		HF			✓
WATFORD NORTH	Hertfordshire					
WATFORD WEST	Hertfordshire		HF		✓	✓
WAVERTREE	Lancashire		HF	1958		✓
WEDNESBURY TOWN	Staffordshire		FF	1964	✓	✓
WELFORD & KILWORTH	Leicestershire	2 line	FF		✓	✓
WELLINGBOROUGH LONDON ROAD	Northamptonshire	2 line				
WELLINGBOROUGH MIDLAND ROAD	Northamptonshire	2 line	HF	1964	✓	✓
WEM	Shropshire		FF		✓	✓
WEMBLEY CENTRAL	Middlesex		HF		✓	✓
WEMBLEY HILL	Middlesex		FF		✓	✓
WEMBLEY STADIUM #	Middlesex		HF			✓
WENDOVER	Buckinghamshire		FF		✓	✓
WENNINGTON	Lancashire					
WEST ALLERTON	Lancashire		FF		✓	✓
WEST DERBY	Lancashire			1960		
WEST END LANE	London		HF			✓
WEST HAMPSTEAD MIDLAND	London		HF		✓	✓
WESTHOUGHTON	Lancashire		FF		✓	✓
WESTHOUSES & BLACKWELL	Derbyshire	2 line	FF	1967	✓	✓
WEST KIRBY	Cheshire					
WHALEY BRIDGE	Derbyshire				✓	✓
WHALLEY	Lancashire			1962		
WHATSTANDWELL some face drilled	Derbyshire		FF			✓
WHETSTONE	Leicestershire			1963		
WHITACRE	Warwickshire		FF	1968	✓	✓
WHITCHURCH	Shropshire		FF		✓	✓
WHITEFIELD	Lancashire		FF			✓
WHITEHAVEN BRANSTY	Cumberland	2 line	FF		✓	✓
WIDNES CENTRAL	Lancashire	LP	FF	1964	✓	✓
WIDNES NORTH	Lancashire	2 line	FF		✓	✓

Place name	County	Layout	Flange	Closed	Auction	Survived
WIDNES SOUTH	Lancashire	2 line	FF	1962		✓
WIGAN	Lancashire		FF		✓	✓
WIGSTON GLEN PARVA	Leicestershire	2 line	FF	1968		✓
WIGSTON MAGNA	Leicestershire		FF	1968	✓	✓
WIGSTON SOUTH	Leicestershire		FF	1962	✓	✓
WIGTON	Cumberland		HF			✓
WILLENHALL	Staffordshire		FF	1965		✓
WILLESDEN JUNCTION + 4' totems 1 line	London	2 line	FF*	1962	✓	✓
WILLESDEN JUNCTION HIGH LEVEL	London	2 line	FF			
WILMSLOW	Cheshire		FF		✓	✓
WILNECOTE	Warwickshire		FF		✓	✓
WILPSHIRE	Lancashire		HF		✓	✓
WINDERMERE	Westmoreland		HF		✓	✓
WINGFIELD	Derbyshire		FF	1967		✓
WINSFORD	Cheshire		FF		✓	✓
WINSLOW some face drilled	Buckinghamshire		FF	1968	✓	✓
WITTON	Warwickshire		FF		✓	✓
WOBURN SANDS	Bedfordshire		FF		✓	✓
WOLVERHAMPTON HIGH LEVEL	Staffordshire	2 line	HF			✓
WOLVERTON	Buckinghamshire		HF		✓	✓
WOODFORD HALSE	Northamptonshire		FF	1966	✓	✓
WOODLANDS ROAD	Lancashire		FF		✓	✓
WOODLEY	Cheshire		FF			✓
WORKINGTON MAIN	Cumberland	2 line	HF		✓	✓
WORSLEY	Lancashire			1969		
WYLDE GREEN	Warwickshire		FF			✓
WYRE DOCK	Lancashire		FF	1976	✓	✓
WYRLEY & CHESLYN HAY	Staffordshire	2 line	FF	1965		✓

NORTH EASTERN REGION TOTEMS

The North Eastern Region

Introduction

The north-east of England is widely recognised as the birthplace of the world's railways. The area's first wagonway – forerunner of the railways – was already operating in 1608. By 1800 a wagonway network of bewildering complexity had developed in the Northumberland and Durham coalfields, and in 1825 the Stockton & Darlington Railway opened as the world's first public steam-operated railway. This enterprise owed much to the engineering brilliance of George Stephenson. Other railway pioneers including his son, Robert Stephenson, William Headley, Timothy Hackworth, and George Hudson ('The Railway King') were also north-easterners. Much of this history has been recreated by the Beamish Open Air Museum, which accurately portrays bygone times.

(Courtesy National Railway Museum/Science & Society Picture Library)

The history of the North Eastern Region

The North Eastern Railway (NER) was established in 1854, and had a virtual monopoly in the old counties of Northumberland, Durham and North Yorkshire. The NER was an amalgamation of four companies. These were:

The York and North Midland Railway	(Y&NMR)
The Leeds Northern Railway	(LNR)
The York, Newcastle and Berwick Railway	(YN&BR)
The Malton and Driffield Railway	(M&DR)

The Y&NMR included most of the railways within the area bounded by York, Whitby, Hull and Leeds. Their strategic links from York to Altofts Junction (part of the original route from York to London) and that between **Knottingley** and **Burton Salmon**, enabled London to be reached via the Great Northern. One of the oldest routes of the Y&NMR was the Whitby & Pickering Railway of 1836, engineered by **North Wylam**-born George Stephenson, and absorbed by the Y&NMR in 1845. The LNR provided the lines between **Leeds**, **Harrogate**, **Ripon**, **Thirsk**, **Northallerton** and **Stockton**.

The key route between Leeds and Thirsk opened in stages between 1848 and 1849. The YN&BR contributed an intricate system of lines, including the former Great North of England Railway between York and Darlington (opened in 1841), the Newcastle & Darlington Junction (1844), and the Newcastle & Berwick (1847–50). It also contained the Durham Junction (Washington to Rainton Meadows), Pontop & South Shields, Brandling Junction (Gateshead to Sunderland) and Newcastle & North Shields railways.

The final constituent of the NER was the short-lived Malton & Driffield Railway, opening in 1853. The Newcastle & Carlisle had opened in 1838, and this was added to the NER empire in 1862. The Blyth & Tyne Railway, operating between Newcastle and Bedlington, then to Newbiggin and Morpeth (1840–72), was absorbed into the NER in 1874. The North British Railway had to be content with owning the Riccarton Junction to **Hexham** (1862), Reedsmouth to Morpeth (1865), and Scotsgap to Rothbury (1870) lines in rural Northumberland. The NER added the present ECML between Durham and Newcastle via Chester-le-Street in 1868, **York** to Doncaster via Selby in 1871, and the Sunderland to **West Hartlepool** via Horden route in 1905.

Apart from the North British presence in Northumberland, the only other major invader of NER territory was the Hull & Barnsley Railway. Established by Hull businessmen to break the NER monopoly to and from their city, the H&B line to Cudworth opened in 1885, and was taken over by the NER in 1922.

The lines described above were to become part of the London & North Eastern Railway from 1923, at which time, they comprised 6,590 route miles, the second largest of the 'Big Four' and almost twice the size of the GWR. By 1946 this had reduced to 6,333 miles, and British Railways inherited a slightly slimmer North Eastern Region in 1948. The remainder of the region's lines added in the redrawing of boundaries in 1950 were in the West Riding coalfield. They were a complex interlacing of routes owned in pre-Grouping days by the GNR, MR and LNWR. Until 1921 the L&YR served parts of the West Riding. The NER enjoyed a monopoly from 1874 in Newcastle, where one major city station sufficed. However, **Leeds**, **Bradford**, **Dewsbury**, **Wakefield** and many lesser towns had two or more stations operated by rival companies.

Under LNER administration (1923–47) some stations received small cream 'lamp tablets' with brown wording (shown below). These were frequently placed beneath the company's Art Deco 'mint-imperial' electric lamps. Unusual orange tablets were fitted to Durham, Newsham and Corbridge. Where totems had not displaced them, many of these tablets lasted well into the 1970s. Lamp tablets survived on the Newcastle and Whitley Bay loop and Riverside branch, also at Alnwick, Alnmouth, Richmond and South Bank. The final ones to disappear were probably those at Filey Holiday Camp.

At the planning stage, as BR was divided into regions in 1946–7, an eleventh hour decision to create a North Eastern Region was made. An Eastern Region of 4,659 route miles was considered unwieldy, so it was unequally divided into North Eastern (1,823 miles) with its headquarters at York, and Eastern (2,836 miles) managed from Liverpool Street. In 1967, by which time closures had made its timetable books distressingly slim, the North Eastern Region became part of the ER, controlled from **York**. The North East Region was markedly less inclined than other regions to install totems at its stations. Many rural lines closed within ten years of Nationalisation, and re-signing stations with a short life expectancy was presumably ruled out as extravagant.

Consequently the 26 ex-NBR stations in Northumberland (closed from 1952 to 1956) and the 15 stations between **Northallerton** and Garsdale (closed in 1954) never received totems. Coalfield lines such as the Newcastle to Consett loop (17 stations: closed from 1953 to 1955) and the West Riding system, focused on Queensbury (13 stations: closed in 1955) were similarly neglected. However, the likelihood of closure cannot explain one of the greatest puzzles – why throughout 90 miles of the ECML, between **Ferryhill** and **Berwick upon Tweed**, totems were never installed. We have to look east and west of Newcastle to find totems in what was a barren land for the totem collector.

A J71 shunts at York under the watchful eye of a totem under the canopy. (Tony Wright)

In 1960, when one might have expected totems to be in place, seventeen successive stations lacked them – even Durham, Newcastle and Morpeth. On the other hand some lines were lavished with totems: in the mid-1960s 10 of the 12 **Darlington** to **Saltburn** line stations had totems, the only exceptions being Middlesbrough and South Bank. There were little West Riding clusters at the adjacent stations of **Pannal**, **Harrogate**, **Starbeck** and **Knaresborough**, and totems at all three stations in **Pontefract**.

Typical of their economy was the Newcastle to Carlisle line, where in the mid-'60s, 7 of the 19 intermediate stations had totems, installed at various times, with no particular pattern of distribution, except that they were all in the **Hexham** to Newcastle section.

The relative scarcity of totemised stations reflects the reluctance of the North Eastern Region to embark on a major re-signing programme. Compared with the

SR, the NER had relatively few stations with long platforms, so fewer totems were required. What is surprising, however, considering there were only 125 stations fitted with totems, is that we have found survivors from 119 of them! Compared with all the other regions, except perhaps the Southern, this is the highest percentage known to have survived, and we shall take a look at the real North Eastern rarities at the end of this chapter.

Geography of the region

Geographically, this is a region of contrasts and worthy of exploration. The North East corner of England is an area combining dramatic history (aside from the development of railways) with abundant natural beauty, classic castles, cathedrals and bastions of industry. Much of the coast is peppered with historic sites, such as **Berwick upon Tweed**, Lindisfarne, Bamburgh and Alnwick, all of which stand as testaments to a turbulent history. The rugged city of Durham – dominated by the magnificent Norman cathedral and castle – is a seat of great learning. The industrial revolution along the Wear and Tees rivers gave much prosperity in bygone times, benefiting the whole region. To the north lies Hadrian's Wall – the first attempt to keep back the Scots – and a constant reminder of 400 years of Roman occupation. The area as a whole contains some of the most desirable totems of any region.

Much of the western boundary follows the summit of the Cheviot and Pennine hills, with inhospitable expanses of open moorland. Railways used Tweeddale, the Tyne Gap, Wharfedale, Airedale and Calderdale to find relatively gently graded routes through these barriers. However, the courageous **Barnard Castle** to **Penrith** line struggled across the moors at Stainmore, rising to 450ft, to reach the western side of the hills. The **Hexham** to Riccarton Junction and Northallerton to Hawes lines threaded their way up picturesque valleys to reach the remarkably ambitious Waverley and Settle to Carlisle routes respectively. These both passed through desolate landscapes at high altitudes.

The lines to Alston, Wearhead, Middleton-in-Teesdale and Richmond did not push any further up their valleys, despite plans to do so. The more densely populated south Pennines proved too much for the Oxenhope and Holmfirth lines to cross, but the former GNR rose to the Pennine challenge with its 'Alpine Lines' connecting **Halifax**, Keighley and **Bradford** by means of impressive viaducts and tunnels. The **Huddersfield** to Manchester route left the North East Region in a 3-mile tunnel through the Pennines at Standedge, the fourth longest on the British Railways system. Further east, 175 miles of the ECML from Edinburgh to **Kings Cross** pass through the region. Entering at the coastal cliffs just north of historic **Berwick**, it crosses a sparsely populated agricultural landscape, having a last view of the east coast at Alnmouth. Moving south, it reaches industrial Tyneside, once a legendary bustling centre of coalmining, shipbuilding and engineering in more nostalgic times.

Ilkley, 1975. (Alan Young)

Percy Main, 1977. (Alan Young)

The Newcastle to Sunderland axis retains some of its dense network of lines, but minor routes that struck out into the coalfield to Amble, Newbiggin, Blyth and Consett have lost their passenger services. Southward to Darlington over the low Durham plateau the main line follows a tortuous path, partly dictated by earlier colliery lines. Many collieries with their large, unlovely villages demanded a complex network of passenger and mineral lines, almost all now closed. The coastal line from Sunderland to Middlesbrough and the Bishop Auckland branch are all that remain open to passengers. South of **Darlington** and the River Tees the main line enters the low, agriculturally productive Vale of York, with tantalising views of the Pennines to the west and the North York Moors to the east, before reaching the magnificent and historic city of **York**. Widening southwards, the Vale merges with the drained marshlands of the Humber and its tributaries, where the railway builders followed easy, unobstructed routes. Here the main line (diverted for some miles to avoid subsidence in the **Selby** coalfield) leaves the region on a long, straight stretch. To the west of the main line is the Yorkshire coalfield, still Britain's major source of deep-mined coal, where the land gently rises up to the Pennines. Scenically marred by its legacy of mining and manufacturing, the numerous villages, towns, and cities around **Leeds** and **Wakefield** were linked by a profusion of passenger lines, several of which are still open. Standing apart from the industrial towns are **Harrogate**, the genteel Victorian watering place adopted by commuters to York and Leeds, and attractive **Knaresborough**.

Yorkshire, east of the Vale of York, begins with Middlesbrough and the Tees estuary. This is a landscape tortured and tormented by oil refineries, chemical works and steel mills, many now lying derelict. Here we find the totem names of **Cargo Fleet**, **Eaglescliffe** and **Thornaby**. Suddenly this scenery gives way to the North York Moors, with its wide, empty plateau, spectacular coastal cliffs, and the intimate charm of the Esk Valley and Newtondale. Railways from Teesside entered this area to serve the old ironstone mines and villages of the Cleveland Hills, and the attractive towns of Guisborough, **Whitby** and Pickering. The 35-mile Esk Valley branch still offers a delightful journey to Whitby, but sadly the coastal route from Loftus to **Scarborough**, noted for its magnificent views, viaducts and steep gradients is no more.

The North York Moors end abruptly at the Vale of Pickering, through which the York to **Scarborough** line finds a nearly level route. Southwards, the landscape changes once again, with the chalk hills and narrow streamless valleys of the Yorkshire Wolds. This sparsely populated landscape, reminiscent of southern England's Downs, had only the long-closed **Malton** to **Driffield** line passing through its interior, and the **Scarborough** to Bridlington line still clambers over its seaward end close to **Flamborough** Head.

And finally to the coast itself. Although some stretches of the Durham coast were strewn with colliery waste from a once-mighty coal industry (such as at **East Boldon**) and the Tees estuary was polluted by chemicals, the north-east had some fine bathing beaches. Further south at intervals along the coastline the railway encouraged the development of resorts. In Yorkshire **Scarborough**, the self-styled 'Queen of the Resorts', attracted much excursion traffic and even acquired a station dedicated to such trains (shown opposite).

Boldon Colliery. (N. Skinner)

East Boldon. (Alan Young)

In contrast, nearby Bridlington's growth was modest. Only Whitley Bay and Tynemouth benefited from being 10 miles from Newcastle, but still could not rival the two major Yorkshire holiday towns. There were numerous other, smaller resorts, all at one time served by rail, of which **Whitby** and **Saltburn** were probably the most appealing.

Heyday at Scarborough: a hive of activity, with frequent excursions arriving from far-flung places. A D49 'Hunt' class 4-4-0 No. 62770 *The Puckeridge* takes centre stage. (R. Blencowe)

For more than 30 years from the late 1940s onwards summer holidaymakers poured into **Filey** to stay at the Butlin's Holiday Camp, sited on its windswept cliff top. Many arrived at the camp's own terminal station south of the town, which closed in 1977. Thankfully, for those who want the quiet life, the railway failed to reach some stretches of this wonderful coastline, which is still tranquil and unspoilt today.

A familiar scene to many a holidaymaker: Saltburn, 1973. (Alan Young)

North Eastern Region database

Despite its vast size, this region had the fewest number of stations fitted with totems, and 'tangerines' have always been desirable to collectors. Fortunately many different totems have been saved from the clutches of the scrapman, and we have included photos of a high proportion (74 per cent) of these wonderful beasts throughout the book.

A: Opened by the Bradford, Wakefield & Leeds Railway in 1857, **Ardsley** became a locomotive depot under GNR ownership, with a predominantly freight engine allocation. It had the code 37A under ER control, then in 1956 it was handed to the NER and became 56B. The station closed in 1964, and the shed the following year. A totem has never been auctioned, and neither has another Leeds area station, **Armley Moor**, which opened as Armley & Wortley in 1854 courtesy of the Leeds, Bradford & Halifax Junction Railway. BR renamed it in 1950.

B: Although seen at auction, **Barnard Castle** is rare, as the totems allegedly ended up in a bonfire during demolition work in 1964. This would explain their almost brown appearance. Located near **Ilkley** on the edge of the moors is the wonderfully named **Ben Rhydding** – a flangeless totem, with black edged letters. (One of us used to own one and to let it go was a serious error!) The Otley & Ilkley Joint Railway opened the station in 1866. One of our contributors was once offered a **Blackhall Rocks** totem, though pictures of the station mysteriously do not show

them. It closed in 1960, so maybe they were made but not erected. Desirable names would include **Berwick-upon-Tweed** (opened in 1846 as Berwick and renamed as late as 1955), **Blaydon** (of races fame, opened in 1835) and the delightfully named **Burton Salmon** (a former halt on the ECML that closed in 1959). (Stop press – see page 212.)

As shown on the previous page, **Boldon Colliery** certainly had totems. It is a very old station that opened in 1839 as Brockley Whins and was built by the Brandling Junction Railway. It was renamed in 1926 by the LNER, and has not been seen at auction thus far. Neither has **Bolton on Dearne**, which is a Swinton & Knottingley Joint station. Opened as Hickleton in July 1879, it was renamed in November of the same year.

C: All the totems in this section have made very infrequent appearances at auction. Probably the rarest is **Cross Gates**, which the Leeds & Selby Railway opened in 1834. The York & North Midland closed it in 1840, then reopened it in 1850.

D: **Darlington Bank Top** totems were removed and replaced by full-flanged **Darlington** totems. Both survive, but only the latter has appeared in auction (January 2002). As one of the most evocative names in the railway world, it created much interest. There are other rarities, including **Darton**, **Denby Dale** and **Dewsbury Central**, but the scarcest is **Dinsdale**, which opened in 1887. We have spoken to local collectors and the consensus seems to be that they may have all been destroyed.

E: **East Boldon**, which was formerly known as Cleadon Lane (1839–98), has only made one outing in public so far, but even rarer is **Etherley**, which was opened by the Bishop Auckland & Weardale Railway in 1843 as Etherley & Witton Park.

F: We have only seen one **Featherstone** totem so far. The station was opened in 1848 by the Wakefield, Pontefract & Goole Railway and closed in 1967. It has been given a new lease of life since 1992. **Ferriby** is another rarity. The Hull & Selby Railway opened the station in 1840.

G: There is only one real rarity worthy of mention, with no examples found yet – **Golcar**, on the trans-Pennine **Huddersfield** to **Stalybridge** route. The station closed in 1968, but may have lost its totems at an earlier date.

H: Half-flanged **Halifax Town** totems were removed in 1961 when the station became **Halifax**, and full-flanged totems were installed. Remarkably several of the older totems have survived. The one and only **Hebburn** totem in auction appeared over 15 years ago. The station was built by the NER in 1872 and closed in 1981, reopening in 1984 as part of the Tyne & Wear PTE system. One of the most elusive names is **Heddon-on-the-Wall**, which closed in 1958, so if any totems were fitted they were very short-lived. Despite enquiries and rumours, we have been unable to locate a picture of this rare beast – opened by the Scotswood, Newburn & Wylam Railway in 1881. We know of a totem from **Heighington** in a museum, but await one in public auction. They are flangeless.

A few **Howdon-on-Tyne** totems are known, as they were *in situ* relatively late in the 1970s. The station was closed in 1980 for Tyne & Wear PTE work and reopened in 1982. Lastly, **Hunmanby** is a rare totem. It is a York & North Midland Railway station dating back to 1847.

K: **Knottingley** stands out, with scant information on the existence of totems here.

Both the major stations in Leeds had totems, but because **Leeds Central** closed in 1967, and Leeds City being rebuilt by 1966 they are both quite scarce. Our personal opinion is that **Leeds Central** is the slightly rarer of the two, with fewer appearances in the public domain. These were discoloured because of the environment – see page 170.

M: **Marsden** (opened in 1849) is another of those elusive trans-Pennine route totems. This was the last station on the Standedge south-west route out of this region, and we await one in a public auction. Our next port of call is **Menston**, east of **Ilkley**, which was originally a Midland Railway station that opened in 1876 to replace an earlier station further north. This is a rare totem that has yet to make its public debut.

Moorthorpe and **South Kirkby** was renamed in 1961, becoming **Moorthorpe**. Totems carrying both names have been seen at auction. **Morley Top** has only been seen at auction once, back in 1983, when totems really were cheap, by today's standards anyway. This ex-GNR station only had totems for 10 years and it closed in 1961.

N: **Northallerton** is the only real rarity here, with no example ever seen. Totems were only displayed here for six or seven years, because by 1958 the station had electric lighting and the totems disappeared – probably all ending up in the skip again! A colour photo of a totem *in situ* appears in the Ian Allan publication *On North Eastern Lines*.

P: As **Percy Main** was one of the last stations in the region to lose its totems in 1980, it is rather surprising that one has not appeared at auction thus far. The Newcastle & North Shields Railway opened it in 1839, and after brief closure for rebuilding in the early 1980s, it is now part of the Tyne & Wear PTE. Our contributor Alan Young has produced an excellent book on Tyneside's railways, including many of the dates when totems were installed and removed (see Bibliography).

R: One of the oldest stations in this region is **Riding Mill**, which was opened by the Newcastle & Carlisle Railway in 1835. The photo in the database (page 171) is one of Alan Young's *in situ* shots. He informs us that there were very few on the station, so not surprisingly we still await one in a public auction. Another little gem is **Ripon**, a Leeds & Thirsk Railway station of 1848, closing in 1967. This town boasts a market, cathedral and nearby Fountains Abbey. With a population of over 14,000 it is now strangely detached from the railway system.

S: With only one outing in public, **Scorton** is quite rare. It was a York & Newcastle station of 1846 that survived until 1969. Worthy of mention is **Seaburn**, which was not opened by the LNER until 1937. We have not found much information on the totems here; suffice to say that several existed. The last **South Milford** seen at auction was in 1983, and then it did not sell! It may have been heavily or poorly restored. The photo shown here is of one in very good condition. The station was originally opened by the Leeds & Selby Railway in 1834 as Milford, then gained its current title in 1867.

A very unusual and possibly unique double-sided flangeless **South Shields** totem has been seen, although the vast majority were the usual half-flanged variety. The station at **Spennymoor** closed officially in 1952, but the totems remained *in situ* for over 10 years beyond this date, as the station was used for excursion traffic until the early 1960s. We are not absolutely sure whether they were only erected for the benefit of excursionists, or whether they were left over from pre-closure days. It was an NER opening of 1878 replacing an earlier station. **Stanningley**, near **Pudsey**, has never appeared in auction, neither has the former locoshed location of **Starbeck** (50D), once home to several LNER D49 'Hunt' class locos. The shed closed in 1959. The station was originally opened as **Harrogate** by the Leeds & Thirsk Railway in 1848, becoming Starbeck in 1857. Steeton opened in 1847, courtesy of the Leeds & Bradford, and then became **Steeton & Silsden** in 1868, only to be resited in 1892, and closed in 1965. It is quite a rare totem. Since 1990 the station has reopened, giving it a new lease of life.

Two for the price of one: we cannot even find one! (Alf Miles Collection)

T: Only **Thornaby** is worthy of special note, as despite no totems have appeared at auction yet, several are known to exist. It is probably best known for its large locomotive shed (51L) at the south end of Tees Yard. The shed opened in 1958 to replace the old Newport and Middlesborough depots. The station was known as South Stockton until 1892.

W: Of the two **Wakefield** stations, we have found **Westgate** to be much rarer than **Kirkgate**, because of earlier re-signing. The York & North Midland Railway opened the station at Wetherby in 1847. It closed in 1902 as a new station was provided further south, which only lasted until our old friend Dr Beeching came along and dictated that it was unviable in 1964. Lastly we must mention **Whitby West Cliff**, which was obliterated from the railway map in 1958, long before Beeching came along. This was because of its poor siting relative to the town.

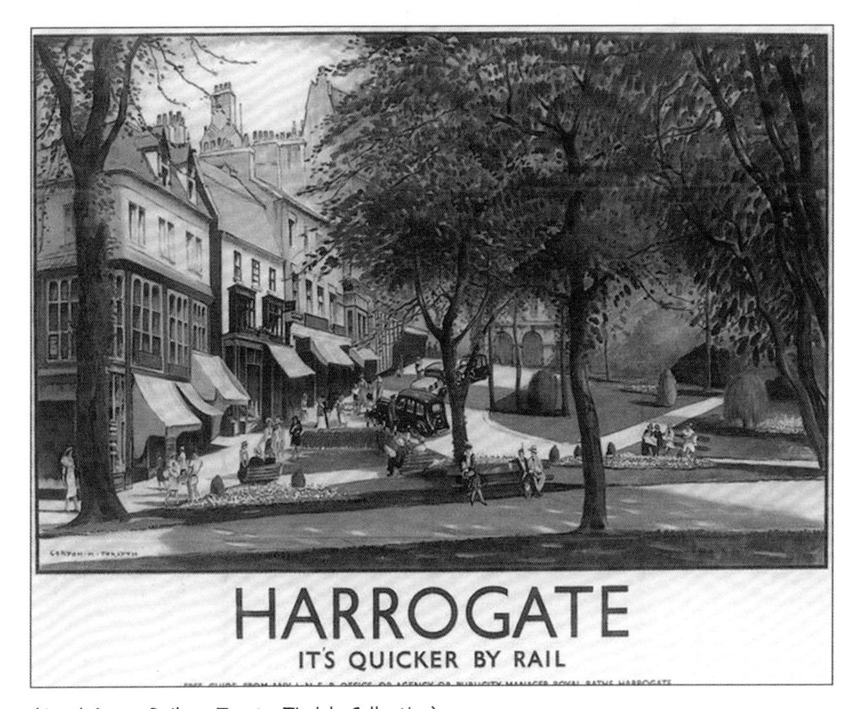

(South Devon Railway Trust - Tindale Collection)

We close this chapter with more mouth-watering North Eastern Region images below. The Harrogate poster is nicely framed with four wonderful tangerine gems.

Chapter 10 Totem Listing

** = Black edged lettering: **LF** = large white flange variety

Place name	County	North Eastern Region Layout	North Eastern Region Flange	North Eastern Region Closed	Totem in Auction	Totem Survived
APPERLEY BRIDGE	Yorkshire		FF	1965	✓	✓
ARDSLEY	Yorkshire			1964		✓
ARMLEY MOOR **	Yorkshire		HF	1966		✓
BACKWORTH	Northumberland		FF	1977	✓	✓
BARNARD CASTLE	Durham		HF	1964	✓	✓
BATLEY	Yorkshire		HF/Flat	1964	✓	✓
BEMPTON **	Yorkshire		HF		✓	✓
BEN RHYDDING **	Yorkshire		Flat			✓
BENTON	Northumberland		HF		✓	✓
BERWICK UPON TWEED **	Northumberland	2 line	FF		✓	✓
BEVERLEY **	Yorkshire		Flat		✓	✓
BILLINGHAM	Durham		FF		✓	✓
BLACKHALL ROCKS	Durham		FF	1960		✓
BLAYDON	Durham		HF		✓	✓
BOLDON COLLIERY	Durham		FF			✓
BOLTON ON DEARNE	Yorkshire		HF			✓
BRADFORD EXCHANGE **	Yorkshire	2 line	FF	1990	✓	✓
BRADFORD FORSTER SQUARE **	Yorkshire	2 line	HF		✓	✓
BRIGHOUSE re-opened 2000	Yorkshire		FF	1970	✓	✓
BROUGH **	Yorkshire		HF/Flat		✓	✓
BURTON SALMON **	Yorkshire		HF/LF	1959	✓	✓
CARGO FLEET	Yorkshire		FF	1989	✓	✓
CASTLEFORD CENTRAL	Yorkshire	LP	Flat		✓	✓
CASTLEFORD CUTSYKE	Yorkshire	LP	HF	1968	✓	✓
CLECKHEATON CENTRAL **	Yorkshire	2 line	HF/LF	1965	✓	✓
CROFT SPA **	Durham		HF/FF	1969	✓	✓
CROSS GATES	Yorkshire		HF		✓	✓

Place name		County	Layout	Flange	Closed	Auction	Survived
DARLINGTON		Durham		FF		✓	✓
DARLINGTON BANK TOP		Durham	LP	HF			✓
DARTON' **		Yorkshire		FF			✓
DENBY DALE	to confirm	Yorkshire					
DEWSBURY CENTRAL **		Yorkshire	LP	Flat	1964		✓
DEWSBURY WELLINGTON ROAD		Yorkshire	LP	HF		✓	✓
DEWSBURY WELLINGTON ROAD **		Yorkshire	LP	FF			✓
DINSDALE		Durham		HF			
DRIFFIELD		Yorkshire		HF		✓	✓
EAGLESCLIFFE' **		Durham		FF/Flat		✓	✓
EAST BOLDON		Durham		FF		✓	✓
ETHERLEY		Durham		HF	1965		✓
FEATHERSTONE		Yorkshire		FF	1967		✓
FELLING' **		Durham		HF	1979	✓	✓
FERRIBY		Yorkshire		HF			✓
FERRYBRIDGE' **	also HF	Yorkshire		FF/LF	1965	✓	✓
FERRYHILL		Durham		HF	1967	✓	✓
FILEY **		Yorkshire		LF		✓	✓
FLAMBOROUGH **		Yorkshire		HF/LF	1970	✓	✓
GARFORTH	orange flange	Yorkshire		FF		✓	✓
GOLCAR		Yorkshire		HF	1968		
GOOLE		Yorkshire		HF		✓	✓
GRANGETOWN **		Yorkshire		FF		✓	✓
HALIFAX	from 1961	Yorkshire		FF		✓	✓
HALIFAX TOWN	until 1961	Yorkshire		HF		✓	✓
HARROGATE		Yorkshire		HF		✓	✓
HEBBURN		Durham		FF		✓	✓
HECKMONDWIKE		Yorkshire		FF	1965	✓	✓
HEDDON-ON-THE-WALL		Northumberland		FF	1958		✓

Place name	County	Layout	Flange	Closed	Auction	Survived
HEIGHINGTON	Durham		Flat			✓
HEXHAM **	Northumberland		HF		✓	✓
HIGH SHIELDS	Durham		FF	1979	✓	✓
HOWDEN-ON-TYNE	Northumberland		FF			✓
HUDDERSFIELD **	Yorkshire		HF/FF		✓	✓
HUNMANBY	Yorkshire		HF			✓
ILKLEY **	Yorkshire		FF		✓	✓
KNARESBOROUGH **	Yorkshire		FF		✓	✓
KNOTTINGLEY to confirm	Yorkshire					
LEEDS CENTRAL	Yorkshire		HF/Flat	1967	✓	✓
LEEDS CITY	Yorkshire		HF		✓	✓
MALTON **	Yorkshire		HF/LF		✓	✓
MARKET WEIGHTON	Yorkshire		HF	1965	✓	✓
MARSDEN	Yorkshire					✓
MARSKE **	Yorkshire		FF		✓	✓
MENSTON **	Yorkshire		HF			✓
MICKLEFIELD **	Yorkshire		FF		✓	✓
MIRFIELD	Yorkshire		HF		✓	✓
MOORTHORPE	Yorkshire		FF		✓	✓
MOORTHORPE AND SOUTH KIRBY**	Yorkshire	2 line	FF		✓	✓
MORLEY LOW **	Yorkshire		HF/LF		✓	✓
MORLEY TOP **	Yorkshire		Flat	1961	✓	✓
NEWLAY & HORSFORTH **	Yorkshire		HF	1965	✓	✓
NORMANTON	Yorkshire		FF		✓	✓
NORTHALLERTON	Yorkshire		HF			
NORTH WYLAM	Northumberland		FF	1968	✓	✓

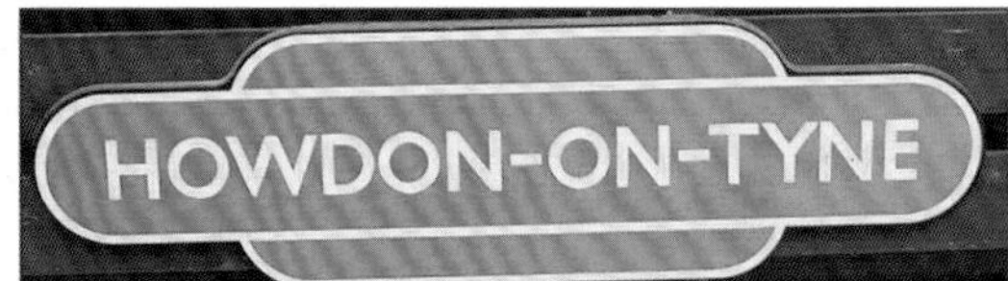

Place name		County	Layout	Flange	Closed	Auction	Survived
PANNAL		Yorkshire		HF		✓	✓
PELAW **		Durham		FF	1979	✓	✓
PERCY MAIN		Northumberland		FF			✓
POCKLINGTON		Yorkshire		HF	1965	✓	✓
PONTEFRACT	orange flange	Yorkshire		FF		✓	✓
PONTEFRACT BAGHILL		Yorkshire	LP	HF/Flat		✓	✓
PONTEFRACT MONKHILL		Yorkshire	LP	Flat		✓	✓
PONTEFRACT TANSHELF		Yorkshire	LP	Flat	1967	✓	✓
POPPLETON **		Yorkshire		FF		✓	✓
PRUDHOE	orange flange	Northumberland		FF		✓	✓
PUDSEY GREENSIDE **		Yorkshire	LP	Flat	1964	✓	✓
PUDSEY LOWTOWN **		Yorkshire	LP	Flat	1964	✓	✓
REDCAR CENTRAL **		Yorkshire		FF		✓	✓
REDCAR EAST	orange flange	Yorkshire		FF		✓	✓
RIDING MILL		Northumberland		FF			✓
RIPON		Yorkshire		HF	1967	✓	✓
SALTBURN **		Yorkshire		FF		✓	✓
SCARBOROUGH CENTRAL	also HF	Yorkshire	LP	FF/LF		✓	✓
SCORTON **		Yorkshire		FF	1969	✓	✓
SEABURN		Durham		HF			
SEAMER **		Yorkshire		FF		✓	✓
SELBY		Yorkshire		HF			✓
SHIPLEY		Yorkshire		HF		✓	✓
SLAITHWAITE **		Yorkshire		HF	1968	✓	✓
SOUTH ELMSALL **		Yorkshire		HF/FF		✓	✓
SOUTH MILFORD **		Yorkshire		FF		✓	✓
SOUTH SHIELDS		Durham		HF/2side		✓	✓
SOWERBY BRIDGE		Yorkshire		HF		✓	✓
SPENNYMOOR	still up in 1963	Durham		HF	1952		
STANNINGLEY		Yorkshire			1968		✓
STARBECK		Yorkshire		HF			✓

Place name	County	Layout	Flange	Closed	Auction	Survived
STEETON & SILSDEN **	Yorkshire		HF	1965	✓	✓
STOCKSFIELD **	Northumberland		HF		✓	✓
STOCKTON **	Durham		FF		✓	✓
THIRSK	Yorkshire		HF		✓	✓
THORNABY **	Yorkshire		FF			✓
WAKEFIELD KIRKGATE **	Yorkshire	2 line	HF		✓	✓
WAKEFIELD WESTGATE	Yorkshire	LP	HF		✓	✓
WALKER GATE	Northumberland		FF		✓	✓
WEST HARTLEPOOL	Durham		FF		✓	✓
WEST MONKSEATON	Northumberland		HF		✓	✓
WETHERBY **	Yorkshire		HF	1964		✓
WHITBY TOWN ** also HF	Yorkshire		FF/LF		✓	✓
WHITBY WEST CLIFF	Yorkshire	LP	LF	1958		
YORK **	Yorkshire		HF/FF		✓	✓

A fine pair of NER totems from the birthplace of railways. (Author's collection)

Station pillar enamel and totem from a wonderful bastion of steam.

CHAPTER 11

The Scottish Region

Introduction

The Scottish region has arguably the most wonderful scenery and the best names to be found on totems. With names such as **Ballachulish Ferry**, **Boat of Garten**, **Carnoustie**, **Dundee Tay Bridge**, **Fort William** and **Kyle of Lochalsh** to choose from, who would argue? It is a difficult region in which to build railways but has led to some of the greatest railway journeys to be taken anywhere in Great Britain (the West Highland line to Mallaig, or Inverness to **Kyle of Lochalsh** cross-country route). Considering the relatively sparse population over the majority of the country, the Scottish region had a high number of stations (over 450) and the majority were fitted with totems during their lifetime.

(Courtesy NRM/Science and Society Picture Library)

This region also had some very large counties with relatively few stations (Ross & Cromarty or Argyllshire), while the densely populated south Lanarkshire and Renfrewshire had a plethora of stations. The database shows that we have had the greatest trouble in researching the Scottish region to try to determine what has actually survived. We expect this work might stimulate the largest amount of new information to surface – at least this is our hope!

The history of the Scottish Region

The geography of Scotland was largely responsible for the formation of the constituent railway companies. Initially these began in the south and gradually spread north. The NBR had the largest number of route miles (1,378) at the 1923 Grouping, and not surprisingly the GNSR the smallest (334). The five companies were:

The Glasgow and South Western Railway (G&SWR) (covering the counties of Kirkcudbright, Dumfries-shire, Ayrshire and Renfrewshire).

The North British Railway (NBR) (Stirling, Midlothian, Lanarkshire, Peebles, Berwick, Roxburgh, Selkirk, Fife, Kinross, Clackmannanshire, through Argyll and into Inverness).

The Caledonian Railway (CR) (Lanarkshire, Midlothian, Stirling, Dumfries-shire, Argyll, Perthshire, Angus, Kincardineshire and up to Aberdeenshire).

The Highland Railway (HR) (Perthshire, Ross & Cromarty, Morayshire, Nairn and into Caithness).

The Great North of Scotland Railway (GNSR) (Aberdeen, Banffshire and Morayshire).

With its wonderful blue locomotives, superbly coloured crimson and white coaching stock with the Royal Arms of Scotland incorporated into the badge, the Caledonian Railway was the most prestigious of the Scottish companies. At 1,115 route miles, it was just a 'wee tad' smaller than the NBR, but had access into **Carlisle**, Glasgow, Edinburgh, **Perth**, **Dundee** and Aberdeen. It also ran the wonderful route through **Crianlarich** to **Connel Ferry** and **Ballachulish** on the west coast. At its peak it carried over 34 million passengers in a single year. Two of its many stations are shown below.

This company was formed in 1845, and the first line was the famous climb from **Carlisle** to Glasgow via **Beattock**. The company extended the line to Edinburgh in 1848. So successful were these ventures that revenue was generated to allow the CR to grow by acquiring the smaller companies in the central area between Edinburgh and Glasgow. They acquired access rights to **Perth** in 1865 and obtained the route into Aberdeen a year later. On the western side of the country purchase of the Callander & Oban Railway gave the CR the route into the Highlands and the line was extended to **Ballachulish** in 1903. In the 1923 Grouping the proud Caledonian Railway Company passed into the LMS Region.

SCOTTISH REGION TOTEMS

The NBR had lines running from **Carlisle** to Aberdeen and from **Berwick** to **Mallaig**, criss-crossing the whole of southern Scotland. Other railway companies used their routes more than the NBR (up to Aberdeen and down the east coast through **Berwick**). The NBR formed in 1845 and in the mid-1850s built the famous Waverley route from Edinburgh to **Hawick**. This was extended into **Carlisle** in 1865 and a legend was born. The company ran the routes in south-east Scotland with the odd foray into the north and west. They ran the famous West Highland Line through **Fort William** and **Glenfinnan** to **Mallaig**, as well as all the routes in Fife and East Coast routes through **Montrose** and into **Perth**. They were responsible for the building of the first Tay Bridge that so tragically collapsed during a storm in 1879 with great loss of life, and were instrumental in the building of the unmistakable Forth Bridge. Like the CR, the NBR bought small south and central Scottish companies (Edinburgh, Perth & Dundee and the Edinburgh & Glasgow) so by the end of the 19th century their network was complete. In 1923 they passed into the hands of the LNER, along with the GNSR. Two of their many stations are illustrated below.

The GNSR was formed earlier than either of the big two (CR and NBR), being granted a charter in 1844. They built the line from Aberdeen to Inverness and consolidated their route network within Aberdeenshire. They also served the great fishing ports of **Peterhead** and **Fraserburgh**. The line to **Ballater** serviced the Royal estate at Balmoral and other routes followed to **Elgin** and **Boat of Garten**. This region has the greatest concentration of distilleries in Scotland, so somebody in the GNSR knew what they were doing! On passing into the LNER in 1923, rather surprisingly, not many of these unprofitable routes were closed until nationalisation. After 1948 it was a different story, and the only line that survives today is the section from Aberdeen to **Keith**.

The GSWR was concentrated south of Glasgow. It was responsible for most of the southern Glasgow commuter lines. With this revenue base, it was strange that the company did not grow beyond 493 route miles. Two companies (the Glasgow, Paisley, Kilmarnock & Ayr Railway and the Glasgow, Dumfries & Carlisle Railway) merged in 1847 to form the G&SW, giving the towns of **Ayr**, **Kilmarnock** and **Dumfries**, access into Glasgow St Enoch. They also gained lucrative ferry and mineral traffic at **Greenock** (1869), but a price war for this business with the CR

forced an agreement about the lower Clyde estuary routings. Following are two GSWR totems.

The GSWR passed into the hands of the LMS in 1923 and at nationalisation BR's Scottish Region assumed control. Much of the line density in central Ayrshire was reduced, but other traffic in suburban Glasgow saw much electrification investment. Their impressive station in Glasgow, (St Enoch), was demolished in 1977, but much of the central network remains intact today.

The fifth company in the formation of the Scottish region was the famous Highland Railway. It too passed into the hands of the LMS at the 1923 Grouping, after 75 years of operation. The HR has the distinction of operating Britain's most northerly stations (**Wick** and **Thurso**) and the famous **Kyle of Lochalsh**. They do, however, have some other wonderful names on their routes, **Stromeferry**, **Achnasheen**, **Pitlochry** and **Blair Atholl**. These are the epitome of the Scottish highlands for totem collectors. Just two of their stations are shown below.

The company first opened routes between Inverness and **Nairn** (1855) and extended further east to **Elgin** (1858). They eventually finished the famous route through **Aviemore**, linking Inverness to **Perth** in 1898 through some breathtaking scenery. They also opened various branches from their core routes, the most notable being to Aberfeldy, Fortrose, Dornoch and Lybster. The LMS were kind at take-over and the network shrank little (only the Lybster branch being closed). However, it was a different story under BR management, with most of the branches being closed early and even the main line from **Aviemore** to **Forres** was a casualty.

At its peak the HR had just over 500 route miles and the Strathspey Railway has preserved the **Aviemore** to **Boat of Garten** section. Interestingly, at the time of grouping discussions one proposal for Scotland was to operate the railways under a fifth main region. It seems strange today that we now have such a scheme that seems to work very well.

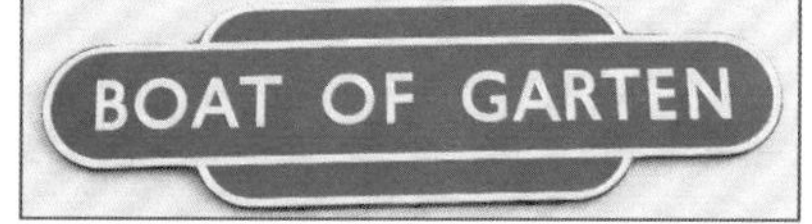

The geography of the region

Scotland sees the greatest variation in terrain in Great Britain with respect to railway construction and operation. The railway companies had to cope with mountains, steep-sided valleys, large swings in climatic conditions, and few customers north of the main southern industrial belt. A look at a map of Scotland shows how the geography has dictated the boundaries and the positioning of railway lines.

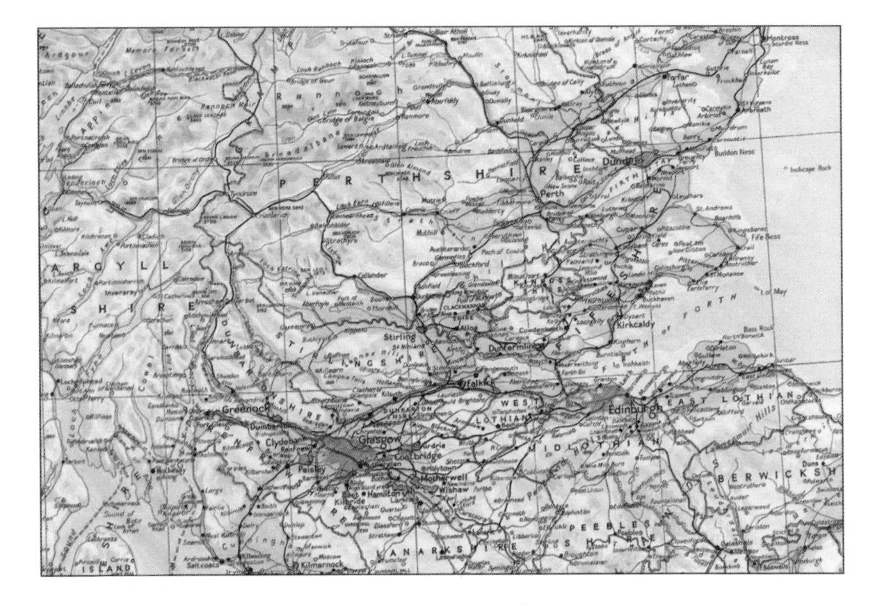

There is a huge concentration of lines from Glasgow to Edinburgh and around both cities. To the north the mountainous interior of Scotland gives rise to only one route through the centre of the country, the Highland route to Inverness. So difficult was the terrain in this area that the track building took over six years! In the south Scotland is characterised by hills falling almost into the sea on the east, rolling border hills in the centre, the picturesque Ayrshire coastline with some wonderful golf courses and Burns country to the west. To the south are the border lands around **Lockerbie**, the land that was the inspiration for some of Burns's poems and Gretna Green the place for eloping couples! West of Gretna are the Galloway hills, looking down on empty beaches and estuaries full of wading birds, but very few totems! The central region is the country of Sir Walter Scott, of wonderful tweed mills, of warriors able to beat powerful English kings (William 'Braveheart' Wallace) and the ruins of ancient abbeys. Here we have the collectable totems of **Kelso**, **Peebles**, **Innerleithen**, **Roxburgh**, **Melrose**, **Tynehead**, **Hawick** and **Galashiels**.

The rolling hills of south Scotland give way to the once busy and prosperous city of Glasgow. Only **Glasgow Cross** and **Port Glasgow** carry this proud name. In recent times heavy industry has taken a beating, with steel mills and shipbuilding yards progressively falling silent. To the east is the city of Edinburgh, with its rich history and one of the most unmistakable skylines in Britain, the famous castle.

Edinburgh is the city of Calton Hill and Waverley station, of military tattoos and of A4s at **Haymarket** shed (64B); it is steeped in railway history. The ECML hugs the coast all the way from **Berwick upon Tweed** through Dunbar and down the Firth of Forth into Edinburgh. North of the industrial belt is the real Scotland. The wooded island area around Loch Lomond soon gives way to high mountains and deep valleys further north. On the West Coast in Argyllshire (the county of long finger lochs) are the castles of the MacDougalls and Campbells, and the territory of Rob Roy. The area has much spectacular loch and mountain scenery. Several quite superb carriage prints show this area to its full beauty. Here we find the high peaks, Ben Nevis and Ben Cruachan. Railway lines snake slowly to the totem towns of **Oban** and **Fort William**. On the east coast, the Forth Bridge carries trains north through beautiful Perthshire, bypassing the impressive **Stirling** Castle, for years the battleground of the English and the Scots.

August 1989. (Author's Collection)

One of the wonders of the railway world. (Author's collection)

The Trossachs are west of here, where many wonderful photographs have been taken. Further north the mountains and moorland around **Rannoch** await. They are the southern outposts of the Grampian Highlands. Just to the north and east are the Cairngorms, rocky sentinels that suffer terrible snowstorms. They form the northern edge of the Grampians. This is not a landscape for either the faint-hearted or the railway engineer! It is home to the best winter sports facilities in Great Britain and mountain scenery that is really unequalled.

To the south-east the tracks pass through the Kingdom of Fife to **Dundee**, then up the coastline through Angus and into the 'Granite City'. In Angus fishing ports and seaside towns, popular in times gone by, fringe the North Sea. Here sandstone cliffs guard pretty bays. Were it not for the cold easterly winds and long winter nights, this would be a perfect place to reside. Just to the west we find large forests and purple heather moorland. The valley of the River Dee is simply beautiful and the summer seat of the Royal Family. It is home to wonder brews of malt and water!

North again in GNSR territory, we find crescents of sand on the coastline of Moray and Banff, once bustling fishing ports with some rare totems for the collector. It is known by some as the 'Scottish Riviera', but is too cold for most! Inverness is known as the capital of the Highlands. Nearby are some of Scotland's greatest attractions – sailing in the Moray Firth, Loch Ness with its famous resident, the Caledonian Canal and a feast of castles for historians. It is also close to the site that saw the slaughter at Culloden in 1746 when Bonnie Prince Charlie's army was cut to pieces in less than an hour. (Since the first book we have confirmed that Culloden Moor did not have totems.) What a great shame, as that would have been quite a totem!

Neither man nor railways alike have really touched the far north of Scotland. The thousands of walkers who seek solitude from time to time are probably the only people to have visited huge areas of Ross & Cromarty and Sutherland. There are no railways at all on the west coast north of **Kyle of Lochalsh**, and it is nearly 100 miles from there to Cape Wrath, the north-western tip of Scotland. The northern coastline is rugged and inhospitable in winter, with cliffs shaped by centuries of nature's fury and small sandy bays, where seals bask in privacy when the sun shines. Stations are found in **Thurso** and **Wick**. Scotland may have been ravaged by wind, snow and station closures, but few can deny the beauty of the land.

The Scottish Region database

Because of the sheer size of the Scottish database, we will restrict discussion to the rarities and the more desirable items. This has been the most interesting region to research, but we know there is still much to learn.

A: **Aberlour** is one of those real gems of a Scottish name in the heart of whisky-making country. Totems from this GNSR station (opened in 1869, closed in 1965) have not been seen in auction. We have yet to confirm any survivors from **Achterneed** or **Addiewell**, but recently found out that totems existed at **Anderston Cross**, an ex-CR station right in the heart of Glasgow. We also have no data from **Ardrossan Town**, **Arnage** or **Auchinleck**. Nine other totems from this section have yet to appear in auctions. We can contrast the old LNER lamp tablet with the replacement totem. Below are the two signs from **Aboyne**, a small station in Aberdeenshire that closed in 1966. For us, the 'new' totems were a vast improvement.

Collectors' names here might include **Achnasheen**, **Achnashellech**, **Arrochar and Tarbert** or **Auchnagatt**. The first two were ex-HR stations that opened within a year of each other (1870 and '71 respectively), **Auchnagatt** was an ex-GNSR station, opened in 1861 and a Beeching casualty in 1965. Below we have included a quality shot of **Arrochar and Tarbert** in the mid-'70s. Notice the distinctive Scottish station lamp.

Arrochar and Tarbert, 1977. (Dawlish Museum)

B: There are quite a few database gaps in this section. We have no survival data on 15 different totems all over Scotland. A few of these are early closures (**Blackford Hill** and **Braidwood**, 1962, for example) but some of these stations are still open. Of desirable items, we could mention both **Ballachulish** and **Ballachulish Ferry** on the northern section of the West Highland line. They both opened in 1903. **Balloch Pier** at the southern end of Loch Lomond is sought after and has not appeared in auction. Rumour has it that most of the totems were dumped into the loch at re-signing! The black and white photo below shows **Balloch Central** *in situ* in late 1959. This station is still open after 150 years. **Banchory** is one of the few totems from the old county of Kincardineshire; the station was another Beeching casualty in 1965.

(Author's collection)

Blair Atholl, on the highland line from **Perth**, has only appeared once in auction. The original name was Blair Athole (opened in 1863). **Borrobol Platform**, on the line north towards Thurso, is the only totem in Scotland carrying the word 'Platform'. This was actually dropped in 1962, three years before plain Borrobol closed. The four totems beginning with **'Bridge of'** (**Allan**, **Earn**, **Orchy** and **Weir**) would make a wonderful quartet on anyone's wall. Only **Bridge of Orchy** has yet to appear in auction. The wonderfully named **Broughty Ferry** (just north of **Dundee**) would also grace any Scottish collection. It is an early station, opening in 1838.

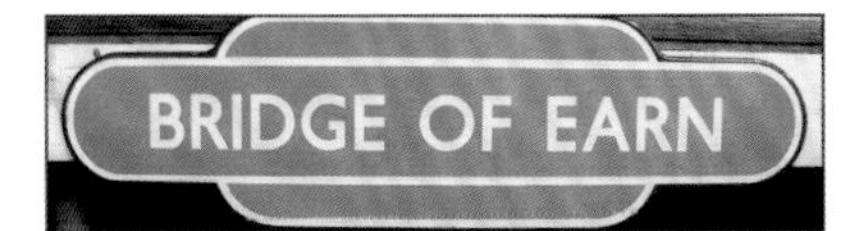

C: This is a large section with 67 totems. On no fewer than 18 of these we have no survival data, even though extensive photo research has allowed us to confirm some of the totem details. A further 12 of the known survivors have not appeared in any auction. **Cambus O' May** (ex-GNSR on the Royal Deeside line to **Ballater**) is among the stations where we have little information – just a super name! Other classics include **Coatbridge Sunnyside** and **Coupar Angus**, and we simply could not leave this brief review without mentioning **Crianlarich Upper** and **Lower**. These stations opened in 1873 and 1894. Lower, ex-CR, closed in 1965, (Upper, ex-NBR is still open. We could not resist putting them alongside each other!

D: During the preparation of this book we were excited when quite unexpectedly a **Dalmuir Riverside** turned up. It was thought this had not survived and a photo has now been used in the database. This still leaves 9 totems out of 36 in this section with no information. Rare items include **Dalbeattie** (ex-GSWR, opened in 1859 and closed in 1965), the ex-NBR stations of **Dalreoch**, **Drumchapel**, **Dundee Tay Bridge** and **Dysart**, the ex-GNSR totem **Dyce** and **Dunragit** on the GSWR line across to Stranraer. A totem from the cathedral city of **Dunblane** is part of the Oliver Neal memorial in the NRM.

E: There are only 16 Scottish totems that begin with 'E', but we have been unable to confirm the survival of six of these, and only six others have actually appeared in auction. We would welcome any data on **Easthaven**, **East Linton**, **East Pilton**, **Eastriggs**, **Eddleston** and **Eyemouth**. **East Fortune** is the most northerly point of the ECML, an ex-NBR station opened in 1849, but axed in 1964. **East Kilbride** is a place one of us (RF) knows well. It is a 'new town' with an elusive totem and the CR opened the station there in 1868. **Elderslie** (ex-GSWR) was one of the first stations to open in the southern suburbs of Glasgow, but it closed in 1966. **Elgin** is just pure Scotland and a station that has been open for almost 150 years.

F: A small select group can be found here and only two, **Falkirk High** and **Fort Matilda**, have yet to appear in auction. The two images below are more for the connoisseurs!

G: This is the section of the 'Glen' totems, but – surprisingly, considering the size and geography of Scotland – there are only six totems with 'Glen' on them and only **Glenluce** with some information lacking. This is one of eight such totems in our listing where the reader may be able to help. The database shows our blanks. There is a real oddball in this section, **Girvan**, which had some plastic totems (as did **Torquay** in the WR). But unlike those at Torquay the totems were in Scottish colours! Desirable totems include **Garelochead**, **Glenfinnan**, either of the totems from **Grantown-on-Spey** and **Guard Bridge**. **Glenfinnan** (for Loch Sheil), to give it the full title, was opened by the NBR in 1901. The shot of the Glenfinnan viaduct that follows is a railway classic.

Glenfinnan Viaduct, West Highland line. (Author's collection)

In early 2001 we found that **Garnkirk**, a north Glasgow ex-CR commuter station, was fitted with totems, a fact not previously recognised, but totems from both it and **Gartcosh** are not known to survive. We close with images of **Garelochhead** (ex-NBR), opened in 1894, and alongside we have included **Garmouth**, an ex-GNSR station that opened in 1884 and closed in 1968.

H: 'H' would normally stand for Highland, but there are not many highland totems in this section. To compensate, there are a couple of 'Waverley' route totems in **Hawick** and **Heriot**. However, on 7 of the 22 totems we have no data, including the Lanarkshire totems of **Hamilton West**, **Happendon**, **Hillington West** and **Hyndland**. Other rarities include the ex-CR stations of **Hairmyres** (opened in 1868), **Harburn** (1848 as West Calder and Torphin), **Hartwood** (1889), **Holytown** (1882) and the ex-GWSR station of **Houston & Crosslee** (which had a variety of names from 1871). The only real northern station in this section is **Huntly**, an ex-GNSR station, opened in 1854.

I: We have no data on nearly half the totems in this section, and only **Insch**, **Inverkeithing** and **Irvine** have appeared so far in auction. Collecting Scottish totems beginning with 'I' is really difficult! A further three totems are known to have survived. Totems from the ex-CR station **Inches** have not been seen since closure in 1964. **Innerleithen** was an ex-NBR station that was open for almost 100 years but an early closure in 1962. **Invergowrie** was opened in early 1847 and **Inverurie** (originally Inverury) is an ex-GNSR station, where we have yet to confirm the existence of totems.

J: All three stations have confirmed survivors, and the rarity of **Joppa** makes this totem collectable. **Jordanhill** has not been seen in auction.

K: Keith, north-west of Aberdeen, had two stations. The GNSR built first (in 1856), followed two years later by the HR. **Keith Junction** (ex-HR) is still open today, but **Keith Town** closed in 1968 and the totem has not appeared yet in auction. We have no data for **Kelvin Hall** or **Kennishead** and **Kilbowie** (ex-CR closed in 1964) has yet to be seen in public. **Kelso** is a lovely border town on the famous Waverley route. Totems from the three Ayrshire towns of **Kilmarnock**, **Kilmaurs** and **Kilwinning** are not thought to have survived, or those from **Kirkcudbright**, **Kirkhill** and **Kirkintilloch**. The classics come in the form of **Kittybrewster** and **Kyle of Lochalsh**. Three other totems, **Kilconquhar**, **Kirkcaldy** and **Knockando** have yet to be the subject of public bidding.

L: **Langbank** (on the south bank of the Clyde) and **Langloan** (near Coatbridge) are both ex-CR stations, with the latter closing in 1964. Any information on totems from these stations is gratefully accepted. This is also the case for **Leith North** (ex-CR but then named North Leith).

We also need data on **Logierieve** (ex-GNSR and closed in 1965) and **Loth** (a rare Sutherland totem, ex-HR station that was an early closure in 1960 and is still to confirm). Totems not seen in auction include Law Junction (opened in 1848 by the CR), **Leuchars Junction** (opened in 1850), **Loch Awe** (opened in 1880 and closed for twenty years, 1965–85), **Lockerbie** (on the WCML to Glasgow) and **Lundin Links** (ex-NBR, opened in 1857 and closed in 1965). Collectors' pieces are numerous, and may include the Scottish highland totems **Lochielside**, **Lochluichart**, **Lonmay** and **Lumphanan**.

M: Several eminent Scottish collectors seek totems from Mallaig, but we have yet to confirm their existence. **Maryhill** is a northern suburb of Glasgow with two stations (NB and CR). **Maryhill Central** (ex-CR) totems are thought to be non-survivors. **Maryhill Park** has been opened three times and closed twice; the last opening was in 1993. (Both totems have lower panel wording.) The Ayrshire totems from **Mauchline** and **Maybole** are thought to have perished, along with Midlothian totems from **Merchiston**, **Morningside Road** and **Murrayfield** (home of the Scottish RFU and one for the sporting collectors). Six other totems beginning with 'M' have yet to make public appearances, including the lovely towns of **Melrose** and **Musselburgh**. **Montrose**, **Motherwell** and **Mount Florida** are on several collectors' shopping lists. Some **Morar** totems did not fare too well, as we can see below!

N: This section finds us with almost as many closed stations as those still open. **Nethy Bridge** is an ex-GNSR station just north of **Boat of Garten** in the County of Inverness. We doubt whether any totems from here have survived. As well as the English **Newhaven** in Sussex, Scotland has its own station of the same name. This is on the ex-CR line to **Leith North** and was an early closure in 1962. Totems from here are not known, as is the case for **New Luce**. **North Connel** is not a common totem. Other rarities include **Neilston Low** (which only held this name for thirteen years, 1953–66), **Newton-on-Ayr** (an early 1839 GSWR station) and **Newton Stewart** (one of the few totems from Wigtown, and a station which closed in 1965).

O: There are only three totems in this section; all are known to have survived, but none have appeared publicly. **Oban** (ex-CR from 1860) is probably the pick of the three, but either of the others **Oakley (Fife)** and **Old Kilpatrick** would be welcome in a Scottish set. **Oakley (Fife)** is unusual, with the county appearing in brackets in the lower panel.

P: There are 31 Scottish totems beginning with 'P', but fewer than half of these have appeared in public so far.

Paisley had five stations, and totems from all of them are very elusive. We do not yet know of survivors from **Abercorn** (ex-GSWR), **Gilmour Street** (also ex-GSWR), **St James** (ex-CR) or **West** (ex-GSWR) stations, and **Paisley Canal** (closed in 1983 and rebuilt in 1990 to the east) is known, but has been auctioned. Totems from nine other stations are yet to be confirmed, including **Partick Central**, **Patna** and **Portessie**. Totems to grace Scottish collections might include **Peebles** (ex-NBR), **Perth** (a joint CR, NBR and HR station named Perth General until 1952), **Pitlochry** (the ex-HR station of 1863) or **Portobello** (a very early 1832 NBR station near Edinburgh).

Q: The two Glasgow totems **Queen's Park** and **Queen Street** are on opposite sides of the Clyde. **Queen Street** only had the larger 4ft totems on the Low Level station, but we do not know of any survivors.

R: Here we have one of the shortest names – **Rhu (**not known) and one of the longest – **Rosewell & Hawthornden**. Only three Scottish totems here have appeared in public (**Renfrew Fulbar Street**, **Rothes** and **Rutherglen**, and two more are thought not to have escaped the builders' skips (**Reston** and **Roy Bridge**). **Riddings Junction** is a really unusual Scottish totem because the station is actually in Cumberland! Below we show a wonderful quartet. Notice the variations in colour and the more 'finished' look of the fully flanged totems from **Renfrew** and **Rosewell**.

S: There are some wonderful names in this section, with a high proportion known to have been preserved, and many already having made appearances in public. You could not get a more Scottish name than **St Andrews** (of golf and university fame, in that order) in the Kingdom of Fife. Just to the south is **St Monance** (which between 1875 and 1936 was named St Monans).

We are still researching to find data for totems from **Scotstoun West**, **Shettleston**, **South Renfrew**, **Stevenston**, both stations in **Stranraer**, **Strathaven Central** and the elusive **Stromeferry**. This is curious because many Scottish totems were still in place well into the early '80s. Rare totems include **South Beach** (an ex-GSWR station that should have been correctly named Ardrossan South Beach), **Strathcarron** (on the Inverness to Kyle line) and **Strathyre** in southern Perthshire. Alan Young's *in-situ* shot below shows the poor state of the 'lamp' at **Spean Bridge**!

Inverness-shire, July 1982. (Alan Young)

T: A high percentage of the totems here are from further north in Scotland and are highly collectable. Names such as **Taynuilt**, **The Mound**, **Thurso**, **Tullibardine** or **Tyndrum Upper** are the epitome of Scottish totem collecting.

The picture below of Taynuilt station was taken in the 1970s. The station is an ex-CR building dating from 1880.

(Dawlish Museum)

We recently confirmed surviving totems from **Thortonhall** (the ex-CR station that took this name in 1944). Previously it was named Eaglesham Road.

U: Only five totems here, four confirmed as surviving, but only **Uddingston Central** has made a public appearance. The other four were victims of the ravages of station closures. We only came across the existence of **Uddingston West** totems during our photo research. Previously this ex-NBR station that closed for two years during the First World War was not thought to have been fitted with totems. However, our photo evidence confirms that it was. The station was an early casualty of BR, closing in 1955, and we do not know of any survivors.

W: The penultimate group contains a couple of classic names in **Wemyss Bay** and **West Kilbride**. The former is an ex-CR station and the latter from the GSWR.

Walkerburn in Peebles-shire, **Westerton** in north Glasgow and **Wishaw Central** have so far failed to show any surviving totems. With the latter totem we are also not sure of the exact layout. Photographic evidence is hard to come by for this station during the totem era.

Y: There are two stations starting with 'Yoker', but in different counties. **Yoker High** is the ex-NBR station that carried this name between 1953 and 1965. **Yoker Ferry** is the ex-CR station that carried its name between 1953 and 1964, when it closed. Both stations initially opened as Yoker, with the NBR station preceding its Caledonian cousin by 14 years (1882 and 1896 respectively).

We cannot leave Scotland without including two superb railway posters that graced many stations throughout Great Britain, and more shots of Scottish stations during the totem era. The poster below shows why this train journey is still as popular today!

(National Railway Museum/Science and Society Picture Library)

The poster that follows shows Royal Deeside, and totems appropriate to this area would include **Ballater**, **Aboyne**, **Glassel**, **Banchory** or **Torphins**. A most desirable totem from this area is **Crathes** (where the royal link on the poster comes from).

(South Devon Railway - Tindale Collection)

During our research we came across many very atmospheric photographs. We simply could not pass up this lovely shot of **Lairg** on a rare sunny day in August 1975. Nor could we pass up the chance to publish a shot of **Kyle of Lochalsh**, showing five totems *in situ*! We have been able to confirm 12 totems existed at this location.

Kyle of Lochalsh, date unknown. (R. Blencowe)

To close we have added a few totem shots that we could not use elsewhere. We have been spoilt for choice because of the quality and wealth of material available to us.

(Alan Young)

(Alan Young)

Chapter 11 Totem Listing

Place name		County	Scottish Region			Totem in	Totem
			Layout	Flange	Closed	Auction	Survived
ABBEYHILL		Midlothian		FF		✓	✓
ABERDOUR		Fife		FF		✓	✓
ABERLOUR		Banffshire		FF	1965		✓
ABOYNE		Aberdeenshire		FF	1966	✓	✓
ACHNASHEEN		Ross & Cromarty		HF			✓
ACHNASHELLACH		Ross & Cromarty		HF			✓
ACHTERNEED	to confirm	Ross & Cromarty			1964		
ADDIEWELL		Midlothian		HF			
AIRDRIE		Lanarkshire		FF		✓	✓
ALEXANDRA PARADE		Lanarkshire		FF		✓	✓
ALEXANDRIA		Dunbartonshire		FF		✓	✓
ALLANFEARN		Inverness-shire		FF	1965		✓
ALLOA		Clackmannanshire		HF	1968	✓	✓
ANDERSTON CROSS	re-opened 77	Lanarkshire		HF	1959	✓	✓
ANNAN		Dumfrieshire		FF			✓
ANNIESLAND		Lanarkshire		FF			✓
ANSTRUTHER		Fife		FF	1965		✓
APPIN		Argyllshire		FF	1966	✓	✓
ARBROATH		Angus					✓
ARDLUI		Dunbartonshire		HF		✓	✓
ARDROSSAN TOWN		Ayrshire	?				
ARMADALE		West Lothian		HF	1956	✓	✓
ARNAGE		Aberdeenshire			1965		
ARROCHAR AND TARBET		Dunbartonshire		HF		✓	✓
AUCHENGRAY		Lanarkshire		FF	1966	✓	✓
AUCHINLECK		Ayrshire		FF	1965		
AUCHNAGATT		Aberdeenshire		FF	1965		✓
AVIEMORE		Inverness-shire		HF		✓	✓
AYR		Ayrshire		FF		✓	✓
BAILLIESTON		Lanarkshire		FF	1964	✓	✓
BALGREEN HALT		Midlothian		HF	1968	✓	✓

Place name	County	Layout	Flange	Closed	Auction	Survived
BALLACHULISH	Argyllshire		FF	1966		✓
BALLACHULISH FERRY	Argyllshire		HF	1966		✓
BALLATER	Aberdeenshire		FF	1966		✓
BALLINDALLOCH	Morayshire		FF	1965	✓	✓
BALLOCH CENTRAL	Dunbartonshire	LP	HF			
BALLOCH PIER early 9.5" high totem	Dunbartonshire		HF	1986		✓
BALMOSSIE HALT wooden only	Angus				✓	✓
BALQUHIDDER	Perthshire		HF	1965	✓	✓
BANAVIE	Inverness-shire		HF		✓	✓
BANCHORY	Kincardineshire		FF	1965	✓	✓
BARASSIE	Ayrshire		FF		✓	✓
BARNHILL	Lanarkshire		FF		✓	✓
BARRHEAD	Renfrewshire		HF		✓	✓
BARRHILL	Ayrshire					
BARRMILL	Ayrshire			1964		
BEARSDEN	Dunbartonshire		FF		✓	✓
BEATTOCK	Dumfriesshire		HF/FF	1972	✓	✓
BEITH TOWN	Ayrshire		HF	1962		
BELLGROVE	Lanarkshire		FF		✓	✓
BELLSHILL	Lanarkshire		FF		✓	✓
BENDERLOCH	Argyllshire		FF	1966	✓	✓
BISHOPBRIGGS	Lanarkshire					
BISHOPTON	Renfrewshire					
BLACKFORD HILL	Perthshire			1962		
BLAIR ATHOLL	Perthshire		HF		✓	✓
BLAIRHILL	Lanarkshire		FF		✓	✓
BLANTYRE	Lanarkshire		HF		✓	✓
BOAT OF GARTEN	Inverness		FF	1965	✓	✓
BOGSIDE	Fife			1967		
BOGSTON	Renfrewshire					
BONAR BRIDGE	Ross & Cromarty		FF		✓	✓
BONNYBRIDGE HIGH	Stirlingshire	LP	HF	1967	✓	✓
BONNYRIGG	Midlothian					

Place name	County	Layout	Flange	Closed	Auction	Survived
BORROBOL PLATFORM	Sutherland		HF	1965		✓
BOWLING	Dunbartonshire		FF		✓	✓
BRAIDWOOD	Lanarkshire			1962		
BREICH	Midlothian		FF		✓	✓
BRIDGE OF ALLAN	Stirlingshire		HF	1965	✓	✓
BRIDGE OF EARN	Perthshire		FF	1964	✓	✓
BRIDGE OF ORCHY	Argyllshire		HF			✓
BRIDGE OF WEIR	Renfrewshire		FF		✓	✓
BRIDGETON CENTRAL	Lanarkshire		FF		✓	✓
BRIDGETON CROSS	Lanarkshire			1964		
BRODIE	Morayshire			1965		
BROOMHILL	Inverness-shire		FF	1965	✓	✓
BROUGHTY FERRY	Angus		HF		✓	✓
BRUCKLAY	Aberdeenshire		HF	1965		✓
BUCKIE	Banffshire			1968		
BURNSIDE	Lanarkshire		FF			✓
BURNTISLAND	Fife		FF		✓	✓
BUSBY	Lanarkshire		FF		✓	✓
CALCOTS	Morayshire		HF	1968	✓	✓
CALDERPARK	Lanarkshire		HF		✓	✓
CALLANDER	Perthshire		FF	1965	✓	✓
CAMBUS	Clackmannanshire		FF	1968	✓	✓
CAMBUSLANG	Lanarkshire		**HF/FF**		✓	✓
CAMBUS O'MAY	Aberdeenshire		HF	1966		
CAMELON	Stirlingshire		FF	1967	✓	✓
CAMERON BRIDGE	Fife		FF	1969	✓	✓
CANONBIE	Dumfries-shire		FF	1964		✓
CARDENDEN	Fife		FF		✓	✓
CARDONALD	Lanarkshire		FF		✓	✓
CARDRONA	Peebles			1962		
CARDROSS	Dunbartonshire					
CARFIN	Lanarkshire		FF		✓	✓

Place name	County	Layout	Flange	Closed	Auction	Survived
CARLUKE	Lanarkshire		FF		✓	✓
CARMYLE	Lanarkshire		HF	1964	✓	✓
CARNOUSTIE	Angus		FF			✓
CARNTYNE	Lanarkshire		FF		✓	✓
CARNWATH	Lanarkshire		HF	1966	✓	✓
CARRON	Morayshire		FF	1965	✓	✓
CARSTAIRS	Lanarkshire		HF		✓	✓
CARTSDYKE	Renfrewshire					
CASTLECARY	Dunbartonshire		FF	1967	✓	✓
CASTLE DOUGLAS	Kirkcudbrightshire		FF	1965		✓
CASTLE KENNEDY to confirm	Wigtownshire			1965		
CATHCART	Lanarkshire		HF		✓	✓
CHARING CROSS	Lanarkshire		FF		✓	✓
CLARKSTON	Lanarkshire		FF	1956		✓
CLARKSTON & STAMPERLAND	Renfrewshire	2 line				
CLEGHORN	Lanarkshire		FF	1965	✓	✓
CLELAND	Lanarkshire		FF		✓	✓
CLOVENFORDS to confirm	Selkirk					
CLYDEBANK CENTRAL	Lanarkshire	LP	FF		✓	✓
CLYDEBANK RIVERSIDE	Lanarkshire	LP		1964		
COALBURN	Lanarkshire		HF	1965		✓
COATBRIDGE CENTRAL	Lanarkshire	LP				
COATBRIDGE SUNNYSIDE	Lanarkshire	LP	FF		✓	✓
COATDYKE	Lanarkshire		FF		✓	✓
COBBINSHAW	Midlothian		FF	1966		✓
CONNEL FERRY	Argyllshire		HF		✓	✓
CORKERHILL	Lanarkshire		HF		✓	✓
CORNHILL	Banffshire		HF	1968	✓	✓
CORPACH	Inverness-shire		HF			✓
CORROUR	Inverness-shire		FF			✓
CORSTORPHINE	Midlothian		FF	1968		✓
COUPAR ANGUS	Perthshire		FF	1967	✓	✓
COWDENBEATH	Fife		FF		✓	✓
COWLAIRS	Lanarkshire			1964		

Place name	County	Layout	Flange	Closed	Auction	Survived
CRAIGENDORAN	Dunbartonshire		FF		✓	✓
CRAIGLEITH	Midlothian			1962		
CRAIGLOCHART	Midlothian			1962		
CRAIL	Fife		FF	1965	✓	✓
CRATHES	Kincardineshire		FF	1966		✓
CRIANLARICH LOWER	Perthshire	LP	FF	1965		✓
CRIANLARICH UPPER	Perthshire	LP	FF		✓	✓
CROFTFOOT	Lanarkshire					
CROMDALE	Morayshire			1965		
CROOKSTON	Lanarkshire					
CROSSHILL	Lanarkshire		HF		✓	✓
CROSSMYLOOF	Lanarkshire		HF			
CROY	Dunbartonshire		HF		✓	✓
CULTER	Aberdeenshire		FF	1966	✓	✓
CULTS	Aberdeenshire		FF	1966	✓	✓
CUMBERLAND STREET	Lanarkshire		FF	1966	✓	✓
CUMBERNAULD	Dunbartonshire					
CUMNOCK	Ayrshire		HF	1965		✓
CUPAR	Fife		HF		✓	✓

Place name	County	Layout	Flange	Closed	Auction	Survived
DAILLY to confirm	Ayrshire			1965		
DALBEATTIE	Kirkcudbrightshire		FF	1965		✓
DALCROSS	Inverness			1965		
DALMALLY	Argyllshire		FF		✓	✓
DALMARNOCK	Lanarkshire		HF/FF	1964	✓	✓
DALMELLINGTON	Ayrshire		FF	1964		
DALMENY	West Lothian		HF		✓	✓
DALMUIR PARK	Dunbartonshire		FF		✓	✓
DALMUIR RIVERSIDE	Dunbartonshire	LP	FF	1964		✓
DALREOCH	Dunbartonshire		HF			✓
DALRY	Ayrshire		HF		✓	✓
DALRY ROAD	Midlothian			1962		
DESS	Aberdeenshire		FF	1966	✓	✓

Place name	County	Layout	Flange	Closed	Auction	Survived
DINGWALL	Ross &Cromarty		FF		✓	✓
DINNET	Aberdeenshire		FF	1966	✓	✓
DOUGLAS WEST	Lanarkshire			1964		
DOUNE	Perthshire		HF	1965	✓	✓
DREM	East Lothian		FF		✓	✓
DRUMCHAPEL	Lanarkshire					✓
DRUMPARK	Lanarkshire		FF	1964	✓	✓
DRUMRY	Dunbartonshire					
DRYBRIDGE	Ayrshire			1969		
DUDDINGSTON & CRAIGMILLAR	Midlothian	2 line	HF	1962		
DUKE STREET	Lanarkshire		FF		✓	✓
DULLATUR	Dunbartonshire		HF	1967	✓	✓
DUMBARTON CENTRAL	Dunbartonshire	LP	HF		✓	✓
DUMBARTON EAST	Dunbartonshire	LP	HF		✓	✓
DUMFRIES	Dumfries-shire		HF/FF		✓	✓
DUNBLANE	Perthshire		HF		✓	✓
DUNDEE TAY BRIDGE	Angus	LP	HF		✓	✓
DUNFERMLINE LOWER	Fife		HF		✓	✓
DUNFERMLINE UPPER	Fife		FF	1968	✓	✓
DUNLOP	Ayrshire		HF	1967		
DUNRAGIT	Wigtownshire		HF	1965		✓
DYCE	Aberdeenshire			1968		✓
DYSART	Fife		FF	1969		✓
EASTERHOUSE	Lanarkshire		FF		✓	✓
EAST FORTUNE	East Lothian		FF	1964		✓
EASTHAVEN	Angus			1967		
EAST KILBRIDE	Lanarkshire		FF			✓
EAST LINTON	East Lothian			1964		
EAST PILTON	Midlothian			1962		
EASTRIGGS to confirm	Dumfries-shire			1965		
ECCLEFECHAN	Dumfries-shire		HF	1960	✓	✓
EDDLESTON	Peebles-shire			1962		

Place name	County	Layout	Flange	Closed	Auction	Survived
EGLINTON STREET	Lanarkshire		HF	1965	✓	✓
ELDERSLIE	Renfrewshire		FF	1966		✓
ELGIN	Morayshire		FF			✓
ELIE	Fife		FF	1965	✓	✓
ELLON	Aberdeenshire		FF	1965	✓	✓
ESKBANK AND DALKEITH	Midlothian		FF	1969	✓	✓
EYEMOUTH	Berwickshire			1962		
FAIRLIE HIGH	Ayrshire	LP	HF		✓	✓
FALKIRK GRAHAMSTON	Stirlingshire	LP	FF		✓	✓
FALKIRK HIGH	Stirlingshire	LP	HF			✓
FAULDHOUSE NORTH	West Lothian	LP	HF		✓	✓
FLEMINGTON	Lanarkshire		FF	1965	✓	✓
FORFAR	Angus		FF	1967	✓	✓
FORRES	Morayshire		HF		✓	✓
FORT MATILDA	Renfrewshire					✓
FORT WILLIAM	Inverness-shire		HF		✓	✓
FOUNTAINHALL	Midlothian		FF	1969	✓	✓
FRASERBURGH	Aberdeenshire		FF	1965	✓	✓
GALASHIELS	Selkirk		HF	1969	✓	✓
GALSTON	Ayrshire		HF	1964		
GARELOCHEAD	Dunbartonshire		HF			✓
GARMOUTH	Morayshire		HF	1968	✓	✓
GARNKIRK	Lanarkshire			1960		
GARROWHILL	Lanarkshire		FF		✓	✓
GARSCADDEN	Lanarkshire					
GARTCOSH	Lanarkshire					
GARTLY	Aberdeenshire		FF	1968	✓	✓
GARVE	Ross & Cromarty		HF		✓	✓
GIFFNOCK	Renfrewshire		FF		✓	✓
GILNOCKIE	Dumfries-shire			1964		
GIRVAN also plastic	Ayrshire					✓

Place name	County	Layout	Flange	Closed	Auction	Survived
GLASGOW CROSS	Lanarkshire			1964		
GLASSEL	Aberdeenshire		FF	1966	✓	✓
GLENBARRY	Banffshire		HF	1968	✓	✓
GLENEAGLES	Perthshire		HF		✓	✓
GLENFARG	Perthshire		FF	1964	✓	✓
GLENFINNAN	Inverness-shire		HF		✓	✓
GLENGARNOCK	Ayrshire		FF		✓	✓
GLENLUCE	Wigtownshire			1965		
GOLF STREET HALT wooden only	Angus		Wood		✓	✓
GOLSPIE	Sutherland		FF		✓	✓
GOREBRIDGE	Midlothian		FF	1969	✓	✓
GORGIE EAST	Midlothian			1962		
GOUROCK	Renfrewshire		HF		✓	✓
GRANGE	Banffshire		HF	1968	✓	✓
GRANGEMOUTH	Stirlingshire		FF	1968		✓
GRANTON ROAD	Midlothian					
GRANTOWN-ON-SPEY EAST	Inverness-shire	LP	HF	1965		✓
GRANTOWN-ON-SPEY WEST	Morayshire	LP	FF	1965	✓	✓
GREENHILL	Stirlingshire		FF	1966	✓	✓
GREENOCK	Renfrewshire					✓
GREENOCK WEST	Renfrewshire					✓
GUARD BRIDGE	Fife		FF			✓
HAIRMYRES	Lanarkshire		FF			✓
HAMILTON CENTRAL	Lanarkshire		FF		✓	✓
HAMILTON WEST	Lanarkshire					
HAPPENDON	Lanarkshire		FF	1964		
HARBURN	Midlothian		FF	1966		✓
HARTWOOD	Lanarkshire		HF			✓
HAWICK	Roxburghshire		FF	1969	✓	✓
HAWKHEAD	Renfrewshire		HF	1966		✓
HAYMARKET	Midlothian		HF		✓	✓
HELENSBURGH CENTRAL	Dunbartonshire	LP				

Place name	County	Layout	Flange	Closed	Auction	Survived
HELENSBURGH UPPER	Dunbartonshire	LP	HF		✓	✓
HERIOT	Midlothian		FF	1969	✓	✓
HIGH STREET	Lanarkshire		FF		✓	✓
HILLFOOT	Dunbartonshire		FF		✓	✓
HILLINGTON EAST	Lanarkshire		FF		✓	✓
HILLINGTON WEST	Lanarkshire					
HOLLYBUSH	Ayrshire			1964		
HOLYTOWN	Lanarkshire		FF			✓
HOUSTON & CROSSLEE	Renfrewshire		HF			✓
HUNTLY	Aberdeenshire		HF		✓	✓
HYNDLAND	Lanarkshire					
IBROX	Lanarkshire		FF	1967		✓
INCHES	Lanarkshire			1964		
INNERLEITHEN	Peebles-shire		FF	1962		✓
INSCH	Aberdeenshire		FF		✓	✓
INVERESK	Midlothian		FF	1964		
INVERGORDON	Ross & Cromarty					
INVERGOWRIE	Perthshire					
INVERKEITHING	Fife		FF		✓	✓
INVERKIP	Renfrewshire		FF			✓
INVERURIE to confirm	Aberdeenshire					
IRVINE	Ayrshire		HF		✓	✓
JOHNSTONE HIGH	Renfrewshire		HF		✓	✓
JOPPA	Midlothian		FF	1964	✓	✓
JORDANHILL	Lanarkshire		HF			✓
KEITH JUNCTION	Banffshire		FF	1968	✓	✓
KEITH TOWN	Banffshire		HF			✓
KELSO	Roxburghshire		FF	1964	✓	✓
KELVIN HALL formerly Partick Cent.	Lanarkshire			1964		
KENNETHMONT	Aberdeenshire		FF	1968	✓	✓

Place name	County	Layout	Flange	Closed	Auction	Survived
KENNISHEAD	Lanarkshire		HF			
KENTALLEN	Argyllshire		FF	1966	✓	✓
KILBOWIE	Dunbartonshire		FF	1964		✓
KILCONQUHAR	Fife		FF	1965		✓
KILMACOLM	Renfrewshire		FF		✓	✓
KILMARNOCK	Ayrshire					
KILMAURS	Ayrshire					
KILPATRICK	Dunbartonshire		FF		✓	✓
KILWINNING	Ayrshire					
KINGHORN	Fife		FF		✓	✓
KINGSKNOWE	Midlothian		HF	1964	✓	✓
KINGS PARK	Lanarkshire		HF		✓	✓
KINGUSSIE	Inverness-shire		HF		✓	✓
KINLOSS	Morayshire		FF	1965	✓	✓
KINROSS JUNCTION	Kinross-shire	LP	FF	1970	✓	✓
KIRKCALDY	Fife		FF			✓
KIRKCONNEL	Dumfries-shire		HF		✓	✓
KIRKCUDBRIGHT	Kirkcudbrightshire		FF	1965		
KIRKHILL	Lanarkshire					
KIRKINTILLOCH	Dunbartonshire			1964		
KITTYBREWSTER	Aberdeenshire		FF	1968		✓
KNOCK	Banffshire		HF	1968	✓	✓
KNOCKANDO	Morayshire		FF	1965		✓
KYLE OF LOCHALSH	Ross & Cromarty		FF		✓	✓
LADYBANK	Fife		HF		✓	✓
LAIRG	Sutherland		FF		✓	✓
LANARK	Lanarkshire		FF		✓	✓
LANGBANK	Renfrewshire					
LANGHOLM	Dumfries-shire		FF	1964		✓
LANGLOAN	Lanarkshire			1964		
LANGSIDE	Lanarkshire		HF			✓
LARBERT	Stirlingshire		HF		✓	✓

Place name		County	Layout	Flange	Closed	Auction	Survived
LARGO		Fife		FF	1965	✓	✓
LARGS		Ayrshire					✓
LARKHALL CENTRAL		Lanarkshire		HF	1965	✓	✓
LAURENCEKIRK		Kincardineshire		HF	1967	✓	✓
LAW JUNCTION		Lanarkshire		HF	1965		✓
LEITH NORTH		Midlothian		FF	1962		
LENZIE		Lanarkshire		HF		✓	✓
LEUCHARS JUNCTION		Fife		HF			✓
LEVEN		Fife		FF	1965	✓	✓
LINLITHGOW		West Lothian		FF			✓
LOCH AWE	re-opened 1985	Argyllshire		FF	1965		✓
LOCHEILSIDE		Inverness-shire		HF		✓	✓
LOCHGELLY		Fife		FF		✓	✓
LOCHLUICHART		Ross & Cromarty		HF			✓
LOCKERBIE		Dumfries-shire		HF			✓
LOGIERIEVE		Aberdeenshire			1965		
LONGMORN		Morayshire		FF	1968	✓	✓
LONGNIDDRY		East Lothian		HF		✓	✓
LONMAY		Aberdeenshire		HF	1965	✓	✓
LOTH	to confirm	Sutherland			1960		
LUGTON		Ayrshire		HF	1966	✓	✓
LUIB		Perthshire		FF	1965	✓	✓
LUMPHANAN		Aberdeenshire		FF	1966	✓	✓
LUNDIN LINKS		Fife		FF	1965		✓
MALLAIG	to confirm	Inverness-shire					
MANUEL		Stirlingshire		FF	1967	✓	✓
MARKINCH		Fife		HF		✓	✓
MARYHILL CENTRAL		Lanarkshire	LP		1964		
MARYHILL PARK		Lanarkshire	LP	FF	1961	✓	✓
MAUCHLINE		Ayrshire			1965		
MAWCARSE		Kinross-shire		FF	1964	✓	✓
MAXTON		Roxburghshire		FF	1964	✓	✓

Place name	County	Layout	Flange	Closed	Auction	Survived
MAXWELL PARK	Lanarkshire					
MAYBOLE	Ayrshire					
MELROSE	Roxburghshire		HF	1969		✓
MERCHISTON	Midlothian			1965		
MIDCALDER	Midlothian		HF		✓	✓
MILNATHORT	Kinross-shire			1964		✓
MILNGAVIE	Dunbartonshire		FF			✓
MONIFEITH	Angus					
MONTROSE	Angus		FF		✓	✓
MORAR	Inverness-shire		HF			✓
MORNINGSIDE ROAD	Midlothian		FF	1962		
MOSSEND	Lanarkshire		FF	1962		✓
MOSSPARK WEST	Lanarkshire		HF		✓	✓
MOTHERWELL	Lanarkshire		HF		✓	✓
MOUNT FLORIDA	Lanarkshire		HF		✓	✓
MUIREND	Lanarkshire					
MUIRKIRK	Ayrshire		FF	1964	✓	✓
MURRAYFIELD	Midlothian			1962		
MUSSELBURGH	Midlothian		FF	1964		✓

Place name	County	Layout	Flange	Closed	Auction	Survived
NAIRN	Nairn-shire		FF		✓	✓
NEILSTON HIGH	Renfrewshire	LP	FF		✓	✓
NEILSTON LOW	Renfrewshire	LP	HF	1966		✓
NETHY BRIDGE	Inverness-shire		FF	1965		
NEW CUMNOCK	Ayrshire		HF		✓	✓
NEWHAVEN	Midlothian					
NEWINGTON	Midlothian		FF	1962		✓
NEW LUCE	Wigtownshire			1965		
NEWMACHAR	Aberdeenshire		HF	1965	✓	✓
NEWPARK	Midlothian		HF		✓	✓
NEWPORT-ON-TAY EAST	Fife		FF	1969	✓	✓
NEWPORT-ON-TAY WEST	Fife		FF	1969	✓	✓
NEWTON	Lanarkshire		FF		✓	✓

Place name	County	Layout	Flange	Closed	Auction	Survived
NEWTONMORE	Inverness-shire		HF		✓	✓
NEWTON-ON-AYR	Ayrshire		HF			✓
NEWTON STEWART	Wigtownshire		FF	1965		✓
NITSHILL	Lanarkshire		FF		✓	✓
NORTH BERWICK	East Lothian		FF		✓	✓
NORTH CONNEL	Argyllshire		HF	1966		✓
OAKLEY (FIFE)	Fife	LP	HF	1968		✓
OBAN	Argyllshire					✓
OLD KILPATRICK	Dunbartonshire		HF	1964		✓
PAISLEY ABERCORN	Renfrewshire	LP	HF	1967		
PAISLEY CANAL	Renfrewshire		FF		✓	✓
PAISLEY GILMOUR STREET	Renfrewshire	LP				
PAISLEY St. JAMES to confirm	Renfrewshire					
PAISLEY WEST to confirm	Renfrewshire			1966		
PARK	Aberdeenshire		FF	1966	✓	✓
PARKHEAD STADIUM	Lanarkshire	LP		1965		
PARTICK CENTRAL renamed 1959	Lanarkshire					
PARTICK HILL	Lanarkshire		FF			✓
PATNA	Ayrshire			1964		
PATTERTON	Renfrewshire		FF		✓	✓
PEEBLES	Peebles-shire		FF	1962	✓	✓
PERTH	Perthshire		HF			✓
PETERHEAD	Aberdeenshire		FF	1965	✓	✓
PIERSHILL	Midlothian		FF	1964	✓	✓
PINKHILL	Midlothian		FF	1968		✓
PINMORE	Ayrshire			1965		
PITLOCHRY	Perthshire		HF		✓	✓
PITTENWEEM	Fife		FF	1965		✓
POLLOKSHAWS EAST	Lanarkshire		HF			✓
POLLOKSHAWS WEST	Lanarkshire	LP				✓
POLLOKSHIELDS EAST	Lanarkshire	LP?				

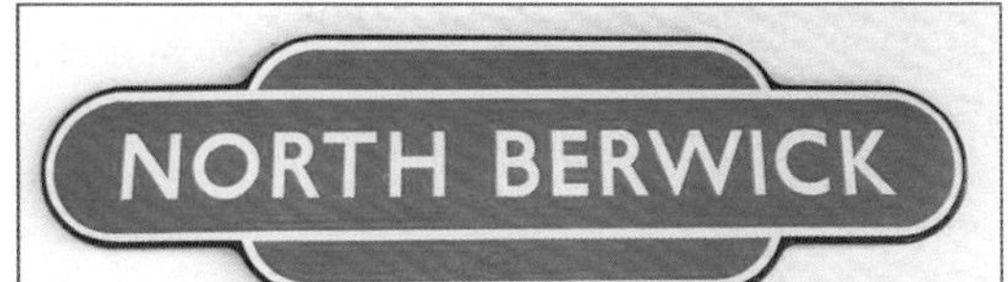

Place name	County	Layout	Flange	Closed	Auction	Survived
POLLOKSHIELDS WEST	Lanarkshire		HF		✓	✓
POLMONT	Stirlingshire		HF		✓	✓
PONFEIGH	Lanarkshire					✓
PORTESSIE	Banffshire			1968		
PORT GLASGOW	Renfrewshire		HF		✓	✓
PORTKNOCKIE	Banffshire		HF	1968	✓	✓
PORTOBELLO	Midlothian		FF	1964	✓	✓
PRESTONPANS	East Lothian		FF		✓	✓
PRESTWICK	Ayrshire		FF		✓	✓
'QUEENS' PARK	Lanarkshire		HF		✓	✓
QUEEN STREET (LL) *(4'totems only)	Lanarkshire		FF*			
RANNOCH	Perthshire		HF			✓
RATHEN	Aberdeenshire		HF	1965		✓
RENFREW FULBAR STREET	Renfrewshire		FF	1967	✓	✓
RENTON	Dunbartonshire		FF			✓
RESTON	Berwickshire			1964		
RHU	Dunbartonshire		HF	1964		
RIDDINGS JUNCTION	Cumberland		FF	1964		✓
ROSEWELL AND HAWTHORNDEN	Midlothian	2 line	FF	1962		✓
ROTHES	Morayshire		FF	1968	✓	✓
ROXBURGH	Roxburghshire		FF	1964		✓
ROY BRIDGE	Inverness-shire					
RUTHERGLEN	Lanarkshire		FF		✓	✓
ST. ANDREWS	Fife		FF	1969	✓	✓
ST. MONANCE	Fife		FF	1965		✓
SALTCOATS CENTRAL	Ayrshire	LP	HF		✓	✓
SANDILANDS	Lanarkshire			1964		
SANQUHAR	Dumfries-shire		HF	1965	✓	✓
SCOTSTOUN EAST	Lanarkshire		FF	1964	✓	✓
SCOTSTOUNHILL	Lanarkshire		FF		✓	✓

Place name	County	Layout	Flange	Closed	Auction	Survived
SCOTSTOUN WEST	Lanarkshire					
SHANDON	Dunbartonshire		HF	1964	✓	✓
SHAWLANDS	Lanarkshire					✓
SHETTLESTON	Lanarkshire					
SHIELDS ROAD	Lanarkshire		FF	1966	✓	✓
SHOTTS	Lanarkshire					
SINCLAIRTOWN	Fife		FF	1969	✓	✓
SINGER	Dunbartonshire		HF		✓	✓
SLATEFORD	Midlothian		HF		✓	✓
SOUTH BEACH	Ayrshire		FF			✓
SOUTH RENFREW	Renfrewshire			1967		
SPEAN BRIDGE	Inverness-shire		HF		✓	✓
SPEY BAY	Morayshire		HF	1968	✓	✓
SPRINGBURN	Lanarkshire		FF		✓	✓
SPRINGFIELD	Fife		HF			✓
STEVENSTON	Ayrshire					
STIRLING	Stirlingshire		HF		✓	✓
STONEHAVEN	Kincardineshire		FF		✓	✓
STOW	Midlothian		HF	1969	✓	✓
STRANRAER HARBOUR	Wigtownshire					
STRANRAER TOWN	Wigtownshire	LP		1966		
STRATHAVEN CENTRAL	Lanarkshire	LP		1965		
STRATHCARRON	Ross & Cromarty		HF			✓
STRATHYRE	Perthshire		HF	1965		✓
STRICHEN	Aberdeenshire		HF	1965	✓	✓
STROMEFERRY	Ross & Cromarty					
TAIN	Ross & Cromarty		FF		✓	✓
TAYNUILT	Argyllshire		FF		✓	✓
TAYPORT	Fife		FF	1966	✓	✓
THE MOUND	Sutherland		HF	1960	✓	✓
THORNHILL	Dumfries-shire		FF	1965		✓
THORNLIEBANK	Renfrewshire		FF			✓

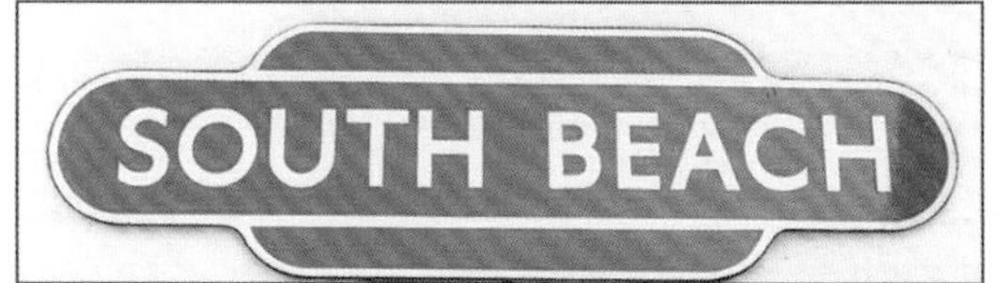

Place name	County	Layout	Flange	Closed	Auction	Survived
THORNTONHALL	Lanarkshire		FF			✓
THORNTON JUNCTION	Fife		HF	1969	✓	✓
THURSO	Caithness		FF			✓
TILLYNAUGHT	Banffshire		HF	1968	✓	✓
TOLLCROSS	Lanarkshire			1964		✓
TORPHINS	Aberdeenshire		FF	1966	✓	✓
TROON	Ayrshire		HF		✓	✓
TULLIBARDINE	Perthshire		FF	1964		✓
TULLOCH	Inverness-shire		HF		✓	✓
TYNDRUM UPPER	Perthshire		HF		✓	✓
TYNEHEAD	Midlothian		FF	1969	✓	✓
UDDINGSTON CENTRAL	Lanarkshire	LP	FF		✓	✓
UDDINGSTON WEST	Lanarkshire	?	HF?	1955		
UDNY	Aberdeenshire		HF	1965		✓
UPPER GREENOCK	Renfrewshire		FF	1967		✓
URQUHART	Morayshire		HF	1968		✓
WALKERBURN	Peebles-shire			1962		
WEMYSS BAY	Renfrewshire		HF		✓	✓
WEST CALDER	Midlothian		FF		✓	✓
WESTERTON	Dunbartonshire					
WEST KILBRIDE	Ayrshire		FF			✓
WHITEGRAIGS	Renfrewshire		FF		✓	✓
WHITEINCH RIVERSIDE	Lanarkshire		FF	1964	✓	✓
WICK	Caithness		FF		✓	✓
WILLIAMWOOD	Renfrewshire		HF		✓	✓
WISHAW CENTRAL	Lanarkshire					
WOODHALL	Renfrewshire		HF		✓	✓
WORMIT	Fife		FF	1969	✓	✓

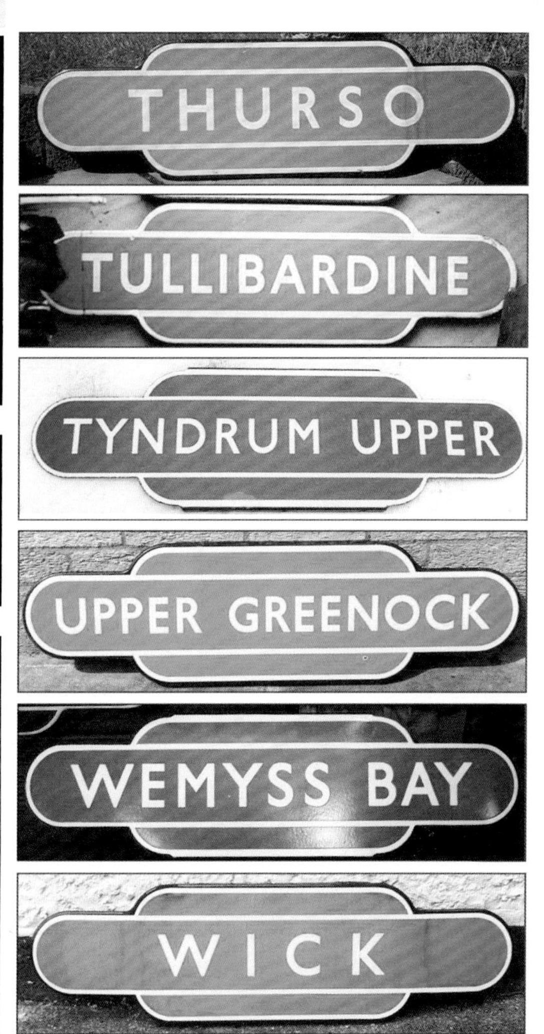

CHAPTER

12 British Railways' Changing Regions

by Alan Young and the Authors

Introduction

This chapter will help throw light on some of the anomalies encountered by the totem collector. Why should **Wolverhampton High** and **Low Levels** have different coloured signs? Why were MR totems installed at stations which only appeared in ER timetables, and SR, WR and ER totems installed at London Underground stations, not served by British Railways? Is it conceivable to find a Welsh, Eastern Region totem, or a Midland totem from the Essex coast? Here follows a history of how the pattern and operation of British Railways regions changed from Nationalisation until Privatisation.

First attempts at regionalisation

At birth on 1 January 1948 British Railways was divided into six Regions, see map (left). They were seen from the outset as subject to review, and the easy option was taken of making them correspond as far as possible to the 'Big Four' companies dating from 1923. Lines previously operated jointly by pre-grouping companies were allocated to single regions, so, for example, the Somerset & Dorset (SR/LMR Joint) joined the SR. Bath, later called **Bath Green Park**, was left as the southern outpost of the LMR, but curiously was bedecked in 'chocolate and cream'. The Midland & Great Northern (LMS/LNER Joint) joined the ER. The Cheshire Lines Committee system remained independent of regional control until November 1948 when it was replaced within the LMR.

A generation of railway enthusiasts had grown up with intense loyalties to the 'Big Four', but the younger generation of the time would form attachments to the new and more colourful regions.

BR's first regional changes

Regional boundaries were re-drawn on 2 April 1950 to remove anomalies such as the intrusion of one region's line into the territory of another region – so-called 'penetrating lines'. Even before 1950 a few adjustments had been made. The **Carlisle** to **Silloth** branch, by dint of being LNER, had been allocated to the NER, even though separated by Carlisle (LMR). By mid-1948 it was in the LMR. Lines in which the LMS had an interest in central and South Wales (including **Merthyr** to **Abergavenny** and **Newport** to Nantybwch) were transferred to the WR in 1948–9, in whose timetable they were awkwardly added as Tables 120a and 120b. The LMR's London, Tilbury & Southend system was handed over to the ER in February 1949. The most remarkable anomaly of the 1948 regions was that the old Great Central lines between Wrexham Central, **Chester** and **Bidston**, as well as **St Helens Central** and Wigan Central to **Glazebrook**, had been allocated to the ER! They were detached from each other and from the rest of the region. So, for a short time, **Gwersllyt**, **Caergwrle** and **Cefn-y-Bedd** were in the Eastern Region: if only they had been given totems! In the redistribution (late 1949) Gwersyllt station was allocated to the WR, and the remainder to the LMR.

The regions defined in the 1950 re-drawing apply to our 'benchmark' year, 1958. The major change made in 1950 was to transfer all SR lines west of Exeter to the WR. The LMR took over the former LNER Great Central main line from the ER between Buckinghamshire and Derbyshire, a prime example of a penetrating line, while London Marylebone to South Ruislip was given by the ER to the WR. The LMR's **Oxford** to **Cambridge** line, which had penetrated into both WR and ER territory, was divided between the three regions. The ER lost its suburban lines east of Manchester to the LMR, while the LMR and ER handed over their lines in the Leeds/Bradford area to the NER. The NER gave the lines west of Barras to **Tebay** and **Penrith** to the LMR in a tit-for-tat swop.

Four hundred years after their defeat by the English at the battle of Solway Moss near Longtown (1542), the Scots gained revenge by annexing the Cumbrian section of the Waverley route, and requisitioning Harker, **Longtown**, **Riddings Junction**, Penton and Kershopefoot stations for the Scottish Region. (This arrangement enabled the Riddings to **Langholm** branch to be attached to the ScR.) The territorial claim brought ScR totems into England at Riddings Junction, but Longtown station returned by stealth to English hands in 1959, and the LMR duly installed totems there – the classic example of 'changing regions'.

In the 1950 regional adjustments the historic division between GWR and LMS lines in the Birmingham/Wolverhampton area was retained, so the WR and LMR continued to cross and re-cross each other. This explains why towns such as **Wolverhampton**, **Wednesbury**, **Dudley** and **Birmingham** had stations in different regions (as in the unique quartet alongside). South of **Selly Oak**, the LMR **Bristol** and **Bath** lines were handed over to the WR. This change brought Bournville into the WR for eight years; regrettably it did not receive chocolate-and-cream totems! It was left to the LMR to install less appropriate maroon signs when it resumed control in 1958!

Some totem enthusiasts might possess British Railways Regional passenger timetable books, and their associated maps, from the 1950s. It seems reasonable to assume that these publications indicate which Region each station was in, and therefore the colour of totems they would have received, but life was not so simple! Only the NER and ScR maps in 1955 showed regional boundaries with any accuracy. Moreover, because of a curious decision in 1950, many train services continued to be provided by the pre-1950 Region, even though new regional boundaries had been drawn up for line and station management purposes. Thus the SR timetable continued to include the lines west of Exeter through the 1950s, even though they had been dispossessed.

The ER continued to operate trains on the former Great Central main line between London Marylebone and **Manchester Central**, and some Manchester suburban lines, until 1959. These lines' services were therefore in the ER timetable, and all were shown as 'their' lines on the regional map. Conversely, the LMR, who owned these lines, disowned them in their timetable and maps. The ER passenger timetable also failed to acknowledge its ownership of lines to Willington (Beds), Ketton & Collyweston (Rutland), and Thorpe (Northants) until 1959. Their neighbours, the Huntingdon (East) to Raunds (Northants) and Bourne (Lincs) to Edmondthorpe & Wymondham (Leics) lines, also ER from 1950, both closed in 1959, so probably never appeared in the ER timetables. Perhaps the division of interests in these lines explains the scarcity of stations with totems in this area – only **Stamford Town** and **Sandy** received them.

This hypothesis collapses, however, when the **Lincoln St Marks** to **Newark Castle** to **Nottingham** line is considered: ER-owned but LMR-operated from 1950 onwards, almost all its stations received ER totems fixed incongruously to LMS lamp standards!

It is rare for signs to survive with the previous owning region's colour on, but we have been very fortunate to have been supplied with a photo of a **Harpenden East** direction sign in ER Dark Blue, which was very short lived and became MR from 2 April 1950.

There were odd arrangements found where BR and London Transport had joint interests. **East Putney** totems hung at a station on the **Wimbledon** to Putney Bridge line owned by the SR, yet served only by District Line trains. Also on the District Line, stations from **Bromley** to **Upminster** were owned and signed by the ER, yet the main user was the Underground. Only Metropolitan Line trains used **Royal Oak** (near **Paddington**), owned by the WR and bearing totems.

Change for the sake of change?

A further modification of regional boundaries took place on 1 February 1958. This principally affected the WR and SR interface, restoring the old Southern Railway lines west of Exeter back to the SR (though not Plymouth Friary). During its eight-year tenure the WR had made little impression on the SR stations, totems appearing only at **Instow** and **Mortehoe & Woolacombe**.

On regaining its lost territory the SR scent-marked it sparingly, so totems were installed for example at some of their Exeter to Plymouth line stations such as **Bere Alston** and **Okehampton**, also at **Callington**, **Bude**, **Wadebridge**, **Bodmin North** and a few others. Targets were left in place at certain stations. A few other minor changes were effected: South Ruislip to London Marylebone changed hands again, this time from WR to LMR. **Luffenham** (Rutland) passed from ER to LMR, Dunford Bridge from LMR to ER, and Blaenau Ffestiniog North as well as stations north of **Blackwell** and Alvechurch (including **Bournville**!) returned to the LMR fold.

The last major regional revision took place on 1 January 1963. By this time totem installation was nearing its close, and BR was in image-modernising mode. The preface to the WR passenger timetable of June 1963 drew readers' attention to the new 'dragon red' cover, replacing the traditional chocolate-and-cream, and announced significant changes in regional layout. A large area in the north of the WR was transferred to the LMR. Stations forming the northern WR boundary would now be Aynho Park Platform, Aynho for Deddington, Milcote Halt, Broom Jn, **Blackwell**, and **Craven Arms & Stokesay**. Thus all lines in the Birmingham/Wolverhampton area and from **Aberystwyth** northwards were now LMR territory.

The WR, in compensation, took over the SR lines west of **Exeter** again, plus the **Exeter** to **Salisbury** main line as far as Dinton and its branches to **Exmouth**, Sidmouth, **Seaton**, Lyme Regis and Chard. Also transferred were the Somerset & Dorset as far as **Shillingstone**, the **Castle Cary** to **Weymouth** line as far as Bradford Peverell & Stratton Halt, and the Bridport branch. Just as GWR enthusiasts found the loss to the LMR of the Cambrian lines and the **Wrexham** to **Dolgellau** route unpalatable, lovers of the Southern regretted the loss of the whole Atlantic Coast Express route west of **Salisbury**, and traditional Southern locations such as **Yeovil** and **Exmouth**, to the GWR's successor. The 1963 reshuffle left a confusing legacy of misplaced totems. WR totems now abounded in the LMR, and SR ones in the WR. Well into the 1970s the 'rogue' totems remained, supplemented by a few 'targets' which somehow survived in WR territory at Exmouth, Exeter Central, Topsham and Crediton.

In 1965 British Railways re-branded itself with the Corporate Identity Programme. As British Rail it ditched the totem and did its best to destroy all evidence of any regional identity. Further adjustments to regional boundaries had no real effect on totems, not even on the zeal with which they were removed. On 3 January 1966, for reasons of improved freight management, the ER/LMR boundary was moved eastwards on the **Nottingham** to **Lincoln** and **Grantham** lines, making **Newark Castle** and Aslockton the ER frontier posts. The absorption of the NER by the ER took place on 2 January 1967. A minor boundary revision occurred in 1974 when the LMR took over all operations south of **Bicester** and **Aylesbury** to London Marylebone; their prize was a fine batch of WR totems at such stations as **Princes Risborough**, **Little Kimble**, **West Ruislip** and **Denham Golf Club**!

By 1990 further tinkering with the boundaries had handed these LMR gains back to the WR, together with the lines from Aylesbury to Amersham (exclusive) and to **Princes Risborough**. The WR had also acquired **Dilton Marsh Halt** and **Warminster** from the SR, but lost Gillingham and **Templecombe** in Dorset, and **Kensington Olympia** to the SR – truly changes for changes sake.

(Tim Clarke) A rare SR totem located just south of Westbury. (Dawlish Museum)

The Regions had already ceased to mean much to most travellers by the early 1980s, except perhaps in Scotland where Scot Rail and Strathclyde signs appeared on lamps. The branding of Network South East with its new livery brought slightly more interesting nameboards to almost half of Britain's stations, but destroyed any vestige of the old regional identity. Network North West, Greater Manchester and West Yorkshire Metro, and Regional Railways liveries were soon to follow. When the regions finally disappeared, who noticed?

CHAPTER 13

De-Totemisation

by Alan Young and the Authors

Opening thoughts

The programme of providing totems for stations was somewhat disorganised, and the process of removing them was equally haphazard. Almost as soon as the installation of totems started at some stations, they were being removed from others! When asked by David and Richard to provide the larger photographs for this book I (AY) took it as a privilege to participate. The picture of **Whittlesea** in the centre of the Eastern Region collage was taken during a weekend 'bash' in the East Midlands in July 1974. On the day of my visit the new electric lamp standards were in place and a week later I returned to see modernisation well underway. This picture was therefore obtained in the nick of time! Two years earlier, in March 1972, I turned up at **South Shields** a few days too late and only buildings and a few totems remained. This made me determined to take as many photos of BR stations as I could before they were 'improved'. I am happy the authors feel such materials worthy of inclusion in this comprehensive new work.

The early years

Totems were the new image of 1948, but even by the mid-'50s (as mentioned in an earlier chapter), an alternative system of signing stations (inscribing the name on fluorescent lamp diffusers) was already being adopted for stations between London Liverpool Street through Shenfield, and on to **Southend-on-Sea Victoria**. The practice was widely adopted on the Eastern Region by the early 1960s, involving the lines from Liverpool Street to Chingford and Enfield Town, **Colchester** to **Clacton** and **Walton-on-Naze**, and **Wood Green** (exclusive) to **Hertford North** stations. On the NE Region's Newcastle Coast circle route, fluorescent lamps displaced gas lamps and totems at **Benton** before totems appeared at neighbouring **Backworth**. Re-lighting of stations continued to be a legitimate excuse for removing totems through the 1970s. In this way the Newcastle Division all but eliminated totems between 1971 and 1973, though a few specimens which were fixed to buildings (as at **Howdon-on-Tyne**) survived until about 1979, and **Percy Main's** were salvaged and displayed on the new lamps until the station closed for Metro works in 1980.

A few 'lame duck' stations that would close in the early 1950s received totems. They were **Golborne North**, **Rickmansworth Church Street**, **St Helen's Central** and **Towcester**, which all closed in 1952. The following year **Aylesbury High Street** and **Stanmore Village** were dealt a similar blow. However, from the early 1960s (and particularly from 1964, when the Beeching cuts began to bite) numerous totem-bearing stations were closed. For example, on the **Leicester** to **Burton-on-Trent** line all seven intermediate stations that had carried totems, including the delightfully named **Ashby-de-la-Zouch**, **Moira**, and **Kirby Muxloe**, were closed in September 1964.

March 1973. (Alan Young)

The modernisation quickens

Following the introduction in 1965 of British Railways' corporate identity black and white signs, this policy was responsible for the sweeping away of all the Southern green livery on the London Victoria to **Brighton** line in 1968. However, for some years, the observant traveller could glimpse totems at **Coulsdon North** on a parallel line. The London **Waterloo** to Southampton line was similarly treated, though **Queen's Road Battersea** (visible also from the Brighton line) clung to its totems until 1979.

Elsewhere in Britain whole line de-totemisation was rare in the early 1970s, **Chester** to **Holyhead**, and **Birmingham New Street** to **Lichfield City** (exclusive) stations being the notable exceptions. Stations on these two routes were stripped of totems by 1974, but LMR nameboards and ancillary signs remained for some time after. Some Glasgow stations, such as **Scotstounhill**, **Easterhouse** and **Clydebank Central** also underwent this half-hearted modernisation, losing totems by 1972. In a tour of almost all of the BR system in 1972–4, the healthiest survival of totems was found in Scotland, and also between Manchester and Liverpool where the **Bolton** to **Wigan** Wallgate and **Kirkby** line had a splendid set of gas-lit stations with totems in 1974.

By the following year totems were becoming a rarity in some parts of the network. The Cumbrian line had numerous totem-bearing stations in 1973, but had been 'purged' the following year. London Liverpool Street to **King's Lynn** and London **Paddington** to **Bristol** lines had few totems left by 1974. Stations in the South Wales valleys, many of them having suffered vandalism after de-staffing, were 'simplified', and totems in place in 1973 at **Treherbert**, **Porth**, **Ystrad Mynach** and **Taffs Well** soon gave way to corporate identity signs.

Hairmyres, Lanarkshire, August 1974. (Alan Young)

In East Anglia many totems could still be admired in 1974. East London had them at **Stratford**, **Lea Bridge**, **Silvertown**, **Forest Gate**, **Woodgrange Park** and several stations on the **Bromley** to **Upminster** section until 1977. There were many survivors on the London Marylebone to **Princes Risborough** line, with its curious mixture of LMR and WR totems (not forgetting the unusual black and white ones) remaining until 1975. Cambrian line stations between **Shrewsbury**, **Pwllheli** and **Aberystwyth** retained their WR totems until at least 1975.

Since 1972 the railway network has more or less stabilised, with few line and station closures. However, uncertainty about the future of some lines may have delayed the removal of totems; the **Bedford St Johns** to **Bletchley** and Ashford to **Hastings** lines were cases in point, the former having a fine crop of totems as late as 1977. The next year pockets of resistance in the west of England had largely yielded to corporate identity, and former NE Region totems were scarce. The earlier zeal of the Southern Region to modernise had abated, and at least fifty stations retained totems. In Scotland, with the exception of some Glasgow suburban stations and the **Carlisle** to **Carstairs** to Glasgow main line, there was little loss of totems. The West Highland stations (Glasgow to Mallaig) succumbed in 1979 followed by the Inverness to **Kyle of Lochalsh** and Inverness to **Wick** lines, where by 1982 black and white signs had been installed.

During 1979–80 many Southern Region stations that appeared to have been overlooked were finally modernised. Isolated examples such as **Kenley**, **Beddington Lane Halt** and **Elmstead Woods** lost their totems, together with the sequence of stations at **South Merton**, **Morden South**, **St Helier**, **Sutton Common** and **West Sutton**. Even **Coulsdon North**, **Coombe Road** and **Bingham Road** on the **Elmers End** to **Sanderstead line**, threatened with closure that eventually took place in 1983, had their totems prematurely removed. In 1979 a few WR totems clung on at **Droitwich Spa**, **Lostwithiel**, and **Cradley Heath & Cradley** (some in very poor condition). The over-painting below is courtesy of BR and the shaping courtesy of a local vandal!

Not a pretty sight! July 1979. (Alan Young)

Totem collecting was reaching almost manic proportions by 1980, and the grotesque but useful verb to 'de-totemise' began to gain currency. With the dwindling number of survivals *in situ*, covetous eyes were focused on what remained. Less scrupulous collectors went to some lengths to help themselves to choice specimens. The last NER signs at **Ilkley**, **Driffield** and **Percy Main** had gone; on the LMR **Harpenden Central** and **Hendon** totems disappeared; and on the SR only **Abbey Wood**, **Coulsdon North**, **Tunbridge Wells West**, **Polegate**, **Stone Crossing Halt** and **Swanscombe Halt** retained them. (The suffix 'Halt' had disappeared from the SR timetable in 1969, so the survival for over ten years of totems bearing the forbidden word was remarkable!)

The East Suffolk line was one of the last ER outposts; **Saxmundham** and **Halesworth** totems were removed by 1981, leaving survivors only at **Brampton** and **Woodbridge**. The Norwich to Lowestoft route still had totems at **Haddiscoe** and **Oulton Broad North**. As late as 1982 a **Reedham** (Norfolk) to **Lowestoft** to **Westerfield** journey included only one station with corporate identity signing, and that was on the newly built **Saxmundham** down platform. **Goxhill**, between Barton-on-Humber and **Habrough**, also retained totems, and was to be the last survivor on the ER – and, it is believed, on the whole BR system. Scotland proved to be the last rich hunting ground for totems: in July 1984 **Neilston High**, **Newton-on-Ayr**, **Troon** and **Whitecraigs** each had at least ten, while one or more could be seen at **Bearsden**, **Broughty Ferry**, **Carnoustie**, **Cowdenbeath**, **Dalry**, **Kilmarnock**, **King's Park**, **Lochgelly**, **Markinch** and **Thorntonhall**. They were also at **Balmossie Halt** and **Golf Street Halt**, where the unusual wooden totems, clumsily repainted in black on cream, remained. The formation of ScotRail saw the final demise of totems by 1986.

Authentic totems may have disappeared from British stations, but it is a delight to see some new ones added on preserved lines and on the national network. The Severn Valley has 'new' Bridgnorth totems even though they are a strange shape.

Severn Valley Railway, April 2001. (Author's collection)

The Keighley & Worth Valley Railway installed some LMR-coloured specimens at Keighley (where totems were not a feature in BR days). Also **Settle** and **Dent** stations on the Settle & Carlisle have had LMR totems fitted, while in the far north of Scotland specimens in authentic ScR colours may be seen now at Scotscalder, and at the disused Watten, reading 'Station House'. The totem logo has also been widely used on railway related signs, for example on the board beside the A59 directing visitors to the reopened Bolton Abbey station.

The removal of totem signs

I (AY) was fortunate to be at several stations in various parts of England when station modernisation was taking place. One of the most interesting was **Hanwell** in Middlesex. The set of photos below was taken between 1975 and 1992.

Hanwell, 1975. (All pictures by Alan Young) Hanwell, 1992.

This station is on the main line from **Paddington** to **Reading**, which was a thrilling trainspotting place in steam days. The two right-hand shots taken 17 years later show that the rebuilding in this case was actually done tastefully, thanks to the involvement of a local pressure group of residents. Contrast the running-in boards, though, in the upper two shots: the red and white sign of 1992 seems strangely out of place in GWR territory!

Sandy (on the ECML) fared less well and as part of the main line upgrade a wholesale change of image was made, including more efficient lighting and no dark blue enamel! This town's station had separate Great Northern (ECML) and LNW (**Bedford** to **Cambridge** line) platforms that opened in 1850 and 1858 respectively. (They are shown as separate stations on OS maps, but were really combined.) The photos of lamps and totems that follow were on the GNR line. The grime- and soot-covered brickwork of the station is superbly captured in the first of three shots. (Compare this first photograph with that shown on page 13, where the fluorescent tube is in place.)

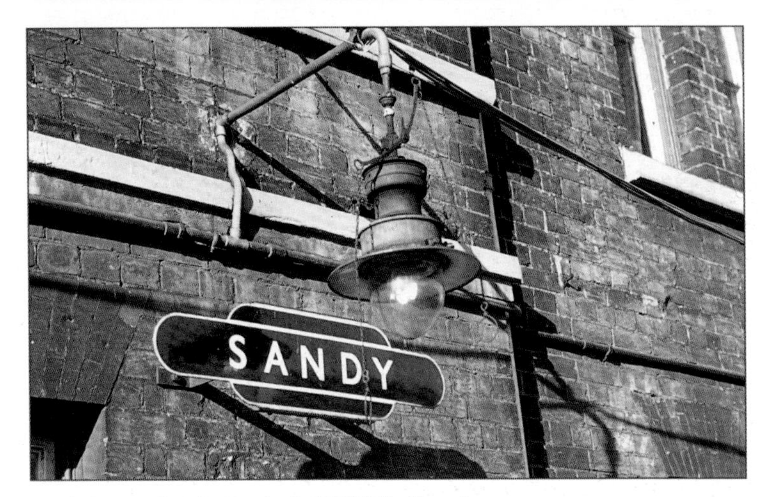

At the start of modernisation in 1977! (Alan Young)

Modernisation underway: note the HST poster.

A classic shot. (Alan Young)

Further south on the ECML is **New Southgate**. This station only officially carried the 'totem name' from 1971 onwards. Before that it was known as New Southgate and Colney Hatch (1876–83), New Southgate for Colney Hatch (1883–1923), and finally New Southgate and Friern Barnet (1923–71). The left-hand photo that follows below shows the south bridge and RIB with the full station name in the 'totem era'. Alongside below is a picture of the station looking north with modernisation underway. Sadly, the bridges at each end of the station were removed during the rebuilding.

Looking south, December 1975.

Looking north, December 1975. (Alan Young)

Notice in the right-hand shot all the new concrete posts on the right-hand platform and holes beginning to appear in the platforms to take the new lighting. One of us (RF) recently paid a visit to **New Southgate** station and it has to be said that the 'rebuilding' of this station is poor compared to the Hanwell 'restoration' seen earlier in this chapter. In the photo below we just love the old LNER-style globe lamp, and the contrast of the deep blue of the totem sign against the two-tone brickwork of the 1880s.

Totem and lamp about to be removed. (Alan Young)

Now north to the modernisation of the WCML. The wonderfully evocative photograph that follows of **Leyland** station was taken in the mid-'70s. We feel this is one of the best shots in the whole work and captures the very essence of this book in a nutshell.

Leyland, Lancashire, April 1974. (Alan Young)

Leyland station, September 2001. (Author's collection)

The new grey lamp standard is poised for installation, as the totems are ready to fall. On the far platform the modernisation is proceeding rapidly, with no LMR maroon totems, just black and white signs and grey lamp standards. What a contrast to the platform from where this shot was taken. It seems odd that a few days later the totems would be gone. Even with the modern overhead power lines, the totems seem perfectly in keeping with the buildings and those wonderful old passenger benches.

I (RF) returned to **Leyland** in September 2001 and an even greater transformation had taken place since Alan's evocative 1974 picture. The lovely old buildings have almost all gone, replaced by a concrete wall and bus shelter-type structure on the central platform. The building by the bridge is still intact (this is the booking office), but the bridge itself has been refurbished since 1974. The whole scene today is much more stark and functional, with the passenger benches resembling those found in bus stations. It is fitting, however, that the benches have been painted red, almost in homage to the lovely red totems taken down nearly thirty years ago. But almost nothing of the old charm of the station is left today. The same can be said of many WCML stations.

The present day station was originally opened by the Northern Union (joint LNWR/L&YR) as Golden Hill (which also would have made a lovely totem name) in October 1838, but within a few weeks it was renamed Leyland. (The North Staffs Railway opened another Goldenhill in 1874, and this too was renamed – as Newchapel and Goldenhill in 1913.)

The final place to look at briefly is **Goxhill**. Quite why **Goxhill** should have been the last station reputed to have totems in place is a mystery, but was probably just chance. This quiet corner of north Lincolnshire, north west of Grimsby, was rarely visited by any of the railway senior decision-makers, so perhaps they simply forgot! The two shots that follow were taken by Alan Young in the summer of 1984, and we have evidence that these totems finally came down in the autumn of 1988.

A full four years before removal, July 1984. (Alan Young)

It took twenty years to put all the totems up and about the same amount of time to take them down – all in the 1949–88 timeframe. The era of the totem may be short in railway terms, but to us it was *the* time. We close this work with a few images of totems *in situ* towards the end of their lives. The last photograph on the withdrawal of train services sums up everything very nicely!

We hope the readers find our work rewarding and useful in defining and refining your collections. We have pored over loads of books and maps, had magnifying glasses over old black and white photos, and made our computers work damned hard moving all these digital images around to fit the pages! There were well over 1,800 images for us to work from, and we trust the 1,380+ we have selected meet with readers' approval. It has been hard work but real fun, and our hope is that this book brings as much new information forward as the original paperback did in the ten years since its publication. Good totem hunting, everybody!

Above: (R. Blencowe)
Left: A classic totem (or two in this case). (Alan Young)

Opposite, top left: (Alan Young)
Opposite, top right: (Alan Young)
Opposite, bottom: (Tim Clarke)

Appendix

Totems in the USA

with input from Michael Brooks and David Wood

We mentioned at the start of the book that many totems and their owners are to be found outside British shores. Over the years many totems that found their way to the USA could be seen in a variety of locations. David Wood, a current US resident, visited two restaurants in the Boston area in 1995. These were part of a large chain that has had a chequered history over the past twenty years. The chain is called Victoria Station, and the New England restaurants were a spin-off from a very large chain that went bankrupt in the early 1980s. During the visit the following totems were to be found on public display:

Burlington MA	Salem MA
MR Kentish Town	**MR Poynton**
MR West Hampstead Midland	**MR Old Roan**
MR Attenborough	**MR West Allerton**
MR Layton	**MR Leyland**
MR Allerton	**MR Apsley**
MR Leagrave	**MR Maghull**
MR Rochdale	**SR Vauxhall**
MR Adlington	**SR Grove Park**
MR Moreton	**SR Shortands**
SR Cobham & Stoke D'Abernon	
SR West Croydon	
SR Lewisham	

(Data from David Wood, June 1995)

Both photographs taken at Salem MA, April 1995. (David Wood)

However, further research led us to an even greater uncovering of treasures. The Victoria Station chain also had restaurants in other parts of the USA, in Canada and in Japan. They had 'raided' CC very extensively in the early '70s, and many hundreds of totems ended up leaving these shores. Mike Brooks has been particularly helpful in piecing together an important part of totem collecting with respect to the USA operations. Mike actually saw containers filled with totems from Collectors Corner arriving in California for use in their restaurants. Most were LMR, but there were additions from the other regions and his information fits well with the New England data. Later in this appendix we have included a listing of the totems in just 8 of the 100 restaurants they had in the USA. Almost certainly the **Hough Green** that was found in Sydney had come from this chain. The 'Aussie' owner informed me (RF) that the totem had been seen in an antique shop in Los Angeles and was taken to Australia. By the time it eventually returned to Britain this had become the world's most travelled totem – unless somebody knows differently. It now resides in a collection close to its original home – a fitting end to the wandering totem!

On its way back from Australia to the UK, June 1995. (Author's collection)

By 1981 the chain was in financial difficulty and Mike tried to repatriate some of the gems languishing over on the US West Coast. Items he helped to bring back included six **Henley-on-Thames** and a whole host of LMR totems, mainly from Manchester and Liverpool. He estimates less than 10 per cent of those items shipped to the USA eventually returned. Nothing came back from the Japanese chain, so we conservatively estimate about 700 items may have been lost when this chain went bankrupt. On the following page is an official photo from the Victoria Station Restaurant at Universal Studios in California.

Victoria Station restaurant, Universal Studios, CA. (Mike Brooks collection)

Much of the information for this appendix has been pieced together by Michael Brooks. From his private library he kindly supplied the following, so that readers may appreciate just how many totems were moved abroad during the '70s. At that time he was working for a major transatlantic airline and spent some time each month in the USA. Being knowledgeable on railwayana, he acted as an advisor for Victoria Station purchases.

At its 1980 peak Victoria Station had around 100 restaurants in the USA. If each of these had seven totems, you are looking at a significant proportion of the total that passed through Collectors Corner ending up stateside. The lists below relate just to a few restaurants in and around Los Angeles California. Note how many of each there were in some cases, and note the geographic spread of the items. There are no dark blue, tangerine or light blue totems, so collectors from these regions can breath a sigh of relief!

Torrance (July 1972) *23805 Hawthorne Blvd, CA*

Blundellsands & Crosby
Broad Green
Castleton
Dane Road
Hall Road
Henley-on-Thames (poor)
Hightown
Kettering
Luton Midland Road
Manchester Victoria (poor)
Oxford Road
Prestatyn (poor)
Roby
Streatham (excellent)
Vauxhall (excellent)

Woodland Hills (March 1974 *20621 Ventura Blvd, CA*

Bangor
Blythe Bridge
Capenhurst (excellent)
Dane Road
Grove Park (excellent)
Kettering
Lewisham (excellent)
Manchester Victoria
Oxford Road (excellent)
Prestatyn
Roby
Rose Grove
Streatham Hill
Three Bridges (excellent)
Vauxhall (excellent)
West Norwood (excellent)
Wilmslow

Newport Beach (June 1974) *990 Dove Street, CA*

Bangor
Bootle Oriel Road
Broad Green
Castleton
Dane Road
Hall Road
Hightown
Hillside
Kettering
Luton Midland Road
Prestatyn
Roby
Rose Grove
Streatham
Wilmslow
Witton

West Covia (date not recorded) *3145 East Garney Ave, CA*

Bognor Regis (original brackets)
Flitwick
Garswood
Hellifield (original brackets)
Hoylank
Peckham Rye (excellent)
Tamworth
Tunbridge Wells Central
West Croydon (excellent)

Northridge (date not recorded) *19325 Londelius, CA*

Apsley
Bramhall
Bromborough
Grove Park
Hellifield
Peckham Rye (excellent)
Salisbury (excellent)
Vauxhall
Willesden Junction

Sunnyvale (date not recorded) *3850 Lankershim Blvd, CA*

Bradley Ford (screws through front face)
Prestatyn (poor)

Laguna Hills (date not recorded) *24231 Avenida de la Carlotta, CA*

Acton Bridge
Blackburn
Chorley
Eastbourne
Hellifield
Penrith
Squires Gate
Shortlands
Vauxhall

Sepulveda (August 1972) *20015 Sepulveda Blvd, CA*

Blundellsands & Crosby
Bognor Regis
Bradley Ford
Hillside
Luton Midland Road
Oxford Road
Prestatyn
Radcliffe Black Lane
Warrington

Unversal Studios (date not recorded) *Hollywood Frwy, Universal City, CA*

Albany Park
Grove Park
Meols
Pluckley
Styal
Vauxhall (excellent)

In early 1981, when the food chain went belly-up (we could not resist that one!), Michael removed some totems he thought valuable and took them to a warehouse in Wood Island where a container was being loaded with railwayana for return to the UK. (This apparently included some 30 locomotive nameplates.) The Flying Tigers Airlines supplied the container free of charge, and items from the USA and Canada were sent to California. He personally helped load some items, and below is part of his original documentation of a list of the totems that returned, and the order in which they were unloaded on arrival.

The spelling of Kentish Towan, Hyde Centre, Harlington (with a 'B') and Orell Park amused us, but in this list are a few quite rare items. We could name **Holmes Chapel**, **Salford**, **Manchester Victoria** and **Shaw & Crompton** among these.

WEST ALLERTON	FLITWICK	ALLERTON
MAULDETH ROAD	SHORTLANDS	MOSSLEY
HYDE CENTRE	BEESTON	GODLEY JUNCTION
UTTOXETER	DRIGG	HABLINGTON
WALLESEY VILLAGE	HOLMES CHAPEL	MANCHESTER VICTORIA
OXFORD ROAD	HELLIFIELD	MANOR ROAD
ALLERTON	KETTERING	HELLIFIELD
KENTISH TOWN	KENTISH TOWAN	STYAL
HOLMES CHAPEL	HENLEY-ON-THAMES	CARNFORTH
HENLEY-ON-THAMES	HENLEY-ON-THAMES	WEST ALLERTON
KENTISH TOWN	MAULDETH ROAD	HENLEY-ON-THAMES
OLD ROAN	HENLEY-ON-THAMES	SHAW & CROMPTON
WILLESDEN JUNCTION	WILLESDEN JUNCTION	ORELL PARK
SALFORD	BEESTON	WEST HAMSTEAD MIDLAND
HARTFORD	KINGS LANGLEY & ABBOTS LANGLEY	PENRITH
HENLEY-ON-THAMES		

(NOTE : Any misspelling is by HM Customs who prepared a detailed list of the contents but only charged £33 for handling and clearance!)

Notice how so many from **Henley-on-Thames** were involved! And how did the **Drigg** totem from Cumberland get mixed up with all the Lancashire and Cheshire items! Below are four of the LMR items that returned safely home:

Many of the restaurants in California were made from American railroad cabooses, and when the chain finally closed most of these cabooses and their contents were razed to the ground. Michael estimates that as many as 90 per cent were 'trashed', so that more than five hundred escaped the 'skipman' here, only to perish at the hands of American 'garbage collectors'. We also know that nothing was ever recovered from the chain in Japan, so we may therefore speculate that at least six hundred LMR and over 100 SR totems were lost in this way. This may account why some have never appeared in auction.

Because a high percentage of the LMR totems were from Manchester and Liverpool, we could speculate that **Brooklands**, **Clifton Junction**, **Droylesden**, **Fallowfield**, **Heaton Mersey**, **Hest Bank**, **Neston South**, **Prestbury**, **Warwick Road** and a few more may have met their fate this way. Notice in our LMR database the number of stations in Cheshire and Lancashire where we have no data. We stress again, all of this is speculation on our part, but it is plausible!

When I (RF) visited the Grand Central Station in Toronto a few years ago there were totems for sale in a collector's shop on the main concourse from **Pluckley**, **Hillside**, **Old Roan** and a couple more. These may have come from the Canadian restaurants, from the New England restaurants, or simply other imports from the UK, as the owner was linked with the railwayana stall at the Bath Antique Centre.

The Victoria Station chain came out of bankruptcy for a while in the 1980s, with a few restaurants operating. However, the banks foreclosed again in 1991. A new owner acquired seven restaurants in New England and Florida, and three of these are still operating in 2001. Totems can still be seen at two locations in the Boston area (Burlington and Salem) and at a third location – in Miami, Florida. (One of the restaurants is close to Boston's Logan International airport.) David Wood was able to uncover these additional pieces of information just as we were completing this book.

There is still more research to be done, but we have a better picture now on what may have been lost compared with when we started writing the book. It may well be, therefore, that those of you waiting to complete a Manchester area collection may not be able to do so. We close this short appendix with further images of some very 'lucky' totems.

Stop Press!

Readers may be amazed to learn that during the final few days of completing this book a real gem turned up. It had been rumoured that **Bradford Forster Square** was fitted with totems early on, but photo evidence was inconclusive. It was also rumoured they were taken down in about 1956, but none survived. To our delight, one has survived, and appeared in the first KRA auction of 2002. We thank Mike Soden for allowing us to make the unique shot below, literally a day before we went to press.

The history of the station is interesting. It was an ex-Midland railway structure opened in 1890 as Bradford to replace the 45-year-old Market Street station that was immediately adjacent. In 1924, just after the formation of the 'Big Four' ,the LMS re-named it **Bradford Forster Square**. It was closed in 1990, when the area was re-developed and a new Forster Square opened, again on an adjacent site.

Bibliography

Aerofilms, *British Railways from the Air – Then and Now*, Ian Allan (1998)
Body, Geoffrey, *PSL Field Guide, Railways of the Eastern Region*, Patrick Stephens Ltd (1986)
—–, *Railway Stations of Britain*, Thorsons (1990)
Bolger, Paul, *BR Steam Motive Power Depots*, Ian Allan (1982)
Borley, H.V., *Chronology of London Railways*, Railway & Canal Historical Society (1982)
Brennand, D., *British Railways Totem Signs*, Connor and Butler Publishing (1991)
Buck, Gordon, *A Pictorial Survey of Railway Stations*, Oxford Publishing Co. (1992)
Butt, R.V.J., *The Dictionary of Railway Stations*, Patrick Stephens Ltd (1995)
Coleman, R. and Rajczonek, J., *Steaming into Birmingham and the West Midlands*, Wharton (1997)
Cooke, R.A., *Atlas of the Great Western Railway as of 1947*, Wild Swan Publications (1997)
Connolly, W.P., *British Railways Pre Grouping Atlas*, Ian Allan (1958, 1998 edn)
Connor, J.E., *Stepney's Own Railway* Connor and Butler (1984)
Dent, David, *150 Years of the Hertford & Ware Railway*, Rockingham Press (1993)
Ferneyhough, Frank, *History of Railways in Britain*, Osprey Publishing (1975)
Freeman, M., and Aldercroft, D., *The Atlas of British Railway History*, Croom Helm Publishing (1985)
Hutchinson Encyclopedia of Britain, Helicon Publishing Ltd (1999)
Joby, R.S., *Forgotten Railways, East Anglia*, David & Charles (1977)
Jowett, Alan, *Jowett's Nationalised Railway Atlas*, Atlantic Publishing (2000)
Kay, Peter, *The London, Tilbury & Southend Railway* (vols 1 & 2), P. Kay (1997)
Maggs, Colin, *GWR Principal Stations*, Ian Allan (1987)
Railway Clearing House, *The Handbook of Railway Stations 1956 edn*, David & Charles (reprint)
Simmons, Jack, *The Railways of Britain,* (Macmillan (1961, 1986 edn)
Vaughan, A., *Pictorial Record of Great Western Architecture*, Oxford Publishing Company (1977)
Wignall, C.J., *Complete British Railways Maps & Gazetteer 1825–1985*, Oxford Publishing (1985)
Young, Alan, *Suburban Railways of Tyneside*, Martin Bairstow (1999)

SOUTHEND-ON-SEA
VICTORIA
LIVERPOOL ST
28s